D1114098

ST. GERMAIN

EARTH'S BIRTH CHANGES

ST. GERMAIN THROUGH AZENA

TRIAD
PUBLISHERS PTY LTD

© Copyright 1993 By Triad Publishers Pty Ltd.

All rights reserved under International and Pan-American Copyright Conventions.

No part of this book may be reproduced or transmitted in any form, by any means, electronic or mechanical, including photocopying or recording or by any information storage or retrieval system, without express permission in writing from the publisher.

For information address:

TRIAD Publishers Pty. Ltd.
P.O. Box 731, Cairns
Qld. 4870
Australia
Ph: 070 930121 Fax: 070 930374

Book Title:
EARTH'S BIRTH CHANGES

Author: St. Germain channelled through Azena
Edited and narrated by Peter O. Erbe
Book and cover design by Peter O. Erbe
Typeset by Thomas Williams (018) 107 297

First Edition
National Library Of Australia: ISBN: 0 646 13607 0

Printed by Kaleidoscope, Perth, W.A., Australia

Triad Publications aim at aiding and
inspiring a spiritually unfolding humanity.

PUBLISHER'S NOTE

The 'Earth's Birth Changes' material represents a compilation of St. Germain's teachings, received during group sessions (held in the U.S.A. and Australia) within the period of 1986 to 1989, and channelled through Azena Ramanda.

All editing efforts were aimed at retaining St. Germain's particular style of expression, while simultaneously affording smooth reading.

The reader may take note of the fact that only as recent as November 1992, St. Germain requested this material be published; quote: *'for it is now in the ripeness of time'.*

We at Triad Publishers are honoured for having the privilege of extending our publications with this material. We express our appreciation to the people who made it all possible:

Azena for her selfless service in channelling St. Germain; Ramanda for being the driving force behind the organization of group events and for recording St. Germain's words; David John Ward for bringing St. Germain to Australia; Diane Cummings for her co-operation and her prompt response in releasing this material; to Gitanjali for being the connecting link; and last - but by no means least - to St. Germain himself.

From a river born of God I come forth to reflect your divinity. Hear my call. We of the Council of Light have come so that you may know our joy as One.

I come because you have called the essence of the Brotherhood of the Light unto you. I come as an equal brother, divine being of light that recognizes your divine beingness of light. I come to share with you. I come because I love you! I love you beyond your imaginings. I wish not to be revered or captured within any image that will be placed upon your wall. That I do not desire. I desire to free you unto your own vision of God and, indeed, you are becoming One with GOD I AM.

ST. GERMAIN

It is nigh unto the ripeness of time - indeed - a culmination of eons of times unto the harvest. The time is now. It is the climax unto the unfoldment - the grand orgasm of the experience of the God that you are. The rapture will allow you to perceive fourth density, which is an exchange of frequency, a shift into a different gear, as it were. Therefore, third density will no longer perceive you, for you will be simultaneously existing, coexisting in the same space/time, but merely not perceived, because it is of a different frequency. You will have visions of grandeur beyond your perception.

The convergence is the climax - the unlimited spewing forth of God I Am into the universe, through the communication of the Earth plane, the birth of the light of the world, the merging of Mankind.

The year 2012 of your time is the apex of it. It is a convergence point into unlimitedness, into the golden era of God. When you transverse this threshold, you shall automatically be at Onement with all that is. The fruits of the labour of love upon Terra will bring humanity into Oneness - a humanity at One with God, where God is known.

ST. GERMAIN

CONTENTS

FOREWORD

by Peter O. Erbe

St. Germain's communications were received through a phenomenon known as 'full body manifestation', a procedure, during which Azena Ramanda left her body to allow St. Germain to totally incarnate into it. This process eliminates a common side-effect of general channelling, that is the blending of the consciousnesses of channel and channelled entity, therefore assuring a pure and 'unfiltered' communication.

Those who had the fortune of participating in St. Germain's audiences would most certainly testify to his powerful, dynamic and very loving exposition. The name St. Germain is a mere label to help the audience identify this entity and refers to one of his previous incarnations, also known a Count Ragoszy. There have been many other incarnations of his, some of which history recorded as Samuel and Noah of the Old Testament, Joseph, father of Jeshua Ben Joseph, Christopher Columbus and Sir Francis Bacon. However, whenever one speaks of incarnations one ought be mindful of the fact that any given incarnation of any soul represents only a fragment, a facet, of a much grander being. This accounts for St. Germain's preference to be addressed as 'I AM' and not as St. Germain. To those partial to an orderly labelling of things, St. Germain refers to himself as a seventh level consciousness, compared to earthly humans, who are of third and transitional fourth level.

As he stands before us and bares his heart in love and compassion, we are humbled and exalted at once and the apex we stand upon becomes the cornerstone for the next structure.

Life unfolds in circles - concentric rings - cycles, to be precise. Such cycles within cycles ultimately converge in major birthing points for new realities. The upheavals, the unrest and torment within humanity at this time are the contractions and labour pains heralding

I

a birth of an incomprehensible, cosmic magnitude. The decade before and after the turn of the century represent the culmination - the harmonic convergence - of a 200 million year evolutionary cycle: Earth and her children - in unison with the Solar system and thousands of galaxies - are birthing into a new dimension.

From the shores of eternal being, from the Council of Light, comes St. Germain to assist in this birthing process. Rekindling an ancient memory, he transforms the prophecies of Old - of looming calamities and trepidation - into shining, new horizons without circumference. His words are carried by an air of urgency for the changes are imminent; quote: *'the acceleration is becoming exponential'*. His gift to us is not approximate statement but the promise of fact: freedom for humanity.

Casting a light across the past 20 million years of Earth's history and evolution, he reveals fascinating facts about our origin, about the star-seeding of humanity, about our brothers and forefathers from the Pleiades, the Orion constellation, Lyra, Arcturus and more. The startling details of the rise and demise of ancient Lemuria and Atlantis leave us in suspense. What is more, he unfolds a vision for humanity of such grandeur, that it renders the uninitiated speechless.

If the historian and the scientist only as much as consider the information presented here, they will have to revise their certainties, for their facts are at risk. If the disciples of religious dogma as much as glance at this material, their degrading symbol of a suffering, tortured, bleeding God - where God is reduced to a personage - will have to be laid aside.

Unravelling a tapestry of dazzling beauty for humanity - the thrilling joy of St. Germain's message is contagious - is of effervescence and jubilance: the transition from separation to the union of Oneness with all Life - the age of Love - the golden age of God.

It is my honour and pleasure and the fulfilment of a long-standing desire, to present to you St. Germain.

Chapter 1

BIRTH & REBIRTH OF PLANET EARTH.

FIRST SESSION.

Genesis - Gene Of Isis.

Greetings my beloved brothers and sisters.

Indeed, I am equal to you and you are equal to that which be I. Understand that your genetic heritage is of God. Your children, your forefathers - who created the universes - All-That-Is, is your heritage. That which you call *you* is God. You are all, all, *all* Gods.

Now, we will speak this day of your time about your forefathers, the elders, and the star battles, the civilization of the Atlantean culture, and all of this. However, before we begin this, I wish you to understand the message.

As we issue forth this understanding, you will recall in your grand chronicle, your Bible, the beginning of the beginnings of humanity: the Genesis. What be Genesis? It is an anagram - gene of Isis. In this tale, this gene of Isis, there was a ray of light issued from the civilizations that are coming yet again upon your plane to re-institute a new Genesis, a new birthing, a new tale of humanity that is God and knows it is God.

The awareness of life upon this plane was spun into the light rays of atom, not Adam, through the creation[1] of a chromosome of crystalline formation within the Pineal gland of your brain.

---

[1] On several other occasions St. Germain refers to this process also as the 'star-seeding'.

You know, my beloved brothers and sisters, your skull has four lobes, four quadrants within your brain. The cortex within your brain carries within it the fluid, the stream, the eternal fountain of the perception of what I speak to you this day of your time. As you stimulate it, you will know this as a truth for you.

Carry forth the awareness. As you unveil more and more, emotions will run forth, tears - indeed nourish yourself with your salt. Allow this river within the cortex to flow within every cell of your being. There is a channel, a hole, if you would call it thus, between your crown area down into the Pineal gland. This is the corridor of communication. This affords the flow of energy and it penetrates into this chromosome of crystalline formation within your Pineal gland, stimulates it and *creates conscious awareness.* It resonates within every other cell of your body. Ye, every cell of your body becomes aware and you flow with the awareness of your Godhood.

The gene of Isis was the institution of feminine, of receptive energy within Mother Earth. That is why she is a mother. Because she herself is of the essence of female energy. Indeed, as this Pineal gland becomes stimulated, becoming receptive of the energies of All-That-Is, it is being penetrated by the masculine, the solar energy, the Sun of God, and you *become through immaculate conception.* Do you know what a Messiah is? It is an anointed one. What is anointed? Your crown. It becomes the glorious illustration of your Christus. You place the crown upon your very being and walk in sovereign dominion of All-That-Is, of all that you create as God from the universe of you and as you create it, you love it, you love it, you LOVE IT! For in the love is the creation and in the creation is the love. It is a constant flow of Isness called Isis. Do you know what Isis is? It is duplicity of is - is IS. The polarities - male/female, masculine/feminine, good/bad, negative/positive - will come to know no polarity at all as they intertwine with the conceptive configuration of the Isness of Isis, becoming God. Partaking of sovereignty, placing the crown upon the breast of you. As this issues forth through your breast into the All-That-Is, your dominion becomes apparent to everyone upon the plane. You will glow, you will resonate, you will be the Christus in illustration and anoint those that come before you, and indeed awaken their cellular memory as well, because their cells will resonate to your cells and so it goes in the unveiling of the New Age, the era of God aware.

Now, you know the grand land of Israel. Many have called this nation [USA] the new Israel, the new Jerusalem. But do you know from whence this word came? Israel is also an anagram: Isis, Ra Elohim. Isis the female energy. Ra, the male energy. Elohim the God I Am awareness that interconnects and transmutes the polarities into wholeness, into holiness, if you will. Israel was not originally a land, although it came to be known as a land within your eastern countries. It was originally a craft, a mother-ship called ISRAEL. And also from the Pleiades[2] came forth the mother-ship called JERUSALEM, and established within the kingdom upon your plane the nation of Israel with an illusion called Jerusalem. But Jerusalem was not a city as you know it. It was a resonance, and the vibration within your world that was the exact vibration to the mother-ship came to be known as Jerusalem.

The elders, within ISRAEL [the craft] and the mother land of Lyra[3] - which we will discuss later in your time - they colonized the Earth and established the peoples upon your Earth plane. You all issue forth as the peoples of Atlantis[4], ISRAEL, JERUSALEM and you will all become aware of a vague urgency to do something, to go somewhere, to be of assistance, but you do not know exactly how. It alludes you.

Many of you would consider life as a grand search for the perfect manilla envelope in which to file yourself, to place yourself in a certain alphabetical order, in order to know where you are. But you know, my beloveds, the stirring within you, to come forth into a

---

[2] Pleiades, a large group of stars in the constellation of Taurus, six of which are visible and represent (in mythology) the daughters of Atlas and Pleione, the seventh being 'lost' (the Lost Pleiad).

[3] Lyra, a northern constellation, containing a white star of the first magnitude, called Alpha Lyra and a blue-white star called Vega, also of the first magnitude.

[4] Webster defines Atlantis as a legendary island or continent supposed to have existed in the Atlantic west of Gibraltar and to have been sunk by an earthquake.

newness of life, a change - a transition - is not only in what you *do*, but what you *are*. You will not be a third density God/Man. You will be fourth density God/Man, and you will transmute this God/Man into God/Light. You will become living light and then you will become thought vibration - the ultimate Isness of All-That-Is. The emanating thought of creation. Therefore *you will acquire the capacity to transport yourself through thought vibration, to precipitate out of the atoms of the atmosphere your thought, to transmute base metals into gold - the ultimate alchemy.*

Now, as you all become in the journey, the seeking, you will notice a restlessness within your beingness. You will notice omnidirectional sight perception. You wish to go in all directions at once; you experience confusion and you give it a negative vibration. Do you know what confusion is? Co-fusion - fusion with All-That-Is. It is not negative. It is grand, to be sure. When you perceive this confusion, this co-fusion, with clarity, you will become multidimensionally aspected, aware of all the dimensions in which you exist. Experiencing, garnishing the wisdom to enlighten yourself with - you will be consciously aware of it and it will all spew forth from this gene of Isis, this chromosome within you that is being stimulated every moment of your being upon this plane. Do you know why? Because there is a ray that is encircling your planet now. It is called a violet ray and it is transmuting the resonance within your atoms.

There is a microcosm within your being and a macrocosm within your world. Every atom within the consciousness of Mother Earth is also being stimulated to become aware, and that is why there is such transition in your scientific awareness, your religious structures, and your bureaucratic structures. It is all becoming stimulated because of the violet ray encircling your plane. It issues forth from the Sun, ultraviolet to be sure. It is no accident the ozone is opening to allow more ultraviolet light - beyond your physical spectrum of light - to penetrate this plane. Ultraviolet rays are not damaging. Ultraviolet rays are the rays of God transmuting your being into your awareness of beingness.

Now, many of you have much fear within your breast about this transition, the rebirth of Earth, as it is called. It is not to be feared, or to be dreaded, no more than that grand event of creating new life upon your plane is to be feared. It is a celebration. It is an event of cataclysmic proportions - cataclysmic, indeed, in a wondrous manner. It will affect many dimensions beyond your perception, many galaxies, many universes will be brought into new awareness.

This land of Earth, it is becoming a sun [metaphorical reference]. It is becoming a star, as you all are, within its own beingness. You are brightening yourselves, enlightening yourselves. Because you are atoms within her own consciousness, she herself is enlightening, becoming of higher vibration in the process of ascension, becoming a star, as it were, a sun, of God. She herself is crowning her own being with Christus. The penetration of light upon your plane is to be reflected back out into the universes, through you - you are the transmitter, you are the receptor and reflector, the mirror. You are the crystal, because your Pineal gland, which was placed by the original elders, is crystalline in structure. It is not a mineral. It is tissue in crystalline formation, it is a spiral of energy within the cortex of this gland.

Your scientists and your miracle doctors have already understood that your Pineal gland is the one gland within the endocrine system that, when certain hormones are released within it, and stimulated, will enable you to perceive telepathically, accessing energies which are beyond the physical. Now, perceive this journey with joy, with jubilance, it is of song and dance and delight! Truly this may be the experience of a dance and not dire circumstance.

Fear, trepidation, doubt, scepticism, doom and gloom - all of these vibrations are of the polarity of alter ego. You have heard of this, no? Indeed. Well, I will tell you a thing about alter ego and we will discuss it further, later in your time.

The alter ego was altered in structure by the light ray, the original thought vibration into light and into density to coagulate into physical matter in order to become God/Man. It is necessary. It is vital. Bless it, for it gives you the opportunity to experience this

5

glorious land of your world and all the stars within the heavens as you perceive them. Bask in their brilliance as they glitter in the dark night of your time. The alter ego is transmuting as well. The polarity of black, of darkness, that you call negative, evil, bad - you have many labels for it - it comes unto this blessed awareness through your reflection, through your vibration within your own atoms. *It will be shifted in the twinkling of an eye - it will come into the knowing of its SELF.* In this knowing, it will become God. It will come into the rapture of its own beingness, of its own divinity. Therefore it will not be in fear of trepidation and separation.

This will take place in a grand and glorious fashion on your plane. You will have an emphasis on dichotomy, an emphasis on polarities; that which is of unlimited perspective, and that which is of limited perspective. They shall come into mutual reflection of one another. The God I Am beingness within the breast of those who are unlimited and perceive their unlimitedness, will allow what is limited to be reflected from their unlimitedness, if they [the limited] so choose to perceive it, if they unmask themselves of their blinders.

Now, as you bring this world into the birthing of its new light, heralding in the New Age, as you go forth within your own life - in the changes that are to come, in relationships, your busiment of the embodiment - and as you go forth into new and wondrous journeys upon the high seas of life, partake of the joy within the breast of every moment.

Breathe the life of God. Allow the gene of Isis, the genesis within you, to be stimulated, to be excited with the adventure. Allow enthusiasm, the exhilaration to be brought forth in your own private journey. As you do this, my beloved, *as you are in joy of this celebration of life,* you will begin, bit by bit, to transmute this world into the violet ray [the ray of freedom], so it may become the star.

Now, many of you will have remembrance of your dreams. Understand that they are partaking of a new vitality. You are remembering vaguely a shadow, but is not really shadow. It is your genetic heritage. You will perceive many a time what you would call your future. But it is not your future. It is your past. The technologies of your past. You are remembering what really can be. Your perception of life is broadening a bit and your horizons are becoming brilliant with new awareness.

Now, all of you in this room were part and parcel of the lineage of the gene of Isis, or you would not be here. In your contemplation, stimulate the Pineal gland and access what it is that you have come from. Access the civilizations and experiences from which you came, from which you are born. You need not that which be I, to bring forth the battles, and civilizations and colonizations, the history of this plane, although I will reflect it unto you, indeed, but you require NO ONE! You are your own God. You have access to everything that ever was and ever will be, because it is all now, anyway.

When you allow this energy, the fountain of love and light and life, to issue forth unto your Pineal gland, and spark within it the genesis of the crystal within it, you will become knowing, consciously knowing, of the multidimensional experiences of which you partake. Now, would you desire an exercise?

Alright. This will be a brief one, for I desire you not to become dependent and reliant on meditation. It is a joyous experience, but it is truly a limitation if it is relied upon. And it will be only so that you know how to bring it forth within yourself - the knowingness, the access of which I will speak later this day of your time. Alright. You may all do this three times: AUMMM - OMBRAEE - INONE - IRAIONE - INONE - AUMMM - I Am! I Am! I Am!

So be it, indeed. Now, what was spoken were merely vibrations which stimulate the Pineal gland. When you are in this state of awareness, resonate to those vibrations, place within your being a thought or desire to know of whatever it is. You may ask yourself: where is home?, who am I?, tell me, of two centuries ago, or two million years ago, or two million years hence. Or what is 350 dimensions beyond this one in the now?

I am not dogmatic about religion, about meditation, contemplation, quietude, ritual or any of those sorts of things. I wish you to understand that you are the power source and I give unto you vibrations, from time to time, which will assist you. Alright? What do they call it in your verbiage? Okie dokie? That is an unusual variant. At one time I was of the impression that 'okie dokie' was the female version of 'okay'. Now I understand that 'maybe' is the female version of 'okay'.

That which be I will bring forth my presence unto you at any moment you desire contemplation or communion with that which be I. But I tell you I am an equal brother. No more. I am your equal and you are my equal. We are one in the same reflection of eternal divinity - one unto the other. I honour you with all of my being. All that I am issues forth in this moment to give unto you all of life with light and love. I spew unto you the blessings of the Gods of the universes and the stars that be you. As I do thus, the waters of living light come rushing forth to nourish you, to supplicate you, to assuage your wounds and heal your soul. I bless you and I indeed revere you, for you are the children of God. You are the Christus, reborn in a new day, a new dawn. A new eternal now.

In this communion, as you contemplate that which be I, if there is ever a hint of control, if there is ever an understanding that is other than the perspective of unconditional love, be sure and know that, my beloved brothers, you do not have that which be I on the line. Indeed, I wish you all to merge with one another, contemplate, speak to one another about your visions of where you have been in your 'before time', if you would desire to separate it into the dimensions of past and future. I will allow you a short, brief respite of what you would call one half-hour or so of your time, to share with one another. Become aware of how many of you have the exact same vision, and you will begin to understand the civilization that I will explain when I return. The civilization of an ancient land called Lyra. The elders. Indeed there were those that populated Lyra, and they were called the Micese. The Micese came forth to institute this universe about 175 million years ago, of your time. However, we will speak of the Lyrians, the Pleiadeans and the Orions[5], the Black

---

[5] Orion, an equatorial constellation near Taurus, containing the first magnitude stars Rigel and Betelgeuse.

League and your Chinese, (who came from the land of Saturn), the land of Atlantis and Lemuria[6], the lands of Pan[7], your ancient Hopi and Navajo, your Hawaii and your southwest of your country. We will speak about Israel, the lands of Europa, and how indeed this world came to be as it is in the heyday of your now, hm? Sounds exciting?

Peoples of the Earth unite, for there is a grand event about to occur.

Also be aware that not all of you have been of your present gender, in that previous civilization, as you are now. For you have not only been both male and female, you have been both, at the same time, upon the same world. Open your horizons, your field of vision, and be unlimited. The soul is not limited by one embodiment, for the soul is all powerful. Fare thee well, for now. We will reunite very soon in your time. Namaste!

The Titans.

Greetings my beloveds.

The respite, it is where you all go to pot, hm? I will tell you, he who laughs, lasts. Your communion, how did you experience it? As an unlimited flow of brother to brother, star to star, light to light? As the river of experience of All-That-Is? You have a tendency to let your clock-face become a grand limitation to you. As you come into the new birthing, you will understand that time is an experience of now. Every moment upon your clock-face will be containing eternity. This is a time for you to begin to experience the release of limitations, the widening and the broadening of your horizons in this manner. As you do thusly for yourselves, you may do thusly also in example to one another. Give forth demonstration unto your brethren of the release of the slave-driver called time.

---

[6] Lemuria, a continent thought to have existed long ago, now supposedly covered by the Indian Ocean.

[7] Pan, a land thought to have existed in the South Pacific region before the time of Lemuria.

Now, so what be history, hm? Heritage. Ancient tapestry of your knowing. You all have vague memories that, at times, haunt you. I will begin to unveil the mystery and unravel this tapestry for you. I will allow you to view into this mirror you already know and there will be many of you who will issue forth streams of awareness and wisdom, because you have touched the truth within your own breast. You have awakened this genetic encoding within you to create a genesis, a rebirth.

Now, we will begin your history about twenty million years ago of your time. There is a system that is grand indeed. It is called the Vegan, or Lyrian system in your heavens. On that world there were grand and wondrous beings that were quite large in stature as you would judge them to be. They were called titans. They were 20 to 25[8] of your feet in height and therefore, because of this, their worlds were quite different. Their planets were larger and, indeed, their life-spans were longer also. Their life-span was generally about 3 to 5 thousand years in that time. They were grand and wondrous in their display of power-lust, warriors epitomized. In their land, they came upon the horizon of technology. They unveiled the mysteries of life enough to develop the awareness of molecular structure. They understood life and the energy it contains, the thought vibration of God it contains, although they did not understand its divinity in that time. They indeed interwove light to create laser and space technology. They had their crafts which travelled upon light beams. But they had not understood hyperspace yet - beyond light speed, the speed of thought. They had interplanetary travel and they established governments and colonies upon several of their planets. Local governments to be sure.

There was not a central body of government to integrate and unify the energies of the planets, and so there were many war-lords, many entities power-thirsty for more and more conquering. They sent forth armies, as it were, to dominionize other areas of your galaxy, other peoples who were not as developed as they. And they went into their kingdom with a flash of brilliance and set their craft upon the ground

---

[8] 25 feet = 7.62 m

and they would utter a command. Their conditions were utter surrender and so they drew many peoples into their armies in this manner and they became a grand body of warrior energy in this fashion. The peoples who were of their dominion, who were ruled, thought of them, indeed, as Gods.

They were 25 feet or so in height. They had the understanding of light technology. In their brilliance they appeared in the heavens in a blazing instant and swept the land with their power. What undeveloped peoples would not think of them as Gods? The alphabetical understanding, in your verbiage, of the names of their leaders, you find in your ancient Hebrew: IHWH, or YHWH, and it came to be known as YAHWEH [also Yahveh]. Indeed the translation of the Hebrew word is Lord God, Lord of the Mighty, and became translated into God.

That is what your Bible refers to when it refers to YAHWEH, or the Lord God. Now, in this ancient understanding, there were many internal strifes. Civil wars, battles, for the leaders were always desirous of dethroning the present leaders to become new leaders. Ye, even the ruled became revolutionary. Therefore, there arose a grand battle, a grand struggle for power. Over half their population was destroyed. Three races were destroyed in the process and they became scattered yet again. It took several hundred years to redevelop their technology to the point it had been in their past. And yet through these hundreds of years, they did not understand divinity within the energy they were developing. They did not see the divine thread of it within the tapestry of their awareness.

Now, when they came forth to conquer other lands, they also became aware of a large destroyer comet that appeared every several thousand years. It emerged within their area of the sky, their heavens, and lit into a grand blaze, destroying thirty of their worlds, over sixty percent of their population and much of their technology. So they became scattered yet again.

So, one of the most feared of the war-lords chose to leave and demonstrate his power in another world to call that world his own, to illustrate complete dominion without the scattering. He took with him several thousand people and many crafts. They went forth into the galaxy and coasted, as you would call it, wandered aimlessly in uncharted, unfamiliar territory, until they came upon a system [within the same galaxy, e.g.: our galaxy] with many blue suns. And as they did thus, they chose to colonize, for there were hundreds of thousands of them.

The leader's successor, who was the daughter of this particular warrior, was called Pleija, and she partook of the throne, or seat of power, changed the name of the star system to 'Pleiades' and this is where the story really becomes interesting.

Now, the destroyer comet, by this time, was re-entering the area of their systems. It did not interfere with them, but they were curious and they chose to follow it to see where it would take them, for it was a light that would be a beacon unto them. And as they followed it, they discovered in its tail fragments of their ancient heritage, their previous civilizations. While disseminating and analyzing this information between them and in their curiosity to discover who, in fact, they were, they came upon a system, a universe, a grand and wondrous illustration of new life. Indeed, this, your solar system.

They set foot upon Mars, Maldek[9] and Earth and the colonizations of these three areas began. Then Pleija took her forces and returned to the Pleiades, while these planets colonized and developed their technology, until the point when there was a desire upon Earth to get themselves hence to conquer other lands and dominionize other civilizations.

Maldek experienced a civil war so intense and so afflicted with powerlust, that they conquered the planet to the point of utter destruction. Indeed, they exploded their planet into millions of fragments and what is now the Asteroid Belt between Jupiter and Mars is what remains of what once was Maldek. It is truly a memorial to the conquering attitude of your ancient Lyrian ancestors.

Mars' revolution around its axis was changed because of the energy released by the explosion of Maldek. Your peoples upon the

---

[9] Maldek, (according to several channeled beings), a former planet of this solar system, which was destroyed - its remnants being our present Asteroid Belt.

land of Mars became extinct. The rest of them, who remained on the other side of the planet, went forth and conquered other lands and therefore the planet called Mars became desolated. In other words, there was no population upon Mars. Maldek had exploded, and your Earth only had a few people, only several hundred thousand, because all the rest of them had chosen to go forth and conquer other lands. So your solar system remained yet uncolonized by a grand civilization.

There came forth a strategy from the Pleiades to create a great space base upon this planet for it to be a grand colony of peace and harmony, because a new structure of government, or power, had arisen upon the lands of the Pleiades. They had chosen, they had desired, to create an era of peace. Enough of this war and battle. They had begun to understand the energy of light, the spiritual energy, as you would call it, when the understanding of hyperspace was developed.

Indeed, the divine understanding of love, the glue of life which holds atoms together, is none other than the thought of God in divine love. So the colonization began on this plane. This resulted in a reign of 10,000 years of peace. It truly became a grand civilization. But alas, in the belly of those who were reigning in that timing, was spawned powerlust also.

Lemuria and Atlantis.

So, yet again, they destroyed themselves and the scattered tribes of this planet abided, for several thousand years, until a grand, grand master of life [from the Pleiades] emerged upon the plane, and his name was Atlas. He was the one who chose to create peace and splendour and glorious exemplification of a light of God upon the plane. He brought his mate and millions of peoples, and millions of craft to this plane. And truly, this was the beginning of an era of splendour upon your planet, the planet you now call Earth. The father of Atlas' mate was called Muras, and he went forth and developed a grand golden civilization called Lemuria, which was a city, which became a continent that developed around a grand craft called Mu. Mu was a craft. Lemuria was the city around the craft.

Now, Atlantis and Lemuria were many, many miles from one another and your Earth's population was becoming accelerated at the time. This was about 33,000 years ago in your time and it was open real estate on Earth.

There were many, many, many civilizations coming forth to colonize here from many areas of your universe. The Orions came, the Arcturians[10] came, those Lyrians who had settled in other areas of this universe came forth. The Pleiadeans came and many interbreedings occurred. Primitive man [Earth-man] became a man [through the star-seeding], a body that could support an ascended consciousness. Truly this was when Genesis became apparent, for this was the time when the leader desired to create an embodiment, a vehicle, that had the capacity to carry ascended consciousness. Therefore the crystalline understanding was placed - through lightwaves - within the Pineal gland [of Earth-man] to enable the flow of the memory that you are God, to pierce the veil of forgetfulness and to understand your divine, creative energy.

This Atlas was a wise and loving entity who desired peace and harmony. Lemuria, truly, was an exemplification of a colony of art, a colony of experiencing the energy through crystalline technology and they shared it with their brother Atlatians. The Atlatians began to fervently advance their crystal technology to enhance their starships, and their fleets progressed grandly so that truly they could spread the illumination of their peace to other lands and create further and further peace.

The Orions.

Now, an embodiment, an entity that was very vengeful, who had been banished to the area of Beta Centauri in the times before,

---

[10] Arcturus, a fixed star of the first magnitude in the constellation Boötes.

returned with revenge in his breast, and he had crafts with him, and he landed in an area called Hyperborea[11], that is what you now call Florida. It was in the northern area of this land, for your planet was not of the axis it is in this time. The axis was different and the continents were situated in a different manner. What is now Russia was the North Pole and what you call Florida, it was truly in the northern area of the northern hemisphere of your world. Therefore, they blazed in with their craft in a flash of light, into an area that was rather undeveloped, called Hyperborea, and took over the peoples of that land and truly, it was their desire to take over Atlantis and Lemuria. They felt it was of their benefit, shall we say, to establish in an area that was of moderate climate, that was rather undeveloped and, therefore, affording others entrance.

They proceeded to the areas of Asia and Asia Minor to conquer their armies, for, indeed, Asia as well had been populated by millions and millions of peoples. 4.6 million peoples in the land of China now in your time are implanted with the gene of Isis and this occurred in that area also. Therefore there were many entities in the areas of Asia and Asia Minor who were aware of crystal technology and they drew them into their armies to conquer Atlantis and Lemuria.

This was the innings of the Orion energy, as they began to take control of the planet. They understood laser technology and the webbing of this laser to create an electromagnetic net across the planet. This was their strategy.

However, they created skirmishes, small embattlements in the border areas of both Atlantis and Lemuria, but to no apparent avail. It was indeed their heartburn, shall we say, and their gut became inflamed with the desire for revenge, to prove they were power sources. But do you know, they were only proving to themselves their powerlessness, not their power-sourceness. They became more and more engulfed with this fire, this hunger, this seething need to create dominion of this planet. Therefore, they hatched a scheme, as it were, to create inner strife, to infiltrate, as you would call it.

---

[11] Hyperborea, in Greek legend a northern region of sunshine and everlasting spring, beyond the mountains of the north wind.

They understood science and so they went forth to communicate with the scientists of both Atlantis and Lemuria, to create controversy between them, to change their belief systems and become embattled with one another. This is what many of your governmental structures do now in your time. They go into an area that is of great power, create strife inwardly, supply both sides with weapons and when there is much chaos and diversity, non-unity, they enter in. When they take the throne and control, they indeed feel powerful.

This was their plot, their desire, their scheme in that timing - to go forth and create inner diversity within both continents. And they did thusly.

It was about one thousand years later, when the appointed people were within the appointed positions and their hearts were aflame with anticipation that after eons of time they, the Orions, could establish their seed within the world, the planet you call Earth, within the continents of Lemuria and Atlantis. Indeed, since eons, for they had desired this already in the Pleiades.

Now, during one blazing and fateful morn, with one all-powerful blast unto an asteroid with all their forces of electromagnetic light laser energy, they destroyed the entire Earth. Indeed through the powerlust, the peoples, the golden crowning glory of this Earth, were destroyed. Through a ricochet blast from that asteroid, it placed its focus within the centerpoint of Atlantis and also within Lemuria. And just before this, an explosion that is indescribable buried itself into the beloved surface of your Earth.

Mother Earth was wounded deep, deep, deep. And indeed she was bleeding and regurgitating fretfully. And her back was broken. She was cracked down to the centre core. Her continents were separated. The oceans were split apart and ripped from one another and there was fire consuming her. Her waters were drowning her. Her rivers of life were running from her in a torrential understanding. Indeed, her cloud cover above her was pierced by this laser light and she was weeping torrential rain upon her horizons. She was in mourning of herself. For indeed, the wounds were deep within the consciousnesses of the peoples herein.

There were many civilizations on Earth at that time and the destruction was implanted within the memory of everyone of them. Within that fateful morn, two grand golden continents of this Earth were destroyed, after 18,000 years of peace. The rending and gaping of the ocean floors swallowed the Atlantean, the Lemurian, and many other continents upon this plane into the tomb within the deep. For there were many other, many Atlantises, shall we say. There was such rising and shifting of the planet that this occurred everywhere. It was mostly focused in Atlantis and Lemuria, but it occurred in diverse fashion everywhere. This is where your deluge occurred. This is where many of your legends originate, from the destruction of the planet through a grand desire for power, through a clouded act of aggression on one fateful morn.

This is your heritage. This is the memory that you carry with you every day of your life. All these wars are what you are remembering now in your time, what you are recreating upon your Earth now, what you are living from your past into your future, what you are living within your daily life, your activity with your mates, with your business houses, with your neighbours, with your children.

These are the wars you remember when you have strife with them. *Remember.* Aware yourself that it is not necessary to have the destruction. You may recreate the future. You may recreate the ending to this tale of woe. The rebirthing is occurring within your very thought, within the very being of every moment of your life - what you do, what you say, how you behave, how you interact with one another, how you vibrate.

This is not the end of the tale. The Atlanteans - the result of interbreeding between Pleiadeans and Lyrians - and the Orions came forth in grand forces upon your plane to do devilry - is that what you call it, dastardly experiences? They created chaos wherever they went. This was the grand personification of the altered ego.

And truly my beloveds, they are wondrous. They are merely not aware that they are wondrous. It is within your power to awaken them to their wonder and their splendour, to become knowing of the equality of both the alter ego and the divine ego, of both male/female, masculine/feminine energies, of both, limited and unlimited perspectives. They are both divine. They are both wondrous. They are both part of the whole. The whole would not be the whole without both of them. So, to sever, separate, divide, reject, rid yourself of anything that you would judge to be undesirable, is creating further separation. Many of those Orions chose to fight fire with fire, as it were, which only creates more fire.

Orion energy is the fire energy, the male energy of power of creation, the thrust for life.

The Pleiadeans developed within them an underground society called the Black League. This indeed was exhibited during your planetary wars and battles of Maldek. The Black League came in their ships and their grand crafts from the Pleiades and desired to bring forth this wisdom within the inner forces of the Orions, to create within them peace, a desire for harmony and non-battle, for the non-warrior element. They are upon your plane now - the Black League and the Orions - for this is a redramatization of your past history. Your Earth is now in the process of presenting this mirror unto you yet again, to give you the opportunity for a different ending, for a different resolution, for a different birthing into a new era. The point of resolution - the flash point - is the moment of transmutation into the New Age, into divine awareness of All-That-Is, into fourth density, fourth dimension and beyond.

Now, the experience of the Atlantean decline and demise caused grand disarray and disruption within your atmosphere - it was heavy with particles within it, density indeed. The blackened heavens drove and scattered the remaining tribes across the Earth into the inner cities in search for light and life. Therefore the colonization of the inner Earth became rampant with the genetic memory of the Lemurians and the Atlanteans.

As they [the inner Earth people] arrive from the pyramidal structures, in your future time, you will recognize them as your brothers of the Pleiades. They have interbred and their physical structure has changed a bit with time. Their skin is a bluish green and aqua because of the copper within the water that flows therein. The hue of their hair and eyes has shifted a bit - has become a bit more Venusian. However, as they spring forth, you will know them. You may identify them by the light upon their foreheads. As you gaze into their auric field, a light will emanate from their forehead. This is how you may identify them.

The tribes that emerged after the decline of Atlantis culminated in three nations of peoples - the Hyperboreans, the warriors who continued indeed. There was the nation called Almus in South America, Central America and North America. There were the Aryans - they were the war-lords who came forth to conquer, causing destruction and controversy within the Lemurian and Atlantean cultures. They partook of the seats of power through default and became the Aryan race. Notice the similarity between Aryan and Orion. Also your Hitler was of Aryan experience. The Hebrews, or the third race - Hebrew translated is wanderer - it was a world-wide alliance of Gypsies. They were indeed the peoples that wandered, lost in the wilderness. They called themselves the victims of holocaust long before Hitler came along. Hitler was a redramatization.

Now, the Hebrew nation came forth in the land of Egypt and in the land of Israel. There was much warring and much dichotomization of the powers, and indeed, the Pleiadeans who abided therein, who were the remaining genetic race of the Pleiadeans at that time, desired to go home. They desired to return to their home star system of the Pleiades, for there was rampant bloody battle within the lands. Icons and idols and human sacrifice. The story of Sodom and Gommorah, which was really a star battle, is an illustration of this. However, the land became utterly destroyed, became utterly hated, by the utmost powerlust of an entity called Jehovah. Indeed, this Jehovah was also of the Aryan race.

Now, the conception of Jeshua, the unfoldment of this God/Man upon the plane of Earth was initiated by the Pleiadeans and the confederation to re-institute and re-establish a light upon this Earth, to inform them of the original understanding of peace and harmony of the lands of Atlantis and Lemuria. To demonstrate unto them the divine principle of love, of God Creative Force. The star of Bethlehem was a mother-ship. Bethlehem is also an acronym. Bethlehem - Be the Elohim. Elohim is God.

Sirius[12], the peoples from the star system called Sirius, settled in the lands of Venus[13] and colonized. Then they brought forth their essence in the land of Egypt and carried with them the seeds of germination to merge with the Egyptian peoples and the Pleiadeans. So the Egyptians are an interbreeding of the Sirians and the Pleiadeans. The star of Sirius - that truly is the star of Jerusalem - it was a craft as well.

The entity that came forth from this grand craft taught the peoples to view and understand electromagnetic energy within the waves of the atmosphere, and how to manipulate it. Anti-gravity and gravity, anti-matter and matter. The polarities again. He demonstrated how to cause a space, a vacuum, a void, between the gravity field of the Earth and the non-gravity field of space, and created, within this vacuum, a space-time continuum upon this plane so that it would create levitation. And in this manner he created the pyramids in a matter of a few days of time. *All of them upon the plane.* Not only the ones of Giza, upon the sands of the golden deserts of Egypt, but all of them. For they were indeed meridian points of the body of Earth. The capstones were somewhat of crystalline formations encased within gold, emphatic representations of the flows of energy through the body of Earth, to open the seals of Earth, to create light force at the ripeness of time when the spaceships came forth. Indeed, to awaken these vestiges of light that are within the containers of the grand paragons of divinity - the sphinx, the pyramids, and the grand wonders of your world. They are all touched by the hand of God I Am. They are all touched by those that came forth to create wonderment upon your plane. Why do you think there are seven wonders of the world? The seven rays of light.

Now, the twelve tribes of Israel were resonant to the twelve rays of light, the seven rays plus five in communion with one another.

---

[12] Sirius, the brightest star in the heavens, located in the constellation Canis Major.

[13] Venus, in this context, is to be understood as physical fourth density Venus and not as physical third density Venus.

They also resonated to the twelve signs of the Zodiac and the birthings of the house of David came forth. And what is the house of David? There is a house of Bethlehem, a house of Judea, a house of Israel, a house of the understanding of all the grand titles within your book called Bible, the houses, the house of God even. What is it? It is a consciousness. Most of the time when they refer to it, it is a craft.

Now, the flow of the electromagnetic energy through the meridian points of Earth would also spark within you a flow of the electromagnetic energy within *your* meridian points, for you are part of it and it is part of you. The carrier wave of the electromagnetic energy as it flows through you, the river the light flows upon - what is it? It is your blood. It is the light force within you. The platelets within your blood carry forth the genetic encoding of the gene of Isis. As the war of Armageddon wages within you, the warrior memory of the gene of Isis comes forth and causes embattlement of the cells of your body. What do you think cancer is? What do you think Aids is? Aids is also an acronym. *AIDS is anti-integration of the divinity of the soul.* It too is of grand assistance. It too creates an opening, a corridor, so bless it. It is not of grand fear. It is of grand celebration. As you embrace it, you embrace anti-everything. You embrace the polarity of the Black League. You embrace the polarity of the Orion energy. You embrace the polarity of the warrior and the peace-keeper. You allow the harmonious balance to occur within your own being. The peoples of the Earth will illustrate it within their own embodiment - the war of Armageddon - within their plane. The war, the battles, all of this that has come forth, the war of the stars - indeed it is coming forth [in embodiments].

The grand trepidation from beyond the North star will excite a few entities upon the Earth. It is alright. One thing about planet Earth, the grand spaceship of Earth: It did not come with a set of instructions. And as you issue forth this birthing, know that the cataclysms are merely the shiftings of the sound-waves of light as it comes forth to bear a new Christus.

Jeshua was birthed from the house of David, Mother Mary - Mother Earth, and Father Joseph, Father Sun - the Sun of God, the grand ball of illumination that is truly your central sun. As this co-creation occurred, and a procreation of the twelve tribes of Israel issued forth, it was breathing a breath of light into God/Man. Light. Light - what is light? It is not only a ray within your skies. It is not only illumination. What is light? Describe it. Do you have a word that will describe it? The power, the pulse of God. You carry the sonics within you to regenerate this light born Christus.

Now, Egypt, it was the land of the creation and the cultivation of the grandest civilization upon the plane at the time. It followed in the footsteps of Atlantis. Many of the Pharaohs were the grand leaders of Atlantis. Inhutep, Tut-ankh-Amun, Ramses - all of these. The golden shields they wore upon their crowns - they represented an interconnection between the top of their spinal cord and the crown area. It was an instrument to place within their own awareness the divinity that be they. A connector, so to speak, between themselves and the rest of the universe. That is how they communicated with the spaceships - with the crafts that hovered above.

As you stimulate this connection between your own crown, and the crown that is the rest of the universe, realize you are the capstone within the capstone within the capstone, into infinity. The ultimate mirror, the ultimate mystery. And whether you are the only ones of the universe or not, the contemplation of either is really staggering, and you will contemplate both polarities for a time, to experience both polarities of your relationships and your careers and your financial situations. That is a hot one these days.

Embracing the polarities, you will be embracing the birth contractions - allowing the waves to flow through you, to pulse with the pulse of God through you, to ride the wave. For indeed, it is an orchestra. The pain of your life, when carried to one higher octave, is joy. All emotion at the higher octave is joy.

The pain of birth, it can indeed be music. Sing the celestial song. Carry the harmonics to the ultimate and pierce the dimension of sound-waves, light-waves, physicality, and you will pierce and interpenetrate the crystal within the Pineal gland. You will pierce and stimulate the remembrance of the warrior and align it with light. That is literal and figurative.

Armageddon - A New Perspective.

The golden civilization that is to come, that is super-consciousness, is when you are of the awareness that the Orions are your brothers! The warriors are your brothers! They love you but they do not know how much they love you. They desire to understand love and the only way they can express to themselves love, is battle. This is the only manner they understand how power exhibits itself - through dominion of others. They are not aware that you are they. That which is you is that which be they!

And they indeed are coming into this understanding. That is why Russia is beginning to have new panaceas of experience - new governmental structures within it. That is why this nation is becoming so restricted, because it is afraid of this union. There are forces within this nation, within the governmental structures, that are of Orion [energy], the men in black[14] - those that are desirous of conquering this world, this planet. There are forces of the Black League infiltrating portions of the men in black, of the Orion energies, and are making their presence known in your government and in the Russian government and in the government of Central America, and in the Israeli forces. All of the battles that are occurring on your plane now have both elements within them.

The Orions and the Black League - both elements. And the struggle is a struggle between these elements. It is not really about people. It is not really about ideas. It is about resonances - about thought.

---

[14] In Chapter 2 - during a question and answer session with the audience - St. Germain clarifies the terms 'The Black League' and 'the men in black'. For the moment, the reader is asked to understand the 'Black League' as the energy of love and the 'men in black' as representing the energy of the alter Ego.

Now, as these two thoughts come into contact with one another, that encounter shall not, in your time, come to be conflict. The one that is of warrior essence, who desires the conflict, will bring forth instruments of battle. Indeed the lasers and the light weapons, your star war equipment in the heavens, are, by the way, already equipped for yet another star battle. The Black League, the God I Am essence that issues forth, comes into this encounter with open arms, of vulnerable breast, and love in their being.

In this encounter, with one disarmed and one armed, what do you think is the result? Would you be afraid if you were the one who were disarmed? How would you respond if a twenty-five foot titan, so to speak, and this is symbolic, not literal, came forth unto you with laser light weapons and spoke unto you to become fearful of him, otherwise he would take your life, or would bring forth horrendous experience unto you? What would you say, how would you feel? What would be your thought? This is what is called the war of Armageddon, the battle of Jehovah, although it is microcosmic and macrocosmic, because you have this battle within everyone of you every moment of your life.

It is called the war of valued life. The battle of Armageddon as it is waged within your own being. How, indeed, shall you intercede and shift the sands of time to recreate the scenario of the tapestry? How, indeed, shall you bring forth a new understanding upon the plane after eons and eons and eons of struggle? There is within your genes soul memory of ancient anger, ancient, ancient hatred and bitterness of those who were in sovereign dominion over you. Ancient, ancient awareness that you are now spilling forth, uttering within your dream states, and interweaving into your reality. Indeed, there was the land of Egypt, the land of Israel, the land of this nation, and we shall speak of it too. But I wish you to capture the awareness of the Atlanteans and the Lemurians from whence you sprang.

They were brother-sister cultures. They were of the same vibration in the origin - love and peace and harmony, and in understanding of the powers of creation. So you are also the same in the origin - one unto another. As an entity comes unto you and says unto you a harshness, an accusation, a bitterness, voicing hatred, pettiness, jealousies, desire to influence and control your life, what shall be your response? What shall be your interaction to change the tide? How can you transmute these eons of memories in one instant? What is the key? What is the word of wisdom? What is the water that you may quench this fire with? Tell me! By loving them. What is love? How does it express itself? What may you reflect to them in love? Acceptance of that which IS. Non-judgment, indeed.

Now, as I spoke to you about these warriors and battle-conscious entities of your past, what thoughts were within your being? Every time a civilization was wiped out, did you think to yourself: 'there they go again. Will they never learn?'. Were you contemplating how you would have done it differently? Did you ask: 'why don't they understand!? Why must they continue in this manner?'.

I will tell you a truth my beloveds. If you asked those questions, you were judging them. For they are your brothers and they are learning as you are learning. They are learning love as you are in every moment of your life. They are learning to be God. And how do you learn to be God? How do you express and experience God? By *experiencing* All-That-Is. What is All-That-Is? ALL-THAT-IS! Everything! Every polarity - slayer/slayee, perpetrator/perpetratee. That which is in sovereign dominion and that which is ruled. Bitterness and hatred and that which is of love.

You have all been them all. For in the experience of multi-dimensionality, you experience the opposite polarity somewhere in the universes, in the multiverses. The opposite polarity of what you are expressing now. So what you judge you are - in another reality. It is vital, it is necessary, to create the wholeness. That is what life in physicality is. To experience the sensations, the pulsations, the vibrations of what anger really is, of what hatred really is, of what jealousy and powerlust and blood-thirstiness is, so that you may also understand its opposite polarity - divine love, peace, harmony, allowance, justice.

When you think a thought of polarity, such as justice, you automatically birth the opposite polarity. Automatically you birth injustice. For within the emerging thought of the whole of a thought are the polarities contained within it. You may focus and emphasize a particular polarity in a given moment, but the other one is still existent within you. Recognized or not. And therefore, as you go forth into this new birthing of your plane, this super-consciousness as it comes forth, *allow* your brothers. The grandest mystery of life is you. Figure that one out.

Do you know when you gaze unto your brother, you gaze unto you? When you seek advice from someone, do you know what this is? It is knowing that you already know the answer but you wish you did not. And indeed, you will look everywhere else until the last resort is you. Do you know this? You are the chalice of life. To this I will toast.

As the waters begin to flow within you - the waters of wisdom, the replenishment of remembrance, the supplication of serenity, the desire, the understanding and discovery of divinity, the awakening of awareness, the understanding of unlimitedness, the perception of peace and prosperity, the taste of the Trinity - the chalice of Christus is born. To this I issue grand celebration. So be it.

(St. Germain and the audience enjoy the refreshment of some water.)

Partake of your water with gusto! You know what gusto is? Zest, the spice of life. Jest with yourself. Life is not all seriousness, heaviness, contemplation of the power of it all. How do you lighten yourself? By lightening up, hm? By becoming light-hearted and jubilant and joyous, in celebration, in dance and song. As you understand this that is in your Pineal gland, you will understand the integration of light and sound waves.

You will understand the Trinity of light, sound and its vibration called curvature, the element of line. It is the sine-wave of this vibration that comes unto your contemplation, whether you are consciously aware of it or not. This sine-wave, shall we say, will be partaking of the ups and downs of life, to experience the highs and the lows, to be upon the peaks and within the depths, the depressions and the ecstasy of experience, the polarities of life, until indeed they become integrated into a line of eternal vibration of harmony. You know this line will be the culmination of all the waves, all the wavelengths, all the vibrations of light, sound and colour. It will be beyond white. It will be golden. It will be such a golden that it will be brilliant beyond your depiction in third density. It will be truly the blaze of brilliance, of God awareness, of the burning bush - thus it will be beyond description.

You may experience it in your contemplation and meditation, or just prior to your slumber, in the hypnogoshic state. You may conjure unto yourself, not an image, but a knowing of a vibration of brilliance. Taste this jubilant glimpse of what you may be, what you may know, what you may understand as your, ye, even physical experience.

Contemplate it. The electro - the positive energy of this plane - will come to understand the magnetic, the negative of this plane, the female energy. The electro is the masculine energy. In this manner, you will be integrating the male and female, for it will be the thrusting and the receiving. The penetration and the being penetrated by.

I will tell you, this experience will create a grand orgasm for you. Sexuality in this new era will be quite different than it is now. We will discuss that in another encounter of a different kind.

Chapter 2

BIRTH & REBIRTH OF PLANET EARTH.

SECOND SESSION.

Questions And Answers - Part I.

Now, be there query at this point?

Q: St. Germain, when you were talking about the titans of Lyra, 20 million years ago, and about the many war-lords conquering the planets, at that point you referred to YAHWEH. Was YAHWEH a specific war-lord at that time, and if so, of what density was he?

This is a grand misconception upon your plane - this that you call YAHWEH of your time. It has led to many mistranslations, misperceptions, as much as the Jehovah energy has. Now, IHWH, YHWY, however you want to translate it, was the verbiage, or the alphabetical translation given to the leader of the Lyrian races at that time, and to the [leaders of the] Pleiadean races. Atlas was a YHWY, his mate was a YHWY. The conquering war-lords of the planes of other worlds, other planets were also YHWYs. It was merely a title.

For example, in your verbiage you call tissue Kleenex. Now, this word depicts a general concept of what tissue is - Kleenex, it also is a specific brand of tissue. The same is appropriate of this description for YHWY. There was one and there was the title of many at the same time. The particular entity you are referring to was indeed an entity of fifth density consciousness that came upon the lands of this plane, upon Maldek and upon Mars and established a grand civilization of his people. We will discuss this when we also discuss the land of Egypt.

Q: At that time, was it a loving energy, or a warring energy?

This particular one was a warring energy that became loving, through many battles, as you all are establishing your own understanding in your now.

Q: Another question. When you were talking about Lemuria and Atlantis, you spoke about an Orion who came from Beta Centauri and conquered Atlantis. Would that be Jehovah?

It was the forefather of the Jehovah energy. He is called Aris, which is where Aries came from, who spawned Jehovah. Jehovah was the grandson of Aris.

Q: Could you help me to accomplish this acceptance within ourselves of both the dark and the light aspects of the positive and negative polarities in all their various aspects? How may we, within ourselves, manifest the God within us, in his wholeness? How may we then also influence our governments, our world leaders, our power-hungry p... - I am being judgmental, I am sorry.

Don't be sorry.

Q: But that is the way I feel presently - the power-hungry people who are creating the chaos here - how may we somehow get them also to acknowledge both the good and the bad aspects of themselves, so that we might have peace on this world?

Wondrous query, my beloved brother. This is what we are all discussing this day of your time. When you contemplate negative energy, the dark forces, as you have termed it, it is allowing you to understand the light, for within the void, there is no light and dark. So bless it, for it is allowing you to know *you,* my beloved brother. It is allowing you to understand *what* you are, and *how* you are experiencing, and the blessings you are garnishing from them. In this blessing of them, you send forth a vibration of I Am into their atoms that resonate to it. *You awaken within them a recognition of this I Am without their conscious awareness.*

All the entities you encounter, before you utter yet a word unto them, bless them. It does not have to be verbal. Bless them with your heart. Even if it is someone with whom you have grand controversy. Before you speak words of anger, you may say 'I bless you, but I differ with you, and this is what I think of you.' Now, as you begin to unfold into your own awareness, you will also begin to align your feelings of anger and the sputtering out of all the judgments against them. I beseech you, do not judge what is within you that is judgmental. You have a tendency to do this. 'Oh, I was judging!' And therefore you judge yourself for judging. And as you encounter this aspect of yourself that is judgmental, all that is required is for you to say to yourself is: 'I was judging. I bless that aspect of myself that judged, for without it, I would not be whole. I blend it and merge it into the wholeness of I Am.' Integrate it, swirl it, caress it with the energies of love. Acknowledge it. Do not relinquish it outwardly of you. Blend it with you. Allow it to be enlightened by your light. Bring it into you. Say unto it: 'This is judgment. This is I. I love this judgment, for it is that which be I and I transmute it in this moment to divine love. So be it.' That is all that is required. If you do this often enough, it will become quite natural to you, and you will not have the experience of judgment out here, as your perception of the world, for you will have integrated it into your being, and it will not be necessary for it to be reflected out here anymore. Do you understand?

Q: You mentioned some beautiful entities. Are they in any way connected to the beings that live in the center of the Earth?

Indeed, for the land of Mu cultivated the grand inner cities. During that time, some 33,000 or so years ago, this was their grand spawning, as it were. Beneath the Gobi Desert there is a grand inner city called Aghopa - Agapa as you would call it. Indeed, the inner cities - some of them are titanic in size, but they are of light form. They are not of physical density form. If you would encounter twenty-five foot titans, you would feel quite belittled by them and quite overtaken. There are some of the inner Earth peoples who are only one foot in height. And this is the same thing. They are quite overtaken by you. It is all very relative.

Q: Do they surface?

From time to time, but they are overtaken with a bit of awe, shall we say, and they retreat. For you still have the warrior spirit, and they do not.

Q: Are they far superior in light than we?

A bit. They are fourth density and you are transitional fourth density. There are some that abide within the colonies of the inner Earth that are of fifth and sixth density. But the ones you hear about in your legends, most of them are of fourth density.

Q: You mentioned Beta Centauri. I also know of Alpha Centauri[1] - but I have never heard of Beta Centauri.

Last three stars within the Centaurian system. These stars create cultures upon the lands of other dimensions, other understandings and other civilizations that are not physical and not part of this time flow. They emerge in your now to share the light of their awareness, of their understanding, to create within your plane the reflection of all humanity, whether it be in the 35th dimension or this dimension, whether it be in another universe, or this universe. Wherever they come from, they are all your brothers and they are all equal and they are all desirous of sharing the light.

Now, Beta Centauri, for a time, was a colony of warriors who had fled to it, who indeed caused much spirit of disaster upon their plane. Those who had fled to it, desired intensely to create their power there, their technology, so that they could go forth and wreak havoc and revenge upon those colonies from whence they fled. So indeed, the divine area of Beta Centauri is now populated by the descendants of these peoples that have led, that have understood the revolution and the harmonization and alignment of the warrior element. So from war and anger came harmony and peace. That is what is upon Beta Centauri now.

All of you are of the genetic lineage of the Pleiades. When Pleija came forth upon this plane, there was within the governmental

---

[1] Centaurus, a southern constellation between Hydra and the Southern Cross; its brightest star, Alpha Centauri, is nearer to Earth than any other known star.

structure a scientist who desired to create a light-wave to interpenetrate the gene of Isis with man upon this plane. That is where the chain of genes became changed [star-seeding]. Primitive man, the Neanderthal[2] and the Cro-magnon[3], all came into transition. That is where the missing link is.

Q: When we come into contact within ourselves with what we have judged and we are moving into acceptance, into non-judgment, what is the role of our expression in that moment of time? Do we need to express that?

First of all, there is no need within God - there is desire. God is not needy. Now, it is not a movement to this really. You are already in it. You are just not aware of it. It is an unveiling. You are not going anywhere. You are awakening. You see? Now, as non-judgment is integrated into the wholeness of you, and judgment is integrated into the wholeness of you, the judgment and non-judgment of your brothers, will be expressed by *allowing* them to be limited, if they so choose.

If an entity comes unto you and says: 'I can't do this. The world is coming to an end. Woe is me, and doom and gloom', you may state unto them: 'Beloved brother, it is all a choice. It does not have to be this way.' And they state unto you: 'Oh, but yes it does.' Then you may state unto them: 'So be it, if you wish.' This is non-judgment. You are *allowing* them the opportunity to know, you are providing the banquet, the feast, for them, but you are not pushing it down their throat. You are not becoming sovereign over them with your desire for them to be free.

The greatest freedom is the allowance of others to be enslaved if they wish. You cannot free anyone from the chains or the bondage they revere. They love their experience or they would not be experiencing it. On one level or another, they are choosing it as their experience. You would say this would apply to aspects that we experience as being internal. What is the difference? It is all one.

---

[2] Neanderthal, designating a race of early man of the paleolithic period, whose skeletal remains were first found in the Neander valley in the Rhine province, Germany.

[3] Cro-Magnon, after the Cro-Magnon cave near Dordogne in France, where remains were discovered belonging to a prehistoric race of men who lived on the European continent, distinguished by their height and stature, and their use of stone and bone implements.

Do you know, my beloved, this is not *the* reality. This is the reflection of *the* reality. There is no difference. All of this is mirror. All of it. All of it. All of it! This room, your artificial lights, your brothers, your attire, your physical appearance. It is all a reflection of your own consciousness in this now moment. And as you shift your consciousness, this reflection shifts. That is what you call travel by thought. You shift your awareness of consciousness and you shift everything around you. You do not go there. In a manner of speaking it comes to you. You create it in an instant - in a twinkling of an eye. Thank you my beloved for this sharing. Indeed.

Q: I would like to clarify further the identity and the relationship between the men in black and the Black League. My understanding from what you said is that the men in black come from the Orion energy and have a negative polarity of hatred, and that the Black League comes from the Pleiades and has a positive polarity of love.

I will explain this further. The Orions are also capacitated with loving entities. There are both within the Orion system, although the ones who caused such grand proliferation of information on this plane are the ones of the negative or disharmonious vibration. Now, contemplate the word black. You judge this word greatly, do you not? 'Black is evil. It is of the devil. It is bad. It is horrendous.' Do you know what black really is? There are several things that it really is. First of all, it is mysterious. It comes forth from the knowingness of the darkness of the womb - the female energy really. The womb from whence all things are created, the void, that which is not known, that which you are afraid of when you contemplate it.

Indeed, there is a power that abides within the womb, that is awesome. Once this power is sensed, it brings forth fear within the breast because entities do not understand the awesomenesss of this power of creative energy. That is what darkness means to certain entities and that is why the darkness of the inquisition and all of this brought itself forth in the burning of witches at the stake, the creation of the Catholic Church, of stamping out what was beyond conscious awareness, what was telepathic or kinetic, what was of spiritual conception. Not physical conception, spiritual conception. What is that, hm? Precipitation, materialization, out of apparent nothingness. That is what you have termed to be magic and it was polarized into black and white magic. Black magic came to be known as bad and white magic came to be known as good. Black is absorbent. It absorbs energies. That is what a black hole is. It absorbs energies of universes into one point of eternalness.

Now, how can you release the judgment of black? By understanding that it is simply a flow in one direction that has not understood the reversal of the polarity into the other direction. It has dammed itself up and created a ceasement, an awareness that has suffocated. All you need do is breathe life into this blackness. Release the flow of the dam. Complete the circuit of the energy by *blending* with it. Reach out your hand, your heart, and complete the circuits, then you will allow the black, the void, the mysterious essence of life, the absorbent energies, to flow into you, the gold of God. The golden aura of Christus. In this flowing through the gold it will transmute itself into white. The white and the black will be blended and intertwined, and they will be brilliant in their intertwining.

Fourth density, according to many of you, does not have the polarities of negative and positive. But in reality, they do. There is a fourth density masculine energy and a fourth density physical energy. But when they are blended with the golden energy of Christus they become lightened, brilliant. They become less dense, less heavy. They become aware a bit more of what they are.

Now, white is the reflective principle, the combination and union of all the colours of the spectrum. It is the rainbow, the prismatic understanding as being altogether undifferentiated one from the other. It is the opposite of separation. It is the opposite of absorbency. It is the opposite polarity. White has been given forth to the masculine energy upon the plane. The sciences, the structures of the churches - why indeed would you consider that they dress themselves in white?

The scientists, your physicians - it is the masculine energy of control, the reflection of power. But they do not absorb the power. They do not understand the black within them at this point. *The key to non-judgment is the understanding that all contain both [polarities].* You are the element of the white *and* black. The Black League *and* the men in black. The Orions *and* the Pleiadeans.

Q: Then the men in black from Orion are of the opposite polarity to the Black League from the Pleiades?

The men in black, as you would term them, are only upon *your* plane. It is a recent structure - since about 1600 A.D. or so - on your Earth.

Q: Are they the same as the Illuminati?

Indeed, the Illuminati[4] sprung from this. However, there are two Illuminati. There are the Orion Illuminati and the Pleiadean Illuminati. The Illuminati has been given negative connotation. At times when I speak about the Illuminati, I speak of it in the connotation that you are contemplating in that moment. The golden Illuminati, the Pleiadean energy, which is the Black League - again upon your plane - are also the ones who are the ascended masters coming forth to interpenetrate from the inner core of your structures - all of them - the

---

[4] The original Order of the Illuminati was a secret order of the Jesuits and the Franciscans and was called the 'Alumbrados', which means 'the Enlightened' or 'the Illuminati'.

The 'Order of the Illuminati' referred to here, of today, (the Bavarian Illuminati) was formed on the first of May, 1776, by Dr. Adam Weishaupt, a German Freemason, a Master Mason. His six main points to form a New World Order state the abolition of: 1. Ordered or nationalistic governments, 2. private property, 3. inheritance rights, 4. patriotism to national causes, 5. social order in families, sexual laws and moral codes and 6. all religious disciplines based on faith in God.

The Illuminati of our present time are found mainly in seven interlocking societies: 1. The Round Table Of Nine, 2. The Council On Foreign Relations, 3. The United Nations, 4. The Trilateral Commission, (America) 5. The Bilderberg Group (Switzerland), 6. The Club Of Rome, 7. The Royal Institute For International Affairs (England).

There are of course further off-shoot societies as there is, for instance, the Fabian Society. It is most interesting to note that the emblem of that particular society is a wolf in sheep-skin. Their major objective is the abolition of private property.

Most members of one society are also members of one or more of the other societies.

It is to remember that the Illuminati's objective is a dictatorial World Government, in other

bureaucratic understandings and your government, to allow the light to be brought forth from the centerpoint, to expand into a supernova.

Q: It seems to me that usually the beings from the Pleiades with a positive polarity are referred to as the White Brotherhood. And I see that there's a potential confusion in the use of the term Black League.

Confusion? Co-fusion, fusion with All-That-Is. Did we not speak of this? We certainly did. The white and the black are really the same. That is what the whole point of this discussion is.

Q: One further question. That is: Are the men in black from Orion and the Black League from the Pleiades third density human beings?

Some of them are and some of them are light beings.

Q: So some are third density and some are fourth and fifth, and higher?

Indeed. The ones who are terrorizing this plane of your now are of the physical density. The war-lords such as your Iatolla, and the ones within the governmental structures who are squelching the information about your brothers in space. There are other things, concerning this which we will discuss later. Indeed.

Q: Could you explain a little further - the daughter of someone who changed the name of the star system to Pleiades, Pleija? Who was she the daughter of, and why was that name change necessary, and then why did she go forth as a warrior?

She learned from her father the only knowingness that her father presented, as you teach your own children. The fearful leader from the area of Lyra - after they destroyed themselves, and after the

---

words *absolute* power. To the uninitiated the names in the lists of members of these societies are enough to make 'one's skin crawl', for many of them represent the most respected and honoured figures of global public life.

To finally and actually implement their *New World Order* a reason, or foe, is needed, like a global disaster of sorts, which would justify the forming of a World Government which then could step in 'benevolently' and 'take care'. Such disaster has been designed by the inner circle of the Round Table Of Nine: A world-wide financial collapse, for this would justify to the masses the implementation of a cashless society, which - in truth - would represent total control, therefore total enslavement.

destroyer comet came forth into this area of your skies - this was a leader that took with him the grand ships and peoples and wandered aimlessly within the cosmos for a period of time. This particular entity is referred to, in certain translations, by quite different names. One of them is Esis.

Q: Why did she change the name to Pleiades?

That is what all leaders do. They change the name of the lands they conquer to their own.

Q: What was her name then and how do you spell it?

Pleija is how you would spell it.

Q: My impression was that the father of Pleija was the fifth density war-lord known as YHWY.

That was the title. All leaders of the Pleiades were called YHWY.

Q: I was thinking about the specific one who...

This is not the same one. The YHWY that you desire to understand was a war-lord that came forth upon Maldek and caused the destruction of Maldek. Indeed.

Q: I have been, in a sense, disturbed, because my desire is to know, through experience, if in fact I have lived before. Is there a technique that you can give me so that I can practice it and eventually come to the experiential knowing of it?

Let me ask you a question? Have you experienced what some call deja vu?

Q: Yes.

That is not always a past experience. At times it is a future experience. At times it is a parallel universe experience. At times it is an experience of your soulmate. Now, living 'before' is only the acknowledgment of the eternality of the soul. If you would consider that you were birthed into this Earth, that you cease your embodiment, and you cease your existence forevermore into a smattering of nothingness, into a black hole of nothingness, then that is alright. You will understand later.

Q: I don't feel comfortable with that conclusion.

Alright. Whatever you wish. Now, this plane reigns supreme with human free will. If it is your utter desire to understand your experiences, focus not upon the past. Focus upon all dimensions. Multi-dimensionality, simultaneity is exhibited within the vibration of any memory. For as you remember one life, you are also remembering concurrent other lives at the same time that are overlaid upon that life. Past life regression and therapy and all of this - it is wondrous. It is what you call a grand springboard or stepping stone but it is not the unlimited manner in which to understand the alignment of your being, and harmonious representation within this life. For when you contemplate the millions of lives that you currently exhibit within, the millions of universes - now - not past, not future, NOW - the millions and millions of diverse experiences that you are having not only through you but through your soulmates, it would take eons of time to explore every life. So you see, when you merge them all into one instantaneous, magnificent, glorious remembrance, you have the element of transition within your palms, within your breast.

Q: How can one do this?

Experience familiarity with everything you do. As you speak a word, know that you have spoken those very words before to the same energy - not necessarily same person, but energy. Know that you have gone forth upon this plane in the very same pathways upon the ground, not only before, but later, and alternate nows - that you visited the inner Earth, and when you have a direct attunement to what you view, such as many have had with the grand tales of the star wars, and the grand tales upon your [television and cinema] screens, of the previous battles in your history of life, and you resonate to them, and you feel familiar with it - know that you have been there.

You would not feel familiar if you did not identify it as your own experience. For there would be no identification if there was not a resonance within your own being to identify with. That applies also to entities that you feel you have known or encountered before. As you come unto them and you ask yourself 'Have I known you before? You seem so familiar.' In this case, the answer is always yes! You would not have the question if it were not so. Indeed.

Q: You have spoken several times of inner Earth beings. I have read that the Earth is hollow and that the openings to the Earth are 1,400 mile wide holes at the North and South poles. Is that true?

There are several understandings of what you term to be the inner Earth. First of all, there is a certain void within the core, the centerpoint of the Earth. However, this is not the inner Earth of which I speak. *The inner Earth that I speak about is a different dimension.* There are corridors from the crust to the core of Earth - electromagnetic connections, through the light rays which resonate from the core to the crust of the Earth. As you pass through such a particular area they transmute you into that time. It is like a time tunnel capable of transporting you to a different dimension that is super-imposed within the center of Earth. Do you understand?

It has the same space as Earth, but not the same time. The space/time is different. Therefore, the experience within it would be perceived as familiar and at the same time unfamiliar, for you are experiencing two dimensions at once. You understand?

Q: So the poles then, of the Earth, are covered?

The poles of the Earth are entrances to these corridors - both of them. The axis of the poles, as it were, is not the same as it was. The corridors have shifted. Some of them have been sealed through the grand transitions of Earth, the catastrophes and cataclysms of Mother Earth in her torrential experience. Indeed, you may transmute the seals and open the rivers of their wisdom unto you through thought. Open sesame. Do you know sesame? Do you know what this means?

Q: Somewhat.

A grand, grand leader of another world came forth and his name was Sesame. The peoples of the land desired to have communion with this entity and yet he remained isolated. And those people, in their earnest desire to have communion with him, would gather together in circles and resonate and would think with their heart - this is the merging of the mind and the soul: 'Open Sesame, open Sesame, open Sesame' to allow communion with their grand leader. For they desired not to be in dominion. They desired to be of equality and they desired not to establish war. Therefore, through thought energy, they brought forth this communion. It is truly a grand thought vibration where you may open Sesame within your own being. Is this of assistance?

Q: Yes, thank you.

Thank you, my beloved brother.

Q: Are there many mountains in Sedona that have a certain frequency enabling ships to go in and out?

The Sedona area is a white hole from whence energy is coming forth. It is spewing forth likened unto a geyser. It is an area that was and is and shall become known as an opening unto the inner Earth. The mountains - there is a reason they are red. The redrock area - here is a tale of curiosity for you. The core of Earth, before she was shattered and wounded by the asteroid during the Atlantean culture, was in the centerpoint of lead, iron and nickel. The very core of the centerpoint was iron. It was the central sun of the Earth. During the chaos of the plane, when the Atlanteans brought forth their destruction unto the depths, there was a shifting of the core and the Earth's surfaces. The iron spewed forth unto the area of Sedona - the central sun is partly exhibited here, that which resonates to light - that is why it is a white hole. It resonates to the vibration of brilliance. The iron that is exhibited within the mountains, the rocks around here in the area of Sedona, is oxidizing. That is why it is red. It is also illustrating a remembrance of the vibration of Atlantis, for the peoples of Atlantis were red. They placed themselves within the vibration of red upon their skin, because red is the ray of war.

So, the red rocks are a monument to an ancient civilization. They do not come from Atlantis, but they were born because of the fall of Atlantis. They come from the central sun of Earth eons ago. Honour them, for all of them are points, are resonances, are vortices, as it were, of energy pulsations that are directly attuned to the central sun vibration within you, allowing the ultimate creation of your own centerpoint into a white hole. Bask within your own central sun as you view these mountains and rocks.

The Navajo and Hopi cultures, they are the peoples who are genealogically and genetically of the lineage of the land of Atlantis. Their ancient records and crystals were brought forth unto America, Central America and South America; they came also forth into North America. They kept and maintained these instruments of wisdom in the sacred storage grounds of their peoples until the time is of ripeness for them to be revealed. They are within what you call Superstition Mountain - why do you think it is so superstitious, hm? They are truly also within the rivers of the area of red rock. They are beneath the water. There are caverns beneath the water - crystal caverns. They were brought into the eastern coastline area and given unto the Iroquois nation which passed it on from medicine man to medicine man to medicine man, through the centuries.

Now it is here within the southwest area of your nation that is the birthing point of Earth, from whence the Earth will begin contractions of labour. Why do you think there is such grand tale about catastrophes - quakers and tremors? This is where the contractions shall begin. But they will emanate all over your world, so there is nowhere that is safe, if you are within a fear vibration. *If you are within a love and power vibration, everywhere is safe.* Everywhere, everywhere! Even the bottom of the ocean is safe, for you can transmute the electrums within the water and partake of the oxygen molecule within it. If you understand your power, you can disconnect the atoms from one another and re-integrate them. You can indeed imbibe the oxygen and exhale the carbon dioxide.

That is how the dolphins existed. The dolphins were upon the land of Atlantis. Do you know this? They did not have the embodiment that they have now. But they understood how to live within the water. They had their craft beneath the oceans - their grand cultures and civilizations were beneath the water. They mingled with humanity and merged and blended with land and water. That is where the aqualung was developed. The Atlanteans were beginning to understand how to breathe beneath the water, how to develop the transmutation of the molecules.

Now the dolphins are here again. They are assisting humanity in the birth process of life. Through their love and joy they remind you who you are. Have you ever watched one of the dolphins? They behave as though they have not a care in the world and truly they do not. They swim along the sine-waves within the waters. They dance. They complete the circles. They dance upon their tail and spin the web of wonder. Laughter is their vibration. Their squeals are really likened unto your giggle and they are light-hearted. They vibrate grandly to the resonance of children, for your children have not yet allowed the veil of forgetfulness to be closed around them. Truly, you will find some of the dolphins being destroyed, but they are not really. It is their desire. There is a plan to all of this. There is not really chaos upon the land. It is confusion - fusion with All-That-Is.

Now, the dolphins are ceasing their embodiments beneath the waters to re-embody upon the land, to bring the light as a brother that you may embrace and understand and identify with. When you see an entity that is joyous and dancing and there is a sparkle in their eyes and they have a desire for the water, and they gaze unto the heavens of the night and allow the diamond glitter to be reflected in their own eyes, in their own awareness of themselves, and they are elfin of soul and they create joy with everyone they come into contact - bringing the light to Earth - this is a previous dolphin. This is a present dolphin. This is a future dolphin.

Now, there is another history, there is another universe, the Daal Universe, from whence the Pleiadeans now gather their assistance. The Daal universe is the origin of the Dolphins. It is *Daal* as you would spell it and it was translated into your present verbiage as dolphin. It is a Daal with fins. There is much wisdom within your language, you know, if you will only but see it.

Now, by the way, do you know English is not really English - it is anglish. The words have a vibration and angle to them, a resonance, a geometric pattern. Language is merely a local version of a vibration. It is a local resonance. The dolphins have a language of their own - do they not? English is only a community consciousness of vibration. It shall become the grand planetary language. It demonstrates more than any other language that which it contains. Such as what I have been telling you - confusion: co-fusion, recognition - ignition of awareness within you. Co-ignition with the awareness with everyone else - re-co-ignition, doing it again, remembering it again. Now, the English language contains many of these vibrations of awareness. Much wisdom is within a word. It is an encyclopedia within itself. The translation from other languages will be brought forth merely by a vibration, and at times translated into a symbol. The Tetrahedron is a symbol. It is an equilateral pyramid, as you call it. Equal, balanced, polarities of fire energy, culminating in a point of unity. The triangle, or pyramid, is a trinity. Male/female God I Am. It is all symbol and it is represented by a translation from another knowingness, from another language. The Egyptians were grand and wise and they wished what they wanted to communicate be understood by all languages, only by a symbol of that time.

The English language, as it demonstrates prolifically across the globe, will eventually disappear. You know why? You will become telepathic in your communication - thought communication. The symbols will be birthed forth within your recognition, and you need not verbiage to relay it. You will be so exhilarated that you will not have to speak as fast as you are thinking. You will be able to communicate in thirty seconds what would take, in your time, thirty minutes to communicate. So your language will begin to disappear and so will the pyramids and so will all the grand monuments upon your plane and so will the globe itself, as they all begin to ascend.

Q: Concerning dolphins - how do you feel about bringing dolphins to a place like Arizona. Is it cruel to take them out of their ocean?

That would be their hearts' greatest desire. Do you know why so many of the whales and dolphins have beached themselves? It is their utter desire to reach out to their brothers, to be known for what and who they are - equal brothers of humanity. They desire communion. That is why they have been so assisting. They are abiding, very patiently and lovingly and allowingly until you recognize who they are. They come unto you to assist you into this knowingness in whatsoever fashion they may offer their assistance. Truly, when swimming within the tanks of the scientists, they at times wonder when their brothers are going to catch on. The dolphins are grand assistants in the birthing processes, for they already have the vibration of children. So when you have your birthings, in the future, have the dolphins within the same water of your birthings, as water birthing becomes prevalent upon the land. Would it not be wondrous to have a sibling with the umbilical cord yet uncut, unsevered, nestling and nuzzling the dolphin? That is the beginning of the awakening of this awareness. And do you know why your babes can exist within the amniotic fluid without drowning? Because they have a valve within their lungs that closes, whenever they are born, within a few moments of when the umbilical cord is severed. But this valve is open when they are in the womb. *They* are open. They are not closed. There is a symbology here.

Indeed, when the dolphin is within the water, this valve is open as well. All that an aqualung is, all that existing beneath the waters and breathing is - is allowing yourself to have conscious awareness of this valve, and have it resonate to your thought at the moment. And as you choose, so it is with that valve. As you open your awareness, all parts of you will open. Indeed, be there query?

Q: What about flying? I feel that in the future I will be able to do that.

You can already do that. Flying - what is it? It is aerodynamics. What is aerodynamics? What is dynamics? Combustion and interaction. Dynamo - what is dynamo? It is an atom that explodes. Dynamics is a thought that explodes. Aerodynamics is exploding awareness of what is in your atmosphere, the molecules, and the molecules within you to allow yourself to be light enough to create your conscious, shall we call it, swimming within the molecules of the air. Soaring is no more than allowing yourself to play with the air in this fashion. You will come to understand this. The lift of the wing - what is that but lightening? Your wing-span is increasing, my brother. You know what allows you to fly? Spreading your wings to allow your breast to be vulnerable. That will allow you to fly. *Only through vulnerability in allowance and love.* Non-fear. Fear will close this flight.

Do you know, the Wright Brothers, when they developed the grand aeroship of your previous times, they were considered quite mad. They were quite pitied by your brothers. They were ridiculed, condemned and ostracized by society. 'The bicycle brothers have gone off the deep end.' But alas, they allowed the universe to understand the culmination of their vision and so can you. You too can pierce the veil of ridicule, injustice, severance and ostracism of society, and be in knowingness of all.

I will toast for a moment, then we shall continue.

Q: A very brief question - can I take your picture?

Where would you take it to? 'Take' will become anachronistic in your verbiage, for 'take' is a word of limitation. You may capture the vision of what you think be I, for this is not that which be I. This is an embodiment that modulates itself according to my energies. But I wish not to be revered or captured within any image that will be placed upon the wall, and become an icon. That I do not desire. I desire to free you unto your own vision of God. If you wish to capture upon film the vision of this embodiment, so be it. But know that it is not I.

(A member of the audience offers St. Germain a glass of water.)

In unison: I AM, I LIVE, ALL IS, I LIVE ALL THAT IS. SO BE IT. It is always a most grand experience to partake of refreshment.

Q: Have you tried wine?

I do not try anything. I am. Indeed I have partaken of your grand ruby. The ascended grape, as some call it. That is a new one for you, eh?

Questions and Answers - Part II.

Indeed, experiencing the separation from your families and the dichotomy within life, is no more than the disintegration in preparation for reintegration - the dichotomization in preparation for the reunion, familial union of the family of humanity. Now, as you feel the separation, know that you are always interconnected by the atom called God, by the resonance and vibration of the I Am within your being. You are connected to everything. You know my beloveds, your family - it is not really a family. It is a relationship that you experience within this physical dimension. But how many families have you had in the millions of lives you have experienced? How many of them have returned again to this plane? All are your family when you pierce the time continuum. As you feel separation and scattered energy, you only feel the grand emphasis on polarities coming forth to complete the circle of I Am. So do not judge it. It is merely preparatory. Notice it. Allow it. Love it and be in joy. Alright?

Q: I have a sense that part of my soul family is in other dimensions, and I would like you to comment on that.

Your soul family is no more than the understanding of the thirteen original separations or divisions into coagulated thought called light. Soul family is no more than all the aspects of soul energies, fragments of your soul energy, soulmates, as you call them, in all the dimensions - every one of them.

Now, there is soul family upon Earth. There is soul family upon the rest of planetary and stellar understandings of the universe. There is soul family within other dimensions of this Earth - the inner Earth, the parallel universe called Earth. As you experience your soul family, as *you*, as cells of the body of *you*, you will not experience division and separation anymore. You will only experience unity. For indeed, labelling is for pickle jars, not humanity. It creates further separation. That is what I meant earlier when I spoke of many of you considering your lives as a grand searching and seeking for the perfect manilla envelope in which to file yourself. You wish to label yourself and your brothers.

Q: Do you know Elizabeth Clare Prophet[5]?

I am aware of this that you are speaking about. This entity is one that comes upon the plane to illustrate a certain fragment, an understanding of wisdom that has come forth in this dimension, this

---

[5] For the convenience of the readers unfamiliar with that name: Elizabeth Clare Prophet claims to channel St. Germain.

awakening process. That which be I is merely a resonance, and she blends her own consciousness with that resonance and allows her own fears and inhibitions to be demonstrated within it. This is alright. There is reason within it if you perceive beyond the limitations.

What you experience before you is the energy *only* of that which be I. For *this* is clarity of that which be I. There is not a blending.

Q: St. Germain, how were the pyramids in Egypt made?

Gravity and anti-gravity. I will discuss it later when we discuss Egypt and Jerusalem and all of this that is the history of the Earth.

Q: St. Germain, I have some questions about crystals. I am fascinated with crystals. I find them in the area where I live.

Alright. Crystal indeed is the mineral version of Christ consciousness, *Christ-all.* It is a reflection of what you are seeking within yourself. *There is nothing ever placed within a crystal unless it is etched.* Consciousness is of yourself - the power source is of *you,* not of the crystal. You are as powerful without it as you are with it. It is an assistant, but it is not necessary. And it is only an assistant if you are aware that it is unnecessary.

Now, your fascination with them is because you are awakening to your own *Christ-all* within you. The crystal tissue here within the Pineal gland and the crystal that your entire embodiment represents, the Christ-all. There is crystal formation within every gene of Isis within your body, within every atom of your body. Of course you are fascinated with it because it *is* you. It is contained within the very essence of you.

Q: St. Germain, I live in a town that is known all over the world - it is Las Vegas. There is a lot of wonderful energy there. There are those that are enlightened who come in and try to talk about how negative it is, and there are those who are enlightened and who, for some reason, can't leave. We know that there is something greater there and that is why we were brought there in the first place, by our vision. Could you please share the energies that are there beyond the strip, beyond the tinsel town?

Tinsel town - the city of silver, hm? Las Vegas - what does it mean?

Q: Tomatoes ?

But where did the word come from? The Vegas - the star system of the Lyrians. This ancient consciousness that established this community within the desert that was not a desert then. It was a garden, a meadow. So was their own land - the Lyrians'. Truly, negative and positive is exhibited within the city of silver. Truly, it is a place, a point that you may acknowledge within your own being by the very essence of the existence around you - non-judgment. What is it that you call strip? What does the word mean? Separation, pulling apart, allowing also the other polarity of the word to come forth - unveiling, peeling. Understand both polarities of this city, of this strip.

Now, what is contained within it will reflect unto you whatever you wish to understand in that moment. It is a mutually accorded encounter. All encounters always are. So whenever you are being judgmental, you are also calling the city negative. And you wish to understand the resolution of this polarity. That is why you call it unto your awareness. Alright? This indeed is a grand opportunity to understand non-judgment, the merging of the polarities.

Q: There's all the testing going on - nuclear testing...

It is no more than the men in black who are splitting the atoms, smashing them into one another. We will discuss that later. The atoms containing the gene of Isis are being propelled into infinite rapidity unto one another, into collision. This is an area, a panacea of time, the land that existed before the Lyrians came forth. Contemplate what I speak unto you. Become aware that you shall be a light, a beacon within the silver. And reflect upon the silver your own lustre. Alright?

Q: St. Germain, since we are talking about the Lyrians again, I am wondering if this presentation would be an appropriate time to tell us more about your incarnations as a Lyrian.

I was before the Lyrians and that vibration created the consciousness of that which be I. I was one of the scientists for a while, I was one of the priests for a while in that time. I always desired the love and peace within that era of time. Also I came to understand war - what devastation it wrought. But know, my brother, that that which was alternate I also was a war-lord, one of the YHWYs. You cannot have God without both polarities.

Q: Do I understand that you were one of the titans at one time?

At one time. But I had collected the fragments together to create the consciousness that you identify as that which be I in your now. The Lyrians, my third generation above - my great, great grandfather, was the establisher of the Lyrians within the area of Vega. Partaking of this, and the long life-spans - thousands of years of life - I had understood culture to culture to culture, civilization to civilization, war after war after war. I have been both a war-lord and a peace-giver, as all of you have been. And indeed, I became part of the Black League within the area of Maldek. I brought forth the light to interpenetrate the area, and I beseeched them to hearken and hear my words, to come to an understanding of peace and harmony with their brothers, to merge and unite as a global nation, within their own being. It fell upon the void of the wall of darkness they had placed before them. Indeed, they destroyed themselves.

This has occurred time after time. Even upon your plane I came forth to plead to the monarchies [as St. Germain] to not bring revolution and rebellion, but indeed to bring peace. This I speak of was within the [French] revolution. But it was not heeded. And I am here again. And I will continue to be here.

I tell you this: Even when super-consciousness occurs I will also return to third density Earth to speak to them of peace and harmony, until this entire universe has become a supernova and explodes into instantaneous ascension. The entire universe.

Q: I would like you to clarify something that you spoke of earlier about Alpha Centauri and Beta Centauri. Were these part of the same civilization at one time?

They were colonized by parts of the same civilization. But they were great distances apart from one another. They had [then] hyperspace travel in the later Pleiadean times. They allowed transition from one area of the universe into another in but a few moments in time, and colonized.

Q: So there is really no relationship between Alpha Centauri and Beta Centauri.

There is, because they are of proximity. It is likened unto Mars and Earth. They are stars which are close to one another. When one is colonized, the others colonized by the same essence.

Q: So it is my understanding that Alpha Centauri is actually closer to us than it is to Beta Centauri.

That is why there were different races springing forth upon Alpha and Beta - because they were also colonized by the races who were upon Earth, who had come from different areas of the galaxies to populate them. It is a grand melting pot - this universe. The severance, and differentiation and labelling of one another will continue separation, for you are really all the same. You are really all one grand colony within this galaxy, within this universe.

It is very much like your United States. When an entity asks you: 'Are you Indian? Are you Caucasian? Are you Oriental? What are you?', and you very defiantly state that 'I am an American.', you are becoming aware that there really is no difference between the races, that you are all One. An American - Am & Can, an I in the middle.

Q: I have a particular book they have banned in Canada. It has to do with the relationship between the United States and Russia - where we have colonies on the back of Mars or something like that. Is this true?

Not only colonies upon Mars, but the Moon as well, to establish them as space bases, but they became disillusioned with this idea after the star wars instruments became implemented within the heavens, and they understood annihilation. Mars has had Pleiadean and Lyrian experience upon it. Your power-brokers have access to this information through the Black League that have been there and given it to them. You see, your grand brothers of the bear country, Russia, they are the opposite polarity of America and the two are converging into the apex, the capstone of the pyramid. They shall become One. The space race - it will not really be a race to accomplish travel in space. It will be an accelerated movement toward merging. The space race will come to be known as a grand scrambling into what you would term to be a hotel when there is no vacancy.

Q: Second question - are the people who live there truly lobotomized?

Not in the sense you refer to, but in a manner. Lobotomized is not the word, the verbiage, for it illustrates a physical scrambling. But what is a scrambling? The Pineal gland - it is an etheric scrambling, a confusion, a co-fusion. Do not judge it, my beloved.

Q: St. Germain, with regard to the colony on the Moon, someone mentioned once to me that his missing children and all these missing people are somehow involved and are being directed in that direction. Could you enlighten that for us?

There are some of the so-called missing children, who choose to go forth to teach the brothers of space about life on the Earth. It is a mutually accorded desire - soul conscious, at times. It is not necessarily always conscious. But some of them go forth into their playgrounds in the evening of time and gaze into the grand heavens in the sky of night and see indeed their reflection and say unto the stars: 'I wish you to come down to me, twinkle, twinkle little star. I would desire to play with you.' The unlimited of your children upon the plane of now will be the grand teachers, reflectors, mirrors, leaders, demonstrators of your future Christs born indeed. For you see, when you place a child within a multi-cultural area, a multi-racial area, they do not become prejudiced. They play with all of them as equal mates. They really are mates. They do the same with the brothers of space. That is why there are so many children that are so-called chosen, although they are really mutually chosen. And you will gaze into the sky and say the same thing: 'Come unto me. I desire to have communion with my brothers of space. I desire to see one of your grand crafts. I desire to partake of the adventure.' But do you know why they do not? Because of your definitions, your labels, your judgments. How can you blend and merge with them in joy when you judge your neighbour of a different colour or education or culture, or even within your own family - a different religion? A different understanding. Learn from your children. They will teach you much. You think you are their teachers, hm? You are teaching them about limitation.

Q: Channels are very popular now. Why does Jesus not come down to talk?

This is a grand illusion - that which you call Jeshua. He indeed is coming forth from time to time, but what is Pleiadean in its origin of origins of origins, is surfacing with emphasis now. You call it popular. It is not really popular. It is identifiable. Resonance of familiarity of an ancient, ancient memory eons ago. And as you are awakening to these thousands of years and millions of years of history that you brought forth unto this genetic code, you will indeed resonate to that which was within you in the moment of that encoding. I was part of that encoding process in that experience of consciousness, which was a grander consciousness than what you call Le Conte de St. Germain. That is a label you place upon a mere fragment of it. That is not what be I. But you may call me whatever you wish.

Q: Do you have another name you would like to be called?

I Am. You are I Am also and so we are One, and mutual reflections of one another. In time, all will come to be known as I Am, including that which is I. Indeed.

Q: I thought for a few moments about space travel. Why would one from the third dimension be taken on board a ship and taken somewhere? What purpose would it serve? Why?

Most of the ones who experience this are simple people. Many of the Peruvians, who are re-embodiments of ancient Incas, all those that are bringing forth new life, new light unto the world. When they experience unfamiliarity, it is human nature to be afraid. Therefore, a capsule is placed around them by their own consciousness. In time, after a few visits, as you call it, it does disappear and not reappear if the fear dissipates. But it is the simple people, because they do not have all these pre-conceived ideas about what the brothers of space are. They do not have the desire to revere them, as in your culture eons ago, when they appeared in the land of Atlantis and ancient

Samara, which is Egypt. They are allowing the brothers of space to abide in equality, after the fear dissipates. It is through these simple people that your brothers of space can allow the flow of wisdom. That is why the American Indians have been the guardians of the tableau of the Atlanteans. The simple ones upon the land, the ones who are in non-conflict, who are uncomplicated, unseparated, are the ones who will be the bearers of light. That is part of the reason this being was chosen as the instrument. [Reference is to Azena]. Simple. Do you understand?

Q: Yes.

Thank you my beloved brother. Indeed.

Q: I understand in Sedona there is a very advanced community of the New Age to be developed here. Can you tell me anything about that?

It is one of them. It is not the only one by any means. For even within the steel curtain, there will be communities of light to be the example to the rest of the world. Sedona is not a chosen place. This is a place. It is only because of the electromagnetic vibrations that are here that it is a place at all. It will allow the flow of all these vibrations from the central sun of the Earth to enable the electromagnetic flow of the Earth to shift. Then you will have the grand tremors. We will discuss this later, as the birth of Earth is realized. Sedona in the time to come will be a civilization beneath the water, within twenty years or so. Do not let that bring fear into your breast, my beloved. Indeed.

Q: What is the relationship between dolphins and porpoises?

They are relatives - one unto the other. The Sumerian race that came to be known as Hebrew, the olive-skinned peoples - they are born of the same awareness. So is the porpoise. It is merely a different configuration of body.

Q: I just have a question about how you are responding to us. Do you see our molecular structure, or are you responding to us in the physical sense, like we choose to experience ourselves?

First of all, when I come into this dimension of Earth, Terra, I bring forth a resonance of thought. When I allow the capacitation of this embodiment with thought vibration, with the intertwining of resonances of that thought vibration, it becomes animated. And when indeed the breath of life is breathed, the energy within the atoms of the embodiment become ignited with the fire of this breath of life. The eyes, as they open and unveil themselves, gaze forth into a brilliant, splenderous display of constellations, intergalactic stellar representations of God. *I see your light.* And as I gaze unto your light, I focus and I see your auric field, the rainbow within the gold. As I focus further into density, I see coagulated matter, your embodiment. As I focus even further, I see the reversal occur, and I see the blood pulsing in your veins, and the wind as it whips through the lungs and indeed, I understand the pulsations and vibrations of your colonic illustration and the waters of life as they purify and clarify themselves within your kidneys. As I focus further, the reversal continues and I see the grand central sun within your being, the origin of your soul. And focusing even focus further, there is no separation. You and I are ONE. The universe, the circle of life is complete, Oneness. Does this answer your question?

Q: Indeed.

Q: The creation of clouds - I know they have great meaning. Would you like to comment on that?

Cloud formations are merely the representations of the waters of life within the sky. The opposite polarity of the oceans as displayed within the density of water in the buoyancy of the clouds. Often, what you consider to be a cloud formation, is not cloud at all - it is a craft. It appears as though it is a cloud, from time to time. But it is not. It is of light and matter, atoms within the energy vortex of the craft itself. Some would call it shrouding or shielding, and some would call it merely a cover of energy.

Q: What is the blue corona?

The covering, or skin, as it were, of your etheric being, your soul. The corona, the energy of anti-matter and matter, shall we call it, around the physical body. Before the auric field is the point of horizon for you, the perception point. That is where the third eye sees. It allows the corona of you to ignite the Pineal gland. The channel I was speaking of before, that which brings forth its hole, its hollowness, between your crown and the Pineal gland, goes forth in a ninety degree angle out at the frontal area of the forehead. It ignites in the moment of its encounter with the blue corona, which allows you third eye perception or telepathic understanding, or vision beyond this density.

Now, I shall depart hence and greet you after your bellies are full. As you thirst, quench that thirst, quench that thirst with your memory. Awaken the eons of dreams of your history. Unveil the life, the light, the love of God that you are. So be it. And again I exhibit unto you my honour and continued joy in the sharing of the gift of you. Thanks be to you, my beloveds. Until another now. Namaste.

Questions And Answers - Part III.

Be there query?

Q: St. Germain, you stated that Jehovah is of Aryan race. Could you clarify that? I don't understand what that means.

It is the vibratory frequency of the Orion energy which we have discussed earlier this evening of your time. When the Lyrians and the Pleiadeans came forth to conquer the Orions, the Orions and the Pleiadeans interbred in the Orion constellation. The Orions came forth upon your land and instituted themselves and they married the daughters of men.

Q: What is the difference between levels and densities? Is this one and the same, or is it..?

The unlimited response to that is: everything is one in the same. Now, I will explain that in an understanding that you can accept and absorb. Levels are variances of vibrations within a dimension. It is a certain frequency band, and the scope of this band consists of many different vibrations, they are all different levels. When you come to the point of merging into a different frequency band, which is called a different density or dimension, then you have other levels within it.

There are levels within levels within levels, as there are chakras within chakras within chakras. Alright?

Q: I have a question basically about fear. Possibly about discernment. Recently I was in a group where we were practicing channelling and an entity came forth and was teaching us. That entity identified himself as being of the Christ line and having a certain work that he wished to share with us. This was very well-received but at a certain point there was a fear response within a particular individual. It may have been wider, but it was voiced through a particular individual. The question I have for you is: Can you tell me as to the motivation of this particular entity that identified himself as Ca, and how we can use our discernment in terms of the teachers and the energies that are coming forth at this time?

I would most joyously share with you your reflection in this manner. Ca is a vibration of the fire energy. Indeed, it brings forth the expression that it is Christus - all is Christus. All contains a polarity of Christus. Awakened or not it is there. Now, how do you discern? Discernment in your definition is clarity. Clarity is perception of all in non-judgment. Now, how do you tell if it is harmonious? Resonate with the reflection. Understand its vibration within you, of excitement. Fear is a sort of excitement, although it is of the vibration of altered ego.

Now, all that is reflected before you, in what you encounter in your teachers, in your brothers, your communion, everything - it is for you to understand as mirror. That is why it is there, or it would not be there - for you to gaze into the reflection of it without judgment, to know *you*. Clarity is the understanding of non-judgment. As you gaze forth into the mirror, understand that they are divine in whatever they are creating and experiencing. Allow them this and you free them and you. Know your own vibration. Know your own power. *Do not become dependent upon another entity for truth*, for all truth is truth. You are the ultimate truth of you. Dependency is allowing yourself further and further and further separation from God.

Always, I come unto you because I wish to share with you as an equal brother, divine being of light that recognizes your divine beingness of light. I allow this communion with joy and celebration, and I wish you to commune with your brothers in like fashion, always.

Now, there are some limited reflections upon the Earth plane, for that is part of the polarity of physicality. But to love them is the ultimate wisdom, regardless. Do you understand? And 'what should I accept, and what should I not?', accept All-That-Is *as you*. Accept all you experience *as you*. It does not mean that that is the only truth, for all truth is truth. Do you understand? Indeed, my beloved.

Q: You say we know all things within us. Could you tell us how to ask ourselves, so that we can get that answer?

The only question is: what is? The only answer is: I Am. In the ultimate understanding, the only question is: I AM? And the only answer is: I AM. Know that you know and you will know. That is a paradox, but it works.

Q: Could you tell us more about Jeshua?

Jeshua Ben Joseph contained the twelve vibrations, the twelve tribes of Israel. In this understanding, all the constellations, all the civilizations, all the cultures came forth within this genetic understanding. Jeshua was the birthing point, the flashpoint, the two thousand year point or so of the shift. This shift was the beginning of the cycle of blending the polarities of consciousness. About sixteen hundred of your calendar years ago, the Pleiadeans came forth again upon your plane and made themselves known to a few, very surreptitiously, very gradually, to re-introduce awareness unto this plane, of what was misinterpreted and mistranslated and misunderstood of the teachings and reflections of Jeshua Ben Joseph. They appeared for a short period of time to seed this awareness within the peoples of Earth, so it would unfold into super-consciousness, into the ultimate birth of it. It is now germinating into grand fruition. The birth is near. In another day likened unto this day of your time, we will discuss birth changes. That is not only the Earth changes, but every sort of change you can encounter upon the plane and beyond the plane. And what it is to really know, to carry the light. Alright? Indeed.

Q: Prior to being human, were we ever animals?

Animal form is a part of a fragment of soul energy that is of divine God essence, but it is created of a different electromagnetic understanding. It does not have the thought process that you term humanoid. That is why Cro-Magnon man and the Neanderthal did not come to fruition. The lobes of their brain were too emphatic with survival energy, warrior energy. The caveman had such a vault of the brain, so large, that it was difficult to birth the female [energy] through it.

It came to extinction because of its own focus upon war and how it responded in the brain area, in the skull, to the formation of consciousness. All animal form has divine knowingness according to the electromagnetics created within their brain area, although they are not the same [energy] as humanoid. They are a fragment of the same energy, but there is not what you would call transmutation and transmigration of this fashion, changing from a woman to a feline, a cat. Now, there is such a thing as light being changing form, but it retains human consciousness. You can have the form of a cat without the consciousness of a cat. That is one who understands molecular structure and the manipulation of it.

The change of shift of form will come to be known as the shift in consciousness. What has been called magic in other cultures is only a shift of consciousness. That is all magic really is. That is what we are exploring this evening of your time. When you understand the essence, the core of what I give unto you, you can experience or have anything you desire in that moment.

Q: What do I do?

You do no thing. You *be*. And in that doing nothing, you do all things. It may sound as though it is a piece of philosophy, but it is really a poem of divinity. What you experience as 'doing' upon the planet, is going forth forever, forever, forever within the busiment of some activity and it becomes quite distracting, unless you understand the beauty within the journey. For the destination is really the pathway. That grand adventure that you call controversy and diversity - that truly is the grandest experience of wisdom, understanding of magic, shift of consciousness. For in the controversy, you encounter the polarities and you have yet again, a gift, an opportunity to blend with the polarities, to enjoy what you previously considered unenjoyable - to love the unlovable.

Q: As we approach the end of this presentation, I would like to ask one more question regarding the subject of the rebirth of planet Earth. Katumi is quoted as making several statements: One is that the planet Earth is the only planet in our solar system in which third density life is active at the time. And he goes on to say that the transition time involves several different transitions, several different completions simultaneously. Not only the completion of a 2,000 year period of the Piscean age, but also the completion of a 26,000 year cycle and he goes on to say that in addition to that there is also the completion of a 206,000,000 year cycle. He says specifically that the cosmic guardians have decreed that at the completion of this 206,000,000 year cycle, which is the period of time that life has existed in our solar system, no life below fourth density will continue to be active in our solar system. Could you give us a reflection as to the validity of these statements?

Alright. Cycles - there are cycles within cycles within cycles. There are many, many, many different cycles that are culminating in this now. The reason for the focus on planet Earth, and for all the galactic confederations coming forth unto this area of your solar system, is because this universe is in the shifting of densities. *Planet Earth is indeed at the exact mid-point of the phase shift.* From evolution to involution, from the creation of the universe through a supernova to the ultimate involution into a sun to be born yet again to create another universe.

This Earth is the exact midpoint of that cycle. That is the two-hundred million year cycle. Now, what you experience upon the plane of your now, the shifting and all that is occurring is not only of third density. It is also occurring to the astral body of Earth, the etheric body of Earth, and the soul body of Earth. Your solar system is indeed the ultimate understanding of a universe of humanity and this planet called Earth is the only one at this point in time - time/space - in which there are third density Earth beings, humans.

Now, I did say within this time/space. There are other third density Earths, parallel universes. There are other third density planets within other star systems, other galaxies. This particular solar system is born of a sun that brings forth its brilliance *as your light reflected*. It is reflecting the culmination of *your* light. It is a memory. That is a paradox. You will begin to understand the art of creation of the universe and how you, yourself have created this universe with your thought. For a moment I would like you to keep the focus on this particular rebirth of planet Earth.

As the Earth births, the universe births. The same thing is occurring within the universe's consciousness. As you are a cell within the body of the consciousness of Mother Earth, Earth is a cell within the body of the consciousness of the universe.

Q: You have recently indicated that 1987 was the completion of the first half of the transition period of approximately 44 years and 1988 is the beginning of the second half of the transition period which will apparently be completed in approximately 2010. Would you care to...?

These particular dates are all the time shifting, because consciousness is shifting all the time. It is a flux. It appears that it is somewhere between 2010 and 2013 of your now. There are many, many, many tales within the tales of your history. Many, many, many histories within your history. And as we continue our communion together in your future time, we shall explore them in detail.

This day of your time was a bit of an overview - what do you call it, preview? And we shall have the debut, as you call it, of your awakening revealed unto you every moment of your future. Listen to your thoughts. Listen to it. It is telling you something about yourself, about from whence you came, about to where you go, about that which you are. Listen to one another. Hear them with your heart. Heed them with your soul, for they are you and you are they.

The ultimate understanding of all of life is I Am and you will come to know this. That is all there is really, in this tale that I tell you. You are God. All the rest is commentary. And how you love commentary!

I am here to allow you to know that you already know. I understand who you are and I am here for *you* to understand who you are. What else is a mirror? And in this reflection, I shall depart. But parting is sweetness and sorrow in the same drop of now. Dance with dire circumstance. Fleece yourself in friskiness. Partake heartily of humanity and heal the wounds with your own wisdom. Heal Earth with the birth of you. So be it.

You know, in departing, in this particular experience of now, I shall take wings unto flight and soar unto the forevermore. Join me, if you will. It will be a journey of jubilation. Go into the night sky. Gaze unto the illumination therein. Blend and bask within the brilliance that is the mirror of you. You are I Am! Forever be I Am! Forever know I Am! The ultimate God of creation, the OM of life. Farewell. I really do not wish to leave. But it is of the ripeness of time. The grapevine of your consciousness is heavy with the words. And as you whisper these words of wisdom to your brothers upon the Earth, remember to tiptoe through these tulips. Tenderly and gently caress your brothers into wisdom, not forcefully.

Love, light and laughter - the trinity of divinity. Your wishbone is my command. Your funny-bone is yours. And always have a laugh up your sleeve because that is where your funny-bone is, you know. Be buoyant, light-hearted, like children. The children of Christ. Namaste, which is an ancient Sanskrit understanding: the God I Am of my soul salutes forever the God I Am within your being. Farewell.

Chapter 3

CELEBRATION OF THE ATLANTEAN CATACLYSM

Greetings my beloved brothers and sisters!

You are all becoming united of your heart seals, allowing the light of you to come forth and enshrine one another with the love of God I Am. That which be I comes forth unto you to reflect unto one another in the lake of love, to allow yourself to perceive the beauty beyond the surface reflections, the treasures of the depths within. Indeed, limitation is becoming unknown, stress, frustration, your endeavours to provide the prince of you with the provisions of prosperity. This is passing away as ancient Atlantis did upon your plane thousands of years ago in your time.

We shall discuss Atlantis in detail. The fall of it, the ruin, the destruction, the utter devastation of it. However, it is desirous to mention at this point in your time a few things for you to understand the wisdom that is to come forth this evening.

There is a grand fire that burns within you all. It is the torch, the light, the God I Am flame. That indeed comes forth in the convergence of the ever now moment, the eternal now, the God I Am of you. This fire is burning brilliantly within you, and *the divine fire always follows the path of the most resistance,* not least in this case. Those aspects of you that are most resistive, that are indeed non-desirous of merging into the All-That-Is, are where the fire desires to burn heartily and glows to be seen and felt within your essence.

Now, this fire will continue in this manner as long as there remain within you aspects of resistance, non-merging aspects, until all is in Oneness, all is attuned in union with the source of you, with the God I Am of you.

This fire also generates fear upon your plane, fear of the dreaded. The dreaded of your now is the financial institution, the economic situation of your kingdoms upon the plane.

That indeed causes frustration within the heart seal of many entities. But you know, you need not be under the weather about your life experience, in a limbo, when you know the essence it represents unto you, the symbol of it.

Do you know who was the grandest financier of the Bible? Noah. He floated his stocks when the entire world was in liquidation.

Now, that you are all aligned with laughter we shall continue. Bouncing of the jest, as it were. You know, the Illuminati, which you also call the Anti-Christ, which is also the attunement to the Jehovah energy, is coming upon your plane. They indeed understand the manipulation of your economy, and how to spawn fear within the entities who are participating in world mass consciousness. Now, many of you judge these entities heartily and heavily. Judgment is not merely a word. It is a sentence. Indeed, only when you partake of this judgment do you require an antidote. And you are all partaking of judgment in your now.

This is the antidote. The Illuminati, the Federal Reserve Board, as it were, is born of yourself as well, the ancient Atlantis. It was the Orion energy that is representing itself here on your plane in order to understand yet again what be the power. It understands not divine love as a grand power source, the connection to the grand creative force. It understands only manipulation and exertion of its sovereign powers, sovereign essence, free will, as it were, over another entity. Indeed, this is a symbol of powerlessness. It [the Illuminati] will come to understand this very soon in your time, and when it does, *it will resort to dramatic oppression,* because it feels and fears its powerlessness folding in on itself. This is the point of harmonious merging. This is where the unification point occurs, the flashpoint of the flame.

There will be a spark igniting the catalyst that will create an emotional chain reaction among the peoples of this Earth. The catalyst, the spark, will be the understanding, the recognition that the separator and oppressor of the peoples is not the Illuminati, is not the Anti-Christ or the Jehovah energy. It is the Separation itself, that is the barrier between the peoples. The Illuminati are merely the symbol that it represents. That which is of physical, tangible, creative essence upon your plane, to demonstrate and experience limitation, are the Illuminati. It is accommodating you in allowing you to understand what it is and to love it, to merge with its essence. To become one unified harmonious whole with it and not to create barriers, boundaries, resistive points or oppression. To create only a harmonious union and release the shackles that it has wrapped around itself all these eons of time. This indeed will be the harmonious resolution of the new Atlantis.

The Illuminati were very instrumental in the Atlantean destruction, the conversion of its essence into the waters of the ocean. It is of vital importance for you to understand how you can bring forth a harmonious resolution for this era of time, this understanding of another illustration of God understood.

You see, the fear broadcast, the warning or prophecy upon your plane, it is not a sentence that has been passed. It is merely an opportunity to understand mass consciousness in that now moment, that now moment only. The next now moment is born anew from the fiery form of the creation of the now moment before. Indeed, all is anew in each moment. You can choose to create what you desire to experience. You need not have the disharmonious collapse of your financial system. *You may have as your experience a very harmonious resolution.* It need not be according to your belief systems of old in your time, the Piscean era. Your belief system, the knowingness you harbour within your breast, which creates your environment, your reality, your experience - it may indeed be the unlimited perception. Nothing else. What you know, you bring forth into your experience by *believing it into being!* Indeed, as you desire to be free from the economic institutions and the threat of collapse, *know* that it shall be harmonious, that it shall be brought forth from your sovereignty *because* of it.

Currency is a symbol. It is not your energy. It is a symbol of your energy. Bring forth direct interaction with one another and it will enhance and facilitate interactive global economy. Indeed, become the grand example with one another. Understand gold as a symbol and understand what it represents: energy, as a symbol of your own energy, your own power to create. You need not it. You need not any sort of symbol. You may create and manifest the experience without currency, gold, or whatever.

In the interim, while you are discovering this for yourself, know only that your oppressors and the manipulators of the economy are merely representing a reflection of you. They are not to be judged. They are your brothers. They sprang forth from Atlantis. They were within the temples beside you when you were bringing forth the light in that era of time. You may allow yourselves harmonious representation upon this plane again in your time, by allowing your love to entorch them into knowingness, to unfold the blinders that are upon them, to allow them unlimited perception as well.

Atlantis, it has come to be known as a crystal cathedral, a citadel, indeed, a celestial citadel. It was very large in continent form, but it was not a continent. It was an island. There is a difference in geo-physical definition here. The island was grand and massive and it spanned an area of approximately 77,000 square miles. There were several islands, multitudes of them, scattered about the large one. Atlantis was located in the Atlantic Ocean. Indeed, it was the Atlantic bridge continent. It brought forth illustrious representation unto the Earth. It was the grand connector-plateau between Europe, Africa and North America.

It was splendid in its representation. It had upon it a grand mountain. This mountain is called Atlas. That is where the term Atlatian came from. Atlatian and Atlantean are synonymous. They are merely different translations of the same derivative. Indeed, Atlas was a grand column and it appeared to hold the sky up, as it were. That is where the legend of Atlas originated. It was cloaked and shrouded and wreathed in a smoky billow of cloud above it. A silvery cloud that was splendid and glowing. It appeared to hold up the sky.

It was in the form of a mushroom top. Many of you have seen them [these types of clouds] within the heavens [mushroom-clouds]. They also are the shrouding of the crafts of your brothers. This has come to be known in your time. It was also the same in that time.

The land of Atlas, the mountain thereof, it was the home of your brothers, the Pleiadeans; it was the temple of the Gods. It was an abode of divine energy, in the form of a Tetrahedron, an equilateral pyramid. Indeed, that was the original pyramid. It was the prototype for all the rest of the pyramids. It was a terraced temple. What you call step pyramids retain the original form of that prototype.

Within the mountain the lava swirled within a glow. It was not an active volcano, but it did glow heartily. The cloud above it reflected that glow and it was also reflected from the snow-capped peaks and so the blaze brought forth the remembrance of burnished gold; it appeared to be capped in burnished gold. This was retained in the pyramids thereafter.

Indeed, that is where the covering of the pyramids in gold, in lavish form, came from - the remembrance of the glow, the remembrance of the divine resonance of light that issued forth in fiery form. That is also the origination of the capping of capital buildings in gold - the capstone of gold.

The grand, glowing summit could be seen from distances untold - the mountain of Atlantis. Indeed it was light. It was a beacon for the peoples of the world. That is what the capital buildings were meant to be - a beacon point, a lighthouse, satellite white houses as it were.

Now, the formation of the pyramids was also retained in your culture that is now represented upon the churches and your religious structures as steeples. In this form it came to be understood as the spires of the cathedrals, the mosques and the minarets.

There is much within the culture of your now that is representative of the Atlantean era. You remember but you do not know what it is that you remember. You do not even know when you are remembering. You merely experience a ghost of a memory. But the sage within you whispers and echos and flickers. Immerse this eternal wisdom of you with the fire of your heart and embrace the fingers of that flame.

Experience your now in harmonious remembrance in the light of the God of you. Drape yourself in the rainment of remembrance this evening of your time. Recall echoes of ancient awareness, and as you do, you will become healed.

You are indeed the healers of humanity and in the healing, you shall also be healed. All shall be absolved, and all shall be brought forth into the resolution of the era of God, the age of Aquarius. It need not be woebegotten. You know, we never promised you a woes garden. Promenade among the gardens of God in the awareness of who and what you are and the power represented within your own being to create, to bring forth merging and not battling and warring - to bring forth love and not hatred and jealousy and pettiness and greed and power-lust. For that is what your fear that your economic situation is a catalyst of. As it is aligned, so also is the rest of the Atlantean memory aligned.

The Orions and the Pleiadeans are rampant upon your plane in your now. They are integrating, to harmoniously interact and interweave their essences. Integrity is integration. It is the integrating of the elements of God in a harmonious fashion so that the integrity of the GOD I AM is maintained.

The God of Atlantis in your legend of time came to be known as a terrible God, came to be feared, came to be known indeed as rampant with hatred and spitefulness. Therefore, the legend carried forth the experience of sacrifice and a thunderbolt was known to be the instrument of his terror. But it was not a bolt of lightening. It was a bolt of laser energy. It was translated into a bolt of lightening in the eras later. The sacrifice was accomplished by slaying the entity with a symbol of a thunderbolt and allowing the burnt, sacrificial offering to be risen up into the temples so that the Gods may be satisfied.

The glow is not all that was contained within the mountain. There was also a smoky mist, as it were. This is the origination of what you now call incense - the smoky mist of this grand mountain. For it poured forth a beauteous fragrance. Its aroma was of sweetness, was of wisdom, was the channel of the God I Am of you.

Now, this sacrifice, it has become known as the lore of Atlantis, it was the origin of what is now called the Hallowe'en celebration. For it brought forth much fear and trepidation within the breast of entities, and much judgment as wickedness, as paganism, as that which is non-God I Am. It was merely an aberration of a different perception of God I Am. And we are bringing it forth into merging in your now, knowing indeed that there is no limitation on the Earth.

The crash of the stockmarket - it was not really a crash. It was merely redistribution of resources. You know, there is no lack upon your plane. There are merely different perspectives - a shifting of perception. This is what is occurring with your judgments of what is evil and what is to be feared; it is to be understood. It is a shifting of perspectives into the wholeness, into the unity of it all. To allow the unfoldment as accorded to the divine desire within your own breast, the birth of the new Atlantis.

The star wars which was implemented by your King called Reagan - there was another star wars. This is the star wars of the new Atlantis, and it can be aligned as the other was not. We will discuss this in detail as well.

There was crystalline technology upon the plane that allowed entities to place their hand within a beam and obtain all the knowledge and technology in that manner, by absorbing the frequencies. This was their school, their university as you call it. They placed their hand within a beam and that is all. Now, that is also attuning the cells of the embodiment, the atoms within the cells, tuning them all up, as it were, unto a grand symphony of wisdom in a particular field.

There was much technology rampant within Atlantis. It was a divine institution for wisdom to be perceived, experienced, and understood in a tangible fashion. Not only in an etheric manner, although they did become a bit - how do you term it? - airy fairy - at times, but indeed, to allow divine experience in the beauteous representation of tangible, concrete form in physicality.

The crystal technology coming forth this time on your plane is but the tip of the iceberg. You will already perceive it in your nation in the next four or five years, for it is indeed the new Atlantis. It is following in the footsteps, as it were, and we will illustrate how in your later time.

The experience of heritage, it is within the breath of Mount Atlas. Indeed, what was housed within the walls of the mountain was the wisdom of eons of the brothers of light. The keepers of this wisdom were the Pleiadeans. It was the original temple, house of worship, as you call it, house of light, love, and divine awareness. Support offered forth eternally in the light of gold of God.

Now, the wisdom contained within the walls was understood by the peoples of the temple, the priests and priestesses. They were the brothers of the light. Then this wisdom came into the hands of the technologists and the governmental officials, those that had power-lust in their breast.

This is where the tale of terror begins. This is the culmination of human nature. Both in the goodness of the heart, in bringing forth light and of the desperation of the Alter Ego, the clinging to fear and hatred and desire, coveting the power of another.

Now, the star wars in your now, it is already instituted within the heavens. It is the crystalline technology, that casts forth laser power as it interweaves in a lattice fashion, covering your nation and the continents of your world, like casting a light net across the nations so that they are captured with laser. They indeed will be brought forth into forbearance if this star wars machinery of your now is not aligned. The star wars of your ancient history was Atlantis understood. An ancient battleground.

There was a celestial body - an asteroid, and it came into an orbital alignment which was in the evening of time, at dusk when the heavenly bodies that you call Earth, Moon and Venus were aligned. This asteroid was deflected into the orbital pattern of this Earth. It was indeed enhanced through the gravitational fields of Venus and the Moon, towards the deflection into the Earth's orbital pattern.

Now, these scientists upon Atlantis, the technologists, they were aware of this uncommon phenomenon, and they were desirous of establishing their crystalline technology on this asteroid and therefore intended to capture it with, what you term, tractor beams. Allowing it to be brought forth into alignment, to hold still, as it were, and be captured into an orbit of the Earth, likened unto another moon. That was the desire of the Atlantean scientists. They felt their laser power was powerful enough to capture this asteroid body to encircle the Earth and place their instruments of war upon it so that the entire Earth plane would be at their submission, would indeed be their kingdom. This was their hearts' desire in that moment. It was a grand one.

There were many who were aware of what their desires were, shrouded as they were. And they counselled them and laboured to bring forth wisdom and love of their brothers, to exist without interference, without dominion. But yeh, these entities voiced powerlust and their desire to rule the empire of the world, and, indeed, it was at the threshold of their fingertips, so they felt.

So they set up their grand instrumentation which was experimental. It was not, shall we say, a laboratory in nature. Therefore, there was no trial. They felt, therefore, that this was to be a great maiden journey for their new laser technology. The dolphin in that period of time was embodied in a different fashion, but it was the same sort of consciousness. They came forth and counselled and pleaded with the entities to give forbearance unto this asteroid and allow it to continue its journey in the celestial heavens. They said nay to this and went forth with much confidence and strength of conviction that they were now the new rulers and masters of the Earth plane.

Your brothers, the Pleiadeans of the mountain of Atlas - the Atlantis of your new era to be born yet again - they held counsel among themselves. They understood what was to occur. They also understood beyond the understanding of these scientists that there was to be a deflection of the laser ray, that, when encountering the asteroid, it would be deflected and collide with Atlantis itself, *in addition to the asteroid.* They counselled whether or not to alert the Atlanteans about this oncoming disaster.

However, they decided to allow the scientists to understand the wisdom about interference and they went forth and brought many of the records of wisdom into the temples of Egypt. The wisdom of the ages encoded in hieroglyphic form, a terminology not understood of your day, not understood of the language of that time, in that era, because they desired not the same occurrence until the wisdom was captured. This counsel was allowed and aligned and so they extended this understanding unto the entity called Noah, to go forth and craft himself a grand ship, a grand ark, as it were, and to go forth in the shining light of his own essence and be patriarch of the new land, to bring the genealogy of the Atlanteans and the Lemurians into the new continents to be dispersed.

This was done and the casting forth of the laser rays, it also was done. It deflected the light of the laser ray and indeed, the asteroid was damaged, it captured the blast, and it brought forth its essence into the atmosphere of the Earth plane in grand fashion.

The asteroid was about six miles in diameter and it was travelling at a rate of about eight miles per second[1]. When it encountered the atmosphere, it lit into a grand blaze. The blaze was blinding. The energy coefficient of it was eighteen thousand degrees Fahrenheit. The Sun's surface is about ten thousand degrees Fahrenheit. That will give you an idea of how blazing the light came to be upon the plane.

It was a flash that existed for about two minutes of your time, and its explosion into two pieces lasted about the same time. It came down over the Atlantic Ocean and embedded itself in the ocean floor near the Puerto Rico plateau. There are two grand holes there now - about twenty-three thousand feet in depth. This is the impact.

The continent of Atlantis was quite in shock. There was much disarray. They frenzied, panicked, and there was some fleeing. Indeed there was some flight by ship. The impact brought forth the rubble of the smaller structures travelling behind the asteroid. Because the impact was loaded with so much heat, so much tremendous potential power, everything it touched immediately vaporized and therefore there was an enormous vapour of gas emission in that area beneath the surface of the Earth. Tremendous sub-terrestrial power was released throughout the Earth plane.

---

[1] 8 miles/s = 28,800 miles/h or 46,080 km/h.

The Earth's crust was brittle and fractured and all this power created rumblings beneath the surface of the Earth throughout the globe and there were risings and lowerings of the Earth's crust in this fashion all over the Earth. That is why there were many Atlantises - the submersion of many continents in some fashion or other - in this timing, until the platform of the islands and the continents gave way, and indeed brought forth a grand volcano, which spewed forth fire into the air.

The impact caused a tidal wave of grand fashion - two thousand feet[2] in height were the waves. But before they could reach the coastal areas, there was the emission of the volcanos in that area. There was a torrent of magma spewing forth unto the heavens. A tower of light, a pillar of fire, going forth beyond the Troposphere into the Ionosphere. It was of such impact that about four hundred and eighty thousand cubic miles[3] of magma were emitted from the volcano of this area called Atlantis. As it spewed forth there was the crashing of the waves and the hissing of the steam quenching the fire and this occurred all over the Earth plane, but in particular in Atlantis.

The magma that spewed into the atmosphere was carried by storms and torrential tornadoes as they enshrouded themselves in mushroom clouds of steam and ash and dust emitted from the volcanoes. What was of volcanic action was set off in a chain reaction. *Every volcano on Earth became active* to release the pressure from the gases beneath your subterranean understanding.

As this came forth into the air, it was swept into massive clouds that became black as night with amber glow because of the ash and the dust. Massive indeed - and they accumulated their size in tremendous speed. They became the size of continents and hovered low across the continent. It was overcast. It was dark as night. Your land, the Earth plane, your beloved Terra, was shrouded in fog for five thousand years after this. There was no Sun to bring warmth into the land.

---

[2] 2,000 feet = 610 m.

[3] 480,000 miles³ = 1,966,080 km³.

The tidal waves crashed into all areas of the Earth plane and funnelled into the glens and valleys and flooded the forests; *and then came the cold.*

The asphyxiating gases travelled across the Bering Strait and were followed by arctic cold. This continued for five thousand of your years, until the warming occurred due to the dispersion of the mists, the shroud of gases, dust and ash. The ash of Atlantis was funnelled through these clouds to all areas of the Earth, so if you, in this day of your time, pick up a clod of clay, it could have been touched by the dust of Atlantis.

The platform of the island of Atlantis sunk ten thousand feet[4], not only the land itself, but the bottom of the Earth floor that supported the island sunk ten thousand feet. It was a gradual disappearance. This occurrence lasted about one and a half of your days and this translates into about one inch per second of your time.

Now, through the impact of this asteroid body, the Earth's axis experienced a rotational polar shift of about two degrees, and this is still so in your understanding of this day. So the temperate primordial forests were brought forth in the south, and the pole of North came northward. The cold was of the northern hemisphere.

The pulse and blast, they were two different ones. The first one caused the jarring and rending of the continents from one another. Until this time they were all connected, they were all unified, harmoniously joined within their essence. The impact brought about their severance. They were ripped and torn from one another and they went eastward and westward, separate. That is where the separate Eastern and Western philosophies came from. That also began the polarities in this fashion, of Alter Ego and Divine Ego, in the manner they are represented upon this plane in your now.

Now, the separation of continents, the continental drift, as it is called, originated from the Atlantean destruction. The second blast went in the opposite direction. It was an echo of sorts and indeed the shock of this created many fragmented islands around the nations because the Earth was brittle in the crust and therefore created a

---

[4] 10,000 feet = 3 km.

fragmented appearance. The second blast caused the widening of the Atlantic Ocean, for it was much narrower in that day of your time. The wailing and mourning on the Earth plane could be heard many, many dimensions from this one. It was the mourning of humanity for a lost civilization of God.

Then there were the storms, the rains, the heavens breaking open their hearts and allowing their tears to run from the breast of the Earth, and allowing Mother/Father principle to mourn for Mother Earth. And indeed she did. The tidal waves and the torrential rains, in their union, they brought forth much flooding and destruction and damage upon the plane. The sea level, around the Earth plane rose approximately an average of about three hundred feet[5] world-wide.

Also the glaciers shifted and broke apart. This was caused in part by the polar shift. However, they did not melt right away in your time, not immediately. It was about five thousand of your years before they dissipated, when the breaking of the dawn came, and the warming of the temperature. The Ice Age was really the Atlantean age. The present era is the birth of a new land of golden warmth in the understanding of God Divine Essence within the Ice Age of your now.

The ice is not apparent upon the plane now. The ice is within your hearts, and it can be melted and merged with, very much like the snow and the fire melt into one another. The fire within your breast can merge with and melt the ice of another's heart, and that is how you become unified. That is how the manipulators become one with God Divine Essence. Their ice is melting.

Now, many of you remember, but you do not remember. This event of cataclysmic proportions has been engraved upon the hearts and memories and souls of all humanity. But they have forgotten. It haunts them. They have dreams about it. There are relics and echoes and shadows within their experience whispering about it. But they do not understand these whisperings of wisdom. This is brought forth before you this day in your time for you to understand, for you to embrace it, for you to capture what it is that you have experienced,

[5] 300 feet = appr. 100 m.

and indeed, enlighten, inflame the world with your new-found knowingness, with your new understanding of what be you and what be your Earth plane, and what be this new Atlantis.

Indeed, to bring the fire of the mountain of Atlantis, and the golden glow of it, to bring it forth for all to see and understand for your own divine example. Burnish yourself with this wisdom and you shall be indeed the refined gold of God.

The entities who were the scientists, who desired to capture this asteroid and bring it forth as a space base, with crystalline formations of laser weapons, these were the Orions. They are your brothers. Indeed, they are also part of the Illuminati, the ones that are - shall we call it - manipulating the financial picture in your time. They are the ones that you must love and embrace, that you must come to understand that it is not their desire to hurt or harm, but their desire to understand their own relationship with the creative essence. They do this in the only manner they understand in their experience of their now. It is for you to reflect unto them a new awakening, a new knowing, a new understanding so that their hearts may be opened and indeed their power may come forth. Not in the manner presented as powerlessness, but as power sourceness.

The dolphins are yet again on this plane to experience, to assist, as they did in your before time. They are your brothers as well. They are also of Pleiadean essence. However, all of you are from many different places in a galactic understanding, so do not place too much emphasis on this. Your origin is your own heart in your own now. What you define as a beginning and an end is placing limitation upon your Isness. You are eternal and so is everyone else. So the labels of Pleiadeans and Orions and Arcturians and Sirians and all of this, are temporary. For they are merely labels, and they too will pass away.

The Sun, for eons of time, has been worshipped and in this worshipping, it is the recognition of the divine power of God - this gold of divine power within you to come forth and bring it unto the Earth, for healing, for warmth, for the creation of new life, the presentation of brilliance. Bring it forth in your understanding. Be the

Sun of God, in more ways than one. That is the new Atlantis exemplified.

Questions & Answers

Is there query?

Q: St. Germain, was there genetic manipulation in a way of engineering at that time to allow physical vehicles or entities to be able to survive underwater or, for example, to be winged in essence - the way the foetus goes through those changes.

Genetic bio-engineering in crystalline technology was rampant at the time.

Q: And would that perhaps be what gave rise to a lot of our mythological beliefs?

That is part of it, but that is not all of it. Within that era were the winged creatures called Pegasus[6]. They came forth to understand merging with humanity. It was a sort of desire to bring forth new light and new knowingness onto the plane after the destruction of Atlantis. There was also some manipulation therein as well, for the Grecian culture was aware of that understanding [genetic engineering] as well. They were born of Atlantis. There were survivors from Atlantis and they went into the Mayan area. Later they indeed sprang up in Greece and Rome. The Egyptians as well were part of the Atlantean culture.

Q: Like maybe pre-Druid in England?

Indeed. The day after the fall of Atlantis is celebrated as the day of the fall of the Druids. Indeed, it is celebrated as the Sabbath of Witches.

The day of the fall of Atlantis, called November the first, that indeed was the understanding called 'All Saints Day'. The day after

---

[6] Pegasus, in Greek mythology, a winged horse, said to have sprung from Medusa when she was slain by Perseus and to have caused to spring from Mount Helicon the fountain of perpetual poetic inspiration called Hippocrene; hence, poetic inspiration. (Webster).

the fall of Atlantis is 'All Souls Day', for it was a commemoration of the departed souls of the grand deluge and catastrophe - the destruction of Atlantis. It has come to a celebration of many sorts of commemorations now in your time.

There is much wisdom to be understood through these celebrations. When you understand what occurred in Atlantis, you will understand many of the legends upon your plane now. The Greek legends and those of the Romans, the Mayans, and what is contained within the Mahabharata[7], that which is contained within the Indus Valley, the Hindu tradition, the Moslem and Islamic tradition. All of your folklore - indeed, all that exists upon the plane now in your time - was spawned of Atlantis.

Q: Could you explain the relationship between Atlantis and Lemuria?

They were dichotomized representations of the Source. The Divine Ego of you, the unlimited allowing love energy of you, is represented by Lemuria. The Atlantean understanding is sovereign, power-oriented. It was of the left brain understanding, rigorous in attitude called scientific technology. It was the masculine aspect and Lemuria was the feminine aspect.

Q: If Atlantis was affected as it was, was Lemuria not also?

Indeed. However, Atlantis is given so much credence in your literature and culture. They are both together at-one-ment in bringing forth wisdom unto you. Atlantis was a continent. Lemuria was a grand ship.

Q: A what?

A ship of light [star-ship]. It had its partaking upon this land. It did bring forth its presentation within the heavens. The land called Mu was a ship. That is why you shan't find it upon the Earth plane as a civilization. Atlantis is buried beneath lava, soot and mud upon the bottom of the ocean. It indeed may be excavated. When Atlantis falls, does it rise again? Indeed. [Metaphorical reference]. You are living proof of this. When the rain falls, does it rise again? In due time.

---

[7] Mahabharata, one of the two great epics of India, written in Sanskrit about 200 B.C.; it combines stories and poems with history and mythology.

Indeed, all is cycle of life. All is a resplendent journey yet again and again.

Q: St. Germain, how did the Earth become populated?

The grand entity Noah went forth unto the land. There were other civilizations that were not so dramatically affected as that of the Atlanteans and the Lemurians. and they re-populated also. The American Indians are your red-skinned peoples, witnesses to the genealogy of Atlantis that was dispersed. The Atlanteans were also red-skinned in a manner. The Egyptians, the Peruvians, the Incas, they also came forth from the land of Atlantis.

Now, Noah brought forth his siblings to create many of the races that are now upon your plane. He brought forth, when reaching dry land, a covenant, a knowingness, with the God divine creative essence that is All-That-Is within the seven-fold spectrum of the rainbow. Seven-fold. There has been a documentation in one ancient record that is housed within the archives of this nation, within the Smithsonian Institute, that links that which be I to that which be Noah[8], as the patriarch of the world. But it is not documented in your history books. Neither is any of this other wisdom that is being brought forth. This too will change.

Q: After such a violent happening in the world, it surprises me that civilization still existed throughout the five thousand years of the ice age.

They were hardpressed. The mammoths were frozen in the ice. Many of the smaller animals - the insects that crept upon the ground, they were swept away by the floods and incinerated immediately by the volcanic ash. You see, the heat within the atmosphere was heavy-laden upon this plane. There was a golden glow within the wind of the Earth. The atmosphere is now clearing in a manner that it can be clarified in union with the celestial heavens without the Ionosphere. You see, you all dread the Ionosphere's disappearance because you fear radiation. But do you know, the Ionosphere[9] will disappear and

---

[8] During another discourse St. Germain mentions Noah as having been one of his incarnations.
[9] Ionosphere, the outer part of the Earth's atmosphere, extending far beyond the stratosphere and consisting of a series of constantly changing layers of heavily ionized molecules. St. Germain refers here specifically to the dreaded disappearance of the ozone (O_3) layer.

you will not be harmed because you will be in alignment with the Sun.

Q: What is the Ionosphere?

It is a protective layer of the Earth that absorbs the radiation of the Sun. You know the ash and the dust within the clouds that were dispersed upon the plane - they are quite rapid in the accumulation of electrostatic particles. Therefore, they became charged. There was lightening and thunder rampant within the skies all over the plane. It rendered the heavens quite enormously brilliant through the golden glow; the amber glow of the lava spewing forth and the lightening as it illuminated the devastation upon the land.

I was desirous of speaking about the Atlantean culture, this evening of your time, and the demise of it, as it were. The Phoenix is born of the ashes, the dust of the volcanic ashes of Atlantis. It rises again in its splendour, its purple-hued plumage, indeed, in its wonderment, in awe of new life. A new adventure. New heart rumblings within its belly bring forth excitement within its breast. It goes forth into the etheric understanding, the heavens, the firmament, until the next fire is to be cast of its nest and is consumed in its flames, to be born yet again. This is the experience of each now moment being born from the fire of the moment before. You are all Phoenixes. Understand this reflection and you will understand living in joy. This is a rebirthing time.

You have carried the torch of this wisdom of Atlantis for eons of your time and handed it from one to another, heart to heart. But you did not understand the brilliance you were bearing. You did not understand the power of divinity within this fiery flame. You did not understand that the torch was you. And you are understanding it now.

You are all coming forth to herald in the golden era of God, the Aquarian age, as it is called. Do so with joy and celebration. Elaborate festivity of heart. Fleece yourself in playfulness and friskiness. Wiggle your rumpuses, as it were and become unfettered. This is not for doom. This is for the understanding of delight. You are the peoples of Atlantis, children born of this plane in this timing to be the peoples of Atlantis again, reborn. America is the new Atlantis. Hold the torch high. Cast forth your light. Be divine freedom exemplified. Freedom from the shackles of fear and doubt. That includes fear about your monetary circumstance. I reiterate it because it is quite an important issue upon your plane in this timing, and it is of vital importance for you to understand what has been spoken of.

It is the witching hour, as they call it, hm? We will resume here on another day in your time to discuss Lemuria, the Pleiadeans, and the buildings of the cathedrals of Atlantis. And indeed, the crystal technology everyone is chitter-chattering about?

Q: St. Germain, the light that you were talking about where people could put their hand in and it would be their education - I would like to know more about that too.

Many would.

Q: Short education, ha ha.

It is not really an education. It is wisdom received. But in order to receive this wisdom, you must allow the resonance, and in order to do this, you must be powerfully accustomed to opening your seals. You are in what you call training camp now.

Q: St. Germain, talking about the seals - I am sure throughout history you have seen different Indian-like ceremonies, purification ceremonies, using certain substances that open up the seals like peyote or mescaline. I was wondering how you perceive those and what you think about those.

That is a forceful opening of the seals. It brings forth rendings and holes within the auric field. Therefore, those are to be healed. In other words, it is an unnatural, non-allowing sort of a flow.

Q: Why are they here then?

For your experience, if you choose them.

Q: So in other words, they are forcing an opening where perhaps the opening was not supposed to be...

Not 'supposed to be', but it was not harmonious according to your attunement in that moment, for it to be opened.

Q: Is there a sign when they can be?

They can always be attuned. You must desire it. You see, in order to allow the seals of your being to open harmoniously in a flow, in a synchronous fashion, it begins with your heart seal. Not with any of the other [seals], as you may suppose.

Q: I see. After the heart seal, is there another one that opens?

According to your attunement. It is different for different entities. But your heart seal is the spigot.

When we resume at another timing, to discuss further about Atlantis - the technology and the culture, the peoples, the sociology of it all, bring forth with you memory. Allow yourself one memory at least in the bouquet of your gathering. As you remember this memory, expand it to incorporate other memories into it. Not only of Atlantis, but other memories of other dimensional experience, for Atlantis was a channel into the inner Earth that is now covered by lava. But indeed, the inner Earth still exists in the nearness of this dimension of space/time. You do remember the inner Earth if you will allow yourself to.

You are all quite beloved of my heart. Wondrous peoples of the land of Atlantis, Israel, Egypt and America. I would desire a toast, before departing. Are you ready?

Q: Ready.

To the light-bearers, to the love-bearers, indeed, to the new Atlanteans, the Phoenixes, the pyramids, the golden glow of God. I salute you and indeed, in eternal love, I am forever in your gratitude. So be it.

Q: So be it.

I have truly enjoyed this evening of your time.

Q: We have too. Thank you.

It has been my honour to bask in your light. Brings me much pleasure of heart. I desire not to depart. Fare thee well, for now, my dear beloved ones, and remember: easy glum, easy glow. I thought you would like that one. Namaste.

Chapter 4

HARMONIC CONVERGENCE

A Time For Celebration.

Greetings, my beloveds. How be you this day in your time? Brilliant, indeed. Like a glorious jewel of fire within the heavens of the universe. It is indeed magnificent to be here.

The culmination of the 'Harmonic Convergence' is the mass consciousness of the Earth-plane coming forward to become at ONE with all of life. The allowance of God I Am.

It is a celebration, it is the jubilant experience of humanity understanding itself as God. Mother Earth - Terra - she has called out to you through the eons of time. She has called you to come unto her to converge the essence of humanity and the essence of the inner Earth plane - and the essence of your brothers of space - into a unified point of Oneness, an apex of sorts, a summit. It is a jubilant experience for your brethren, the Brotherhood of Light, who love you more than you understand the word 'love', indeed. We are come here to celebrate, to be in Oneness, in love, in unified harmony.

So go forth from here, and sing and dance and make festival, bring forth your voice in song - it is the voice of the Earth. Express her love, you will illustrate the love of God I Am unto the masses.

You know, the convergence itself is not the birthing. Indeed, it is a conception. It is a seed brought forth into fruition, into a merging, an embracement with love understood. Therefore, the conception of this Earth plane into the Harmonic Convergence, will bring fruition from its womb.

Indeed, a grand birthing is about to occur in the year of 2012, near about the month of December. Then it will be a knowing of the Oneness of all life, of the divinity therein.

There will be many other convergences of a sort. The convergence is merely the opening, a window as it were, into All-That-Is. It is not the culmination into an absolute experience. It is an initiation into the Isness that is never absolute because that would indicate 'finite' and the universe is infinite. The harmonic convergence will allow an understanding of the Earth changes to a certain extent. They need not be feared - they need not be dreaded. Indeed, they are to be embraced and understood with joy and love and harmony within the breast.

There will be grand discoveries during this period of time. A tableau [stone-tablet] shall be unearthed to give the scientists of your nations a greater understanding. The pyramids shall be understood by your archeologists. You know what an archeologist is? An entity whose career lies in ruins. *(Audience chuckles.)*

You know, laughter is the grand harmonizer. It brings forth bouncing of the belly and indeed, the glory of God. The sound of laughter, of humour, comedy, divine comedy, indeed, is the experience of life as a God living in joy. Not existing, *living.* There is a difference - a grand one. For one is living death and one is living life.

Nature will bring forth an abundance and resplendence of song, saturated with melody, the brook of laughter, of bubbling, of a jubilance around the rocks. Let us not have grievance and complaint about it.

There are those who call themselves ecologists - a voice crying over the wilderness. They shall come to know peace within their breast, for nature will realign itself during the convergence. *Nature shall resplendorize the world.* It shall be a grand mirror unto the Earthlings, unto humanity, as it blooms into fruition.

Indeed, the earth, the water, the wind and the fire will sing a song through you, introducing their essence to the Earth plane to align the elements into harmony.

There has been much chitter-chatter about the 144,000. It is an illustration of an electro-biomagnetic 'battery' upon this plane. Those entities will indeed assist in the conduction of the energy in its most receptive points into the Earth plane and allow us [Council of Light] to bring forth the current, as you would term it, of the God I Am essence. The alignment and attunement of the 144,000 as you have called them, will become the 'rod of God' as it were, a direct influx of energy into this universe, and all the other multidimensional aspects of you will be influxing in other parts of this universe that you do not perceive, which you would call alternate reality - parallel life.

There are about 550 million entities who shall participate [as helpers] in the convergence of this time flow. Those entities will be likened unto a transformer, affording a 'stepping up' of the energy that has been introduced, to embrace the entirety of the Earth plane - *all* her peoples, *all* her nationalities, cultures, creeds, races, ye, even brothers of other planetary understandings. It is indeed a time of celebration, of love. Know that the love that is issued forth from the heart will wave its magic wand and transform the Earth plane. *The fruits of the labour of love upon Terra will bring humanity into Oneness - a humanity at One with God, where God is known.*

You are all grand representations of the glorious God I Am; you are all mirrors unto one another's divinity. You are all indeed, the splendid flora of the garden of God, the arbour of Earth. Its beauty will emerge during the next twenty five[1] years.

Your visual apparatus will flow into full creativity of perception - you shall begin to perceive beyond the physical senses. You will begin to see colours that you had not known existed before. You will begin to see the glorious halo around the entities you call your brethren, and understand their golden glow of divinity. You will begin to understand the song, conversation and language of the flora, the animal kingdom, the insects, even the Sun and the stars. Indeed, your universe, it will be a galactic community.

You will understand your brethren, of all kinds, coming together as One, as equals, as your peers; you will bow unto one another in

[1] Date of remark is August 15th, 1987.

reverence of your uniqueness, allowing each to be a resplendent representation of the spectrum of the rays of the light of white. Indeed, your light is glorious and it shall become even more so as you perceive *your* light, perceive *your* grandeur, perceive *your* eternality.

In the understanding of simultaneity you will perceive other universes, of the past, the present, the future, all concurrent, simultaneous. You will understand your past lives. There has been much emphatic representation about your past lives. You will understand them merely as different facets of your NOW.

So is also your future. The future and the past exist simultaneously in the tapestry of the forever called NOW - and you will indeed perceive it as you open the conduit of yourself and become a corridor of communication for the Brotherhood of Light. As you introduce their lights into the Earth, you are liaisons or emissaries of the Brotherhood. That is why you are here - that is why you resonate to come unto this gathering, for you have responded to the soul essence desire to come unto a mirror such as this so that you can perceive that which be you.

The 12 days² of preparation before the convergence, it allows grandeur of mirror unto you, so that you may have before you, over and over and over again, that which you judge, that which you deem undesirable. As you deem it undesirable, you judge it. As you do that, it is mirrored unto you again, for you NOT to judge it, to give you an opportunity to perceive its Isness, its Divinity. That is what the 12 days of preparation are all about, for you to clarify and to bring it into harmony within yourself, so that you indeed, may be the 'Rod of God,' the 'Lightening Rod.'

So, it is nigh unto the ripeness of time for this. Indeed the time is NOW, *a culmination of eons of times unto the harvest.* It is the climax unto the unfoldment. The grand orgasm of the experience of the God

---

² To understand this reference to the 12 days of preparation correctly, the reader is asked to discern between two different interpretations: one concerns the prediction of actual 12 days of Darkness followed by 12 days of Light just prior to the transition. The other is an understanding of our present time - the years before the transition - as being symbolically representative of the actual 12/12 day period.

that you are, and the God that all the rest of humanity is as well, and all of life. When you perceive the beauty even in a blade of grass, ye, even the ant upon the ground as it traverses a blade of grass, in the labour of its own experience, carrying a fruit unto its nest - as it participates with its fellowship and its community of Spirit - you shall perceive a mirror there for you as well. Even in your own experience of life, you will understand that which you call man-made - inanimate. It also has consciousness and it also is converging. For atoms would not be held together if there were not a consciousness there. The consciousness is part of your own consciousness. For you have collectively created it to be thus. As you perceive it in its own beauty, you will indeed penetrate collective consciousness. That one penetration of the essence of divinity perceived, the Oneness, the harmonic convergence - it will be likened unto what you call the 100th monkey[3].

You all understand what this is? Then it will become collectively perceived. It will be a grand curiosity for some of the scientists, for some of the religious, ritualistic, dogmatic understandings - for they also are having their own convergence. They also are having their own mirrors, which is grand. In non-judgment you will understand all experience as beauteous and wondrous and be in awe of your creation of them. 'How did I get myself into this one?' you will say, 'What is there for me here?' You will understand. You will know.

Your siblings come unto the Earth plane to be your grand masters and teachers. It is the reversal of roles. You will become *their* students, *they* will be your university. You will understand their beauty and wisdom, for they will be the visionaries of the past, present and future as they understand *no time*. They will teach their parents 'No Time'. The grand slave driver of this Earth-plane is the master called time and it is the convergence for this as well - the release of the slave driver called clock - did I hear 'Amen' somewhere?

---

[3] Reference is to The Hundredth Monkey Syndrome, which - in essence - is the understanding of the frequency of a thought (individual or group thought) stimulating the surrounding resonant body (humanity) into resonance. The interesting phenomenon this syndrome symbolizes, is the capacity of the amplitude of the receiving group to become greater by multiples compared to the amplitude causing the resonance.

The experience of God upon Earth, God understood, God-Man aware, will unfold in its own ripeness, without the expectation of a certain amount of time having to elapse. You will understand the foreverness of NOW, the jewel of NOW. You will perceive it.

This is a convergence point. *History as you have known it to be in your experience, will be no more* - your experience of being only a part of a facet of a God in life - but to be the only life. You will perceive all the other facets of this jewel of life; you will become multi-dimensionally aspected.

Grasp one another heart to heart, and let love penetrate the breast of one another; for that indeed is the grand connector. Love. *That* is the grand convergence. *That* is what will be brought forth on the Earth-plane, peace upon Earth. You call it the Peace Meditation, *Hands Across America,* to let the disharmonious dissipate from your experience. It is merely the harmonic convergence of humanity in one manner after another after another, so that indeed, all discordant experience will pass away.

Indeed, you shall go forth from this time onward, in allowance of yourself to be the channel, the conduit of the God essence of you, so that you may bring it forth unto the Earth. Flower, blossom, open unto the light and let the rose of you come forth and the splendour of the rays warm and caress your petals. Let the sweet nectar of the soul spill upon the softness of your cheek and water the Earth. Be jubilant and joyous. This is a festival! This is indeed, what you have termed, 'party hearty'.

The Alignment.

The Harmonic Convergence is a splendid glorious understanding of the converging of humanity into God. You have mirrors before you over and over again, ye, even before the understanding of the convergence becomes part of your conscious awareness. What you will become aware of will be the aligner, the tuner, the balancer as it were, of discordant experience brought forth, the grand understanding called human.

If you would desire to tickle yourself with the feathers of your experiences, go forth with buoyancy. Float upon the waters of life as they come streaming forth unto you. That is what is meant by 'go with the flow.' That is what is meant by allowing All-That-Is to be in jubilance and bubbling effervescence, letting the flow of life to come forth as the babble of the brook, its joyous expression of going forth over the rocks, around them, dancing as it were, and not fretting about the rock itself.

Now, the tone, the notes within your embodiment: As they force themselves from the seals in your circuit, they will also come into the converging point of your instrument [Pineal gland], the celestial instrument that is indeed the connector, the communicator, the corridor from the All-That-Is unto three dimensional experience that is in transition into fourth. The relationship of the notes, the scales of music, and the relationship of the frequencies emitted by your seals, will also come into an understanding with one another. *Your seals will call forth the manifestation and assimilation of experiences for them to resonate with, to align them, to balance, to embrace them with love unconditional.* That phrase [unconditional love] has a lot of exercise in your time, but people do not understand what it means. The essence is that the entities speaking them, speak them by word, not by understanding.

Now, when your embodiment was in the womb, surrounded by the waters of life of your mother, your heart was in development and had wing-like fixtures, appendages upon either side, very much like a flying heart. From this developed the fingers upon your arms and your hands, as it were. Indeed, your arms and hands grew from your heart. That is what is meant by embracing, allowing the extension to bring forth re-countenance with your soul through your heart. Many of you go about hugging one another. That is when you embrace. A hug, a round about way of expressing affection. But, do you know when you make the heart to heart connection, you are allowing the union of your embryonic understanding yet again? That is love. If you do so from the apex of love of All-That-Is, then you reharmonize with all entities, even those you would consider to be discordant -

allowing the flow of this tone to come through you unto all your seals. So, an embrace is a very, very powerful posture. It is an attitude of latitude. A posture of power. Indeed, *ultimate vulnerability is ultimate power.* When you bare your heart, that is the knowing of ultimate power, for that is the posture of no fear of anything. As you express in a hug, you are one and yet separate. Unique, but in Oneness with the All-That-Is. You indeed become merged with humanity through this expression of symbolic understanding of love. Go forth and kiss the morn.

Do you know that life kisses you on both cheeks as it dances merrily through the day of your experience? It laughs, heartily it does. The kiss? Go forth and give it to an entity that does not expect it. That is a harmonizing agent, a tonic indeed. They ask you whyfor, and you can say, 'it is because I love you!' That is what all entities upon the Earth plane will be doing to bring forth peace upon the land. The harmonic convergence is not only of this world, it is multiversal, more than universal, beyond the systems, the galactic understanding. A kiss indeed is an anatomical juxtaposition of two muscles in the state of convergence. Exercise this state quite a bit and you will find your life to be an harmonious state.

Now to music: You understand many different forms or fashions of it. You have different representations of the tones in their different characteristics of frequencies on this plane and you resonate to it by identification of your own resonance. In other words, if you desire Western music, you resonate to physical rhythm. Physical rhythm, the essence of the vibrations, is experienced through physicality. Melody, Eastern music, likened unto the sitar, is free flowing. It has a free flowing rhythm and not a form rhythm, therefore it is attuned to the frequencies of non-physical experience. As you merge the two, the physical and the non-physical essences merge which indeed will afford the merging of the cultures, and all that culture represents.

You will then understand the uniqueness and beauty and splendour of all that is different than you and you will bless it in its uniqueness as a different aspect of God I Am. You will not come to recognize one particular flavour of the Earth plane to be likened unto you, but *all of them*. You will identify life with All-That-Is, as God.

Now, this opening in opportunity, that you have termed the Harmonic Convergence, is not a point in time. Ye, Jeshua has said the time for the harvest is now, and this is always the case. The time for the harvest is always of your now. The convergence is merely the apex point of the energies as a communicator, or connector as it were, a corridor, unto the All-That-Is.

Each moment coming unto you as a new moment of joy is another convergence. Each moment, each now. If you miss it, it is not a thing that is missed, it is merely the non-perception of that moment, but indeed, it may become a perception in this moment. So, do not feel as though you have to catch a train. It is not a searching for, for if you search for it, and go unto the mountains to communicate with God you will never have awareness of it, for it is here, [pointing to the heart] my dear brethren, it is not there. All that is there is merely the reflection of what is already here. All you need do is perceive and become aware that it *is* you, expressing through you, through your experience of life. By searching to communicate with God in your meditation, you are getting hence from life, or humanity, as it is experienced in third density. You do not understand that *God is everywhere about you and you are in constant communication with it at all times. Once you become aware of that, you have converged.*

Attune to each aspect of God, through the blossom, through the fragrance of the stewpot on your stove, through all of life as it is enhancing you, and you will understand the converging more and more. You will understand the blossoming of you. The garden of God will be perceived.

You will experience feelings, emotions you know not from whence they came. That is because they are converging. Your soul essence is enhancing your knowingness, therefore you capture and embrace the emotion contained within it, even though you do not have outward cognition whyfor it is. You are becoming enlightened of yourself and your experiences. You may compress or inhibit emotion and you will find yourself in situations of indigestion; then you are not allowing the flow of it through your soul essence. Therefore you will find yourself 'upon the hot seat' in many situations, in very discordant circumstances. But, this is alright, for as you recognize the beauty of what is before you, the converging will occur more and more within your own essence and you become a reflection of all the other aspects of God I Am, of humanity. As you embrace them [humanity], they perceive their own essence by their reflection of your harmonics and your knowingness.

Now, the notes and tremors within your being, within the seals, will come into balance and harmony of themselves. The seals will make themselves known to you. You will become choked up as it were, congested of the digestive system, or out of breath at times, frustrated of the belly, the solar plexus. That is what you will call the twelve days of preparation that are coming unto you. When the balance of these emotions occurs, your soul will pour forth. Let the river [of tears] stream forth upon the softness of your cheek. Do not bring stoppage unto it, do not dam it up. Let it flow. You are the conduit. You are the harmonizing agent. You indeed *are* the Harmonic Convergence. As this occurs, do not judge yourself. Many of you have sore faces with lines of the course cloth of judgment. This convergence you may perceive beyond the cloth. Do not judge. Do not be in judgment of your brethren or yourself, but perceive the beauty and the splendour of the dawn, of the dusk, and your brethren as the sunset and the sunrise, and ye, perceive even yourself as this. You are the jewel of the universe, the treasure chest of life. It is filled with the jewels of life but you do not perceive yourself as the pearls and the emeralds and, indeed, the amethyst, of All-That-Is.

When the grand creative essence came forth to create the universe in harmony, it extended its essence into the great abyss of emptiness and brought forth this treasure chest and allowed infinite fantasy to stream forth from its fingers. It spewed forth its galaxies, its constellations, its planetary understandings, indeed, its endless universes. They hung like chandeliers in the heavens garnished with stardust and they all danced to the music of the spheres. Indeed, this is harmonic creation.

You are all searching and seeking for the quest of creation to recreate your life. Understand the quest of creation as the bequest of Christus. That is what it is - bequesting Christus upon everything that exists. You need not recreate it. *It already IS.* You only need to perceive its essence as beauty and Isness of All-That-Is.

All-That-Is need not be attuned to your particular feelings of how it should be, for this is judgment, and your judgment will always be mirrored back unto you. *Allow it to be without judgment and you are allowing the convergence.* Laughter is a grand lifter when there are discordant circumstances about you. Laugh - heartily, until your belly bounces. It will realign All-That-Is. It will indeed harmonize the chakras.

Do you know, your verbiage is indeed harmonic in and of itself. It is melodic. It has rhythm and meter. It will spring as music from the soul if it is enhanced with the love of your soul. For that raises it - and the discordant circumstances you perceive in your life - to higher frequencies to transcend space and time. When you embrace discordance, the vibrations will pour forth, so that you do not perceive it as barrier, but as an opportunity. Through the harmonics of laughter and of sound, your communication will come forth assuaged, soothed as it were. Not rugged, jagged, frustrated, abrupt and brief, for the sound may be silent.

Harmonics do not have to be spoken. They are. They already exist in vibration, without speaking them. Merely a sigh is the harmonic vibration. When you sigh is it silent, or is it a coo? If it is a coo, it is the soothing sound of the soul communicating unto the universe. A sigh is an emotional release. Many of you perceive yourselves as checked - in reign and restraint, not allowing your soul to express through the vibration called sound. The non-allowance of this is the frustration of your tears. You do not allow yourself to cry. Weep forth. You do not express the sound of the soul during your sexual merging experience in physicality. You do not say 'I love you' to a bedraggled gentlemen in a park, or to a child who is in wonderment of a flower. You do not love the entities who are of argumentative nature with you, or when they are giving forth their grievances unto you. *How do you conceive of turning this world into Heaven on Earth if you permit yourself to participate in further discordance?*

Embrace the discordance. Allow it to be, in love. And simply turn to the other entity and say: 'I love you!' This will be a grand tonic. Indeed, until it penetrates into their conscious awareness, continue stating this. And, not only state it. Respond in all fashions through love. Through embracing. Go forth unto an entity who does not expect it and embrace them.

Now, frustration is the divergence of polarities so that they may converge in your time in super-consciousness. Polarization will continue to be of emphatic representation, of unlimited knowingness and understanding, and limited knowingness and understanding called dogmatic, ritualistic, regulatory. All of this - allow it. *Allow it.* Allow it to be known as merely a different aspect of God I Am. Give reverence unto it. Be jubilant for its expression, for in this jubilation you are raising the vibrations of it. Let it go forth into the convergence point of super-consciousness so that harmoniously you may embrace one another when the ripeness of time is at hand.

This that you are experiencing has been known as the war of Armageddon. The war of the different aspects of you. The alter ego and the Divine ego coming forth to encounter one another. Do you know how to harmonize it? Cease weaponry and warlike attitudes, argumentative nature, cease separation. Allow the merging to occur - the blending. Blend with ladles of love. Give forth lavishly your love unto the universe. Spill forth your love into the galaxies unseen. You are a conduit. You are a supply of love and God I Am that comes forth endlessly, eternally, non-ceasingly - you shall not run out. As the river of life spills through you into the universe, you are a fountain. Bubble happily. Happily is buoyantly, floating upon the water, bobbing as it were. Not sinking because of heaviness. Happy. This is a peculiar sensation when you are busy being. It is a choice of every moment, a tickling of the soul of every moment.

You have understood humour from time to time, in an understanding of 'black comedy'? This is alright, but this is of the Piscean Age and the blending of all comedy, of all humour and laughter into the divine knowingness of God I Am, will enable you to flow buoyantly through your life. That will be your life jacket. You may place it upon your breast any time you wish. Reverberate the resonance of joy. Dance is movement of joy - expression of the God I Am - through joy, through the divine creative essence within you. Humour is the state of the art of God. Be *within* the art of God. Every moment. God is you. God is not here - is not upon a mountain - not even within a sunset - but is all of the above, *including you.*

Behold God. *That* is the universe. How else do you think peace will accomplish itself upon the Earth plane, if you do not behold *all* as God? Wisdom is not what you learn and remember from a grand mirror. It is that which you do not forget from your own knowingness. It is not that which you remember, it is that which you cannot forget. For you perceive it over and over again in every moment of your time. In every experience of your life you perceive the wisdom of it, the beauteous gemstones, the necklace of life upon your breast. String your pearls of wisdom. Allow them to be as they are. In non-judgment, joyous, unconditional love.

Listen and hear the brook of life. Hear it singing to you. All you need do is heed the vibration and know its beauty and resonance. Resonance is non-physical.

Do you know that tone can coagulate energy into matter? Merely a tone, for it releases energy similar to atomic energy. Your scientists are on the verge of understanding how matter can coagulate simply through the energy from a tone that is ultrasonic in frequency. You can do this also. That is how you manifest. That is how you create your manifestation. You can precipitate something from apparently nothing - by divine thought energy, for that is the vibration.

Free yourself from the fetters of limitation! Be unlimited. You need not restraint or restrictions. Unlimited knowingness is to be brought forth unto the Earth. Who is to bring it forth if not you? Who indeed, is to unlimit, un-restrain the entities of the slavery they impose upon themselves, if not you? You have desired to be the bearer of light unto the Earth, have you not? Then, do so through your grand example, through your illustration of unlimited knowingness, through which the others may perceive, may experience the grandeur of unlimitedness. They will cast away their clock face eventually, but with much frustration they cling to it for a time. The harmonics of third density are so slow, when perceived from the perspective of All-That-Is, that they intertwine and intermingle themselves into the tapestry which you perceive as solidity. It is a beautiful mural indeed, a tapestry of humanity that cannot be understood through the mere perception of the physical apparatus, for it is beyond that. Its beauty is only perceived when you understand the wholeness of it - not by gazing upon one thread.

Many of you are entrenched in habit. Grand slave driver you call time. That is a grand habit of third density. The habit may be likened unto a cable. All the threads are practiced and perceived every moment of your time, until its strength becomes quite binding unto you. *Free yourself from these fetters - be unlimited!*

You are in the rut and participate in its narrowness. But, you know, a moment encompasses an eternity. You may transcend third density, time and space, as you transcend the heaviness of mass consciousness. Enlighten the world. Illumine the world. Free it of the heaviness. Float to the top buoyantly, transcending restraints, limitation, restrictions, and regulations of others. Respect and allow them to be understood as divine, but do not perceive yourselves as being restrained simply because they are. For that is their choosing, not necessarily yours, unless you choose it too, and that is also divine.

Now, freedom is the converging of non-freedom *and* freedom. It is bringing forth third density *and* unlimitedness, that is, fourth *and* beyond. Go upon the mountain and perceive the valley. You may see it. If you desire to see and perceive the mountain, go into the cloud. But, if you desire to understand the valley, the mountain and the cloud, *be* them. Converge them in your knowingness. *Without* judgment, *without* separation. Therefore you embrace your restrictions and your regulations as divine, without heaviness.

This is what the convergence is all about and why at times it begins to be a congestion in the belly, because you are unaccustomed to it - it is unknown to you.

But, indeed, allow the unknown to be brought forth into the known and into the light. Understand what you have not understood before. It is the grand opportunity for you to become aware of the darkness and enlighten it. Be not afraid of it. Be not in trepidation of it - but embrace it and enlighten it. There may be much love upon the Earth plane only if you *allow* it to be. The war-lords shall be dethroned and peace and harmony is indeed upon the horizon.

The heart can be very much likened unto the beat of a drum. The throbbing of the heart and the beating of a drum are very similar resonances. Understand the beating of a drum, as you rock yourself in emotion - the to-and-fro - the swaying as it were. This is the manner with which you may harmonize frustration. Rock yourself. Hear the beat, the throb, the pulsation, the frequency as it resonates through you. When you have the heaviness of the day - go into the 'time of knowingness' - a moment of joy and experience the movement of sound and motion of the body and you will harmonize it through unconditional love. It comes natural to mothers. That is how they assuage their siblings. It is a natural state of being. By pursuing the convergence you will not perceive it. Convergence is a natural state of being. It need not be perceived. Allow it to be in your own essence.

'From dust you came, and to dust ye shall return.' That is third density knowingness. That is indeed a truth, but you may know beyond this. The convergence of *all* the elements of your life into Oneness - the convergence of *all the relationships in your life* into Oneness, shall be the understanding of harmonious knowingness, from now unto eternity. It is not only a now moment. It is every ensuing now moment. As you contemplate yourself, contemplate what be convergence. It is the coming together and merging, a blending as it were, a harmonizing of all the seasons, of all the different elements of life into the stewpot of you.

The stream of life flows forever. Jump in with both feet. Swim within it, likened unto a duck - paddle heartily in it with joy. Joy is a resplendent experience. Joy is a vibration of love and light. But, this is of fullness for now. Your vessels are full to the brim. You may partake of it joyously. For this has been a banquet, and you have partaken of what you have chosen. This is always the case. Bask in the flavour of your own knowingness in each moment of your experience.

Feast upon yourself and upon one another, through the eyes of God. Go bountifully with a cornucopia of tidings of love unto the Earth. Feed the Earth with your love. Give forth a feast of God and you shall indeed be giving forth the harmony of the world. You are truly loved. Your grandeur is indescribable. You are likened unto the song of the sea. It does not stop at the shore. It continues its resonance, ye, even through the soul. So does my presentation here unto you. Your song continues even unto the soul that you term I. Even when I have departed hence. So I will go forth for now, and I will come yet again before you in another now moment - to partake of your sweetness again. I am always with you, always, even unto the end of time into timelessness. All you need do is harmonize with the frequency you term to be 'I' and I will come unto you - my essence will be made known to you, for I am your equal brother, and I love you as a comrade, as a fellow-God. Fare thee well for now.

Be at Onement. Be God. So be it. Namaste!

Chapter 5

ON THE MOUNTAIN.

Greetings, my beloved brethren.

Welcome unto the mountain called Shasta [Northern California] that is hearth and home of the Brotherhood of the Light, the Council of Light, the light of you. This illustration of you [reference is to St. Germain] coming forth in this manner, is the exhibition of the harmonious reverberations of humanity into the hearth and home of God at rest, in peace, with love upon its breath, indeed. Gaze forth into the beauty and splendour, the magnificence and grandeur of God illustrated before you. For it is your mirror. It is *you*.

We are coming into the Harmonic Convergence, a doorway in time, as it were, a threshold. The God I am of the universe is coming forth in its fullness of blossom unto you. Partake of it. Be free. Let your emotions gush forth, likened unto the rivers of the universe, to assuage the heat and aridity of the Earth. Harmony is the lyrics of laughter. It will align you unto the grandeur of the God of you and you will understand light-heartedness, the vibrations of vivacity.

Every cell within your embodiment contains an atom that is in resonance with every other atom in the universe. As the atom experiences the emotions of life within the cells of your body, all the rest of the universe experiences in Onement with you. It is the fruition of the freedom of God I Am coming forth. The hallmark of God realized is the perception of peace and harmony in the eloquence of life experienced.

The utterance of a sigh, the song from the breast of your heart, will harmonize what you would consider to be discordant. Bring forth your emotions through all the seals in alignment, in attunement. Sigh OOOMMM, I AM.

The seven seals within your embodiment are resonant and attuned to the seven continents upon the Earth plane. As fourth density comes forth upon Earth, so also will come forth the resonance of your seven seals. As you align them, you automatically align the Earth plane, for she is attuned to you in this manner, and you are ONE. *As you feel discordant and disharmonious, so does the Earth.*

If you would desire to bring peace among the peoples of the Earth, among the hearts of humanity, BE at peace, BE at Onement with the seals of your own embodiment. Align them, attune them, resonate to the song of God I Am. In doing so, you will attune the Earth plane. Gaze into the mirror and behold God, for that is the essence of you and that is the essence of the Earth herself. She is embracing the light. She is becoming a sun.

I will tell you: the solar system is one of seven that are also seals within a grander essence - a cosmic being, a galactic understanding. *The solar system is the heart seal of this galactic being.* Therefore, love is becoming resonant across your plane, indeed across the universe, through this that you understand as your Sun.

Mars, it is male energy. It represents the power, the sovereignty of the masculine energy of God I Am. Venus is feminine energy - love, light, beauty, balance, allowance and unconditional love. Earth is embracing the Sun, the masculine energy, into the God I Am of her essence. She is indeed female essence merging with male essence and becoming divine essence. She is becoming a sun. The Trinity in this manner, what you understand as the ascension of the planets, is male energy/female energy/sun, male energy/female energy/sun, ad infinitum, until a grand whirling vortex, a kaleidoscope of energy, is brought forth and the entire universe is merging with the God I Am.

As you express the song of love and peace and harmony within the breast of this heart seal of the solar system, this planet, indeed your being, you will bring forth attunement within every atom within the universes to the same song. For they vibrate. They are interconnected and interwoven into the tapestry of God, of Isness.

Hearkening unto the stairway of heaven is not a climbing up. It is a waking up. You are awakening into the morning mist of the heavenly halo of happiness. The mist is clearing for you. The dawn is breaking. You are beginning to perceive what is eternal, what is beyond the horizon, beyond forever, what is indeed aligned to the eons of time where there is no time.

Many of you would perceive the understanding of God I Am to be a bit egotistical, for you understand not the balance of unconditional love. But you know, egotism is a case of mistaken non-entity. You do not understand the entity and essence of which you are. That is why you would perceive the essence that be you [as God I Am] as aggrandizement of Self. For the essence of God within you understands the essence of God within all other life, within the brilliance and beauty of even a grain of sand upon the shores of the seas. Therefore, you are humbled before it in reverence and awe and wonderment.

When you bring forth humility, understand it as a mutual allowance. Not as a bowing unto another entity, but as a mutual bowing before one another in reverence of the crowning glory of both of you. All of you have crowns upon your head. All of you. You do not understand it yet. You have not perceived the beauty of the jewels that are resplendent upon you, within you, that indeed ARE YOU! But you shall. You are stepping into the grand mirror of life that will afford you this perception *if you choose to perceive it.*

The grandeur of life is thought energy brought into manifestation by the God I Am of you. *It is a choice of every moment!* The harmonic convergence is not a moment in time to be passed and never to be understood again. It is every moment unveiling itself unto you in eternal nowness. Every moment. Every joyous now. As it unveils itself to you, you may choose happiness. You may choose awareness of the jewel of life in eternal perception.

The creative essence within you may bubble in joy and jubilation, or in worrisome effort. You know, the beginning of life is each and every new now! *It is eternally beginning! There is never an end.* That is what is meant by eternal. Every step you take in your life, indeed, every brilliance you bring forth to reflect the divinity that is you, is merely another now, chosen to be experienced, as you decide it in that now moment.

You create your experiences, not anyone else. Prophecy, the foreseen, it is merely foreseen in that now moment. It is changeable every now moment, because the God I Am of you is divine, and is glorious in its creative essence. Seek not for the candle to light your way. Rather, understand and become aware of the illumination brought forth by the brilliance of your brethren upon your own pathway. Perceive their glory, their grandeur.

Understand them *as you,* understand the grains of sand *as you,* the glorious trees, *as you.* Indeed, a tree is a treasure trove of beauty. It majestically embraces eternity. It delights as the gentle breeze caresses its branches and dances within them. It spills forth the delicious fragrance of its fruit. It whispers and laughs to the Earth. It caresses the eye of God with its splendour. Indeed, it is majestic. *It is you.* As it hungrily penetrates the Earth in search of the waters of wisdom and indeed milks the breast of her free-flowing springs, you also are thirsty for wisdom. You also suckle at the breast of the Earth. You also come forth in your majesty embracing eternity, delightfully dancing within the winds of your life, the breezes and the gales, and *understand the beauty even within the tempest.* You will come to know yourself as likened unto a teapot, which sings merrily even though it is up to its neck in hot water.

The essence of the harmonic convergence is a higher resonance, a higher frequency of the creative essence within you, flowing through you. Therefore you may create the unfamiliar, that which you are not accustomed to creating, that you may reflect unto you what you would desire to merge with, to become One with, to be in non-judgment of. Embrace it, and you shall become One with God.

The Golden Nebula.

Now, astronomers, and your quantum physicists, have understood the grand golden nebula[1] at the ridge of this universe, embracing and absorbing all the electrums in this universe. Bit by bit it is absorbing this universe. And they are scratching their heads a bit in non-understanding of what be this grand golden essence that is there upon the horizon of the universe. It has not been seen before. The understanding of the golden essence is the Christus. It is the physical manifestation of the second coming of the Christus. It is indeed a parallel universe.

All of you have experienced parallel universes. There are many of them. One of them is one and one/hundredths of a second in your time behind your time, and you flux to-and-fro between it all the time. You may go hither into a room and have perception of an item therein and go hence and return again and it is not there and go hence and return again and it is. That is experiencing the parallel universe. You are in a constant flux in experiencing this, for you are stepping into the threshold of multidimensional experience.

Now, the parallel universe and the golden nebula is the New Age perceived. *When you transverse this threshold, when you become One with the golden nebula, you are in super-consciousness.* It is a parallel universe, it is coming and it is embracing this universe. It is imminent. It is indeed vibrating at a higher resonance, at a higher speed than it has in your before time. The rapidity of its embrace is reflected in the acceleration of the events in this universe, upon your planet, even within your daily lives. The acceleration is shifting into synchronization, for *the acceleration is becoming exponential* and indeed, it is becoming synchronicity experienced. Synchronicity is no more than alignment and attunement with the vortex of energy of God I Am - that which you would know of as psychic energy upon this plane. However, it is more than psychic energy. It is God essence energy experienced as a flow.

---

[1] Also known as the Photon Belt or the Manasic Vibration or, according to the Pleiadean Semjase, daughter of P'taah, the Golden Radiance.

Partake of this flow. Transcend the density of your lives. Indeed, transform it through the fire of your lives. Partake of the sweet incense of the flame of freedom, for it is sweet as honeysuckle. Hear the sounds behind the silence, beyond the depths, and breadths of quietude. There is a resonance within it.

Within the stillness, there is a symphony. Within the moment, there is an eternity. Within God, indeed, there is you, and within you there is God.

Your planet does not contain you. *You contain it!* Experience flows through you and you through it. Super-consciousness is not an either/or. It is an *and* - always. It is inclusive, embracing All-That-Is! *Cloak yourself with a coat of tenderness, gentleness and compassion. For that is the essence of God understood.* That is the essence of Christus. Christus is not afraid to face the music of mankind. The essence of Christus is the essence of the splaying of the rainbow, the hues, the colour, the tone, the sound of All-That-Is. That is the harmonics of it. Within every essence of you exists the rainbow and a pot of gold. You keep seeking for that pot of gold outward of you. But it is here within your heart. The treasure is within your breast. It is not only below your feet. It *is* you! You are the crowning glory of God. You are the Christus. You are the jewel. You are indeed that which IS.

Listen to the blade of grass as it grows. Hear indeed the symphony as the petal unfolds. Hear the whisperings of your own knowingness - your soul telling you the secrets of the ages. You know All-There-Is. You have all the wisdom there ever was, within your own knowingness, within your own breast. Wear it as a cloak of Christus. Perceive and believe. Knowingness, the harmonics, is the allowance for the universe to create through you, is perceiving the invisible, understanding the incredible and experiencing the impossible. You are coming into the threshold of all of these. *You indeed are becoming One with God I Am!*

You shall experience the perceived impossible and go hence - transcending physical reality - into All-That-Is. You shall go hence into a density that is not understood by your outward perception, for the vortex within you creates awareness, by opening the Pineal gland, to spring forth its rivers of knowingness, its fountain of forever wisdom.

The scientists tell you that you use only ten percent of the brain. What do you think the other ninety percent are, hm? It is the awareness of the geometric patterns that bring forth their essence during astral travel, during slumber, during meditation. The symbolic understandings that are placed therein that are not perceived by verbiage, for they are beyond verbiage. That is what is within the other ninety percent. As you harmonize and attune with the God I Am essence of each one of your seals, in the Oneness of you and of life, the flow will be created into the awareness of your outer consciousness - wisdom regained. Indeed, you shall become quite wise, as it were, and shall become more and more of a prophet as you perceive the wisdom of you.

Now, the creation of your life can be a symphony or it can be out of tune and disharmonious to the ear and the heart. But you alone can choose to re-attune to embrace the discordant chord and to be surrounded with beauty. Your life is magnificent for *you create it*. It is a flower of the field coming unto you. You may pluck it and toss it away, or indeed, you may partake of its essence, its fragrance, understand its beauty that is reflective of your own. Understand its crowning glory, the creative essence within it, as it reflects your own. The lily of the valley, indeed, is what you are. The star of the heavens, indeed, is what you are. The blanket of snow in its essence of warmth and cool together in One, indeed is what you are. You are All-That-Is.

I come unto you because you have called the essence of the Brotherhood of the Light unto you. I come unto you because indeed I love you!! All of you! Beyond your imaginings I love you. You cannot understand love unlimited until you understand the God of you. I embrace you all in love, in peace and tranquillity. Unconditional love - that is the key. When you love unconditionally, you experience serenity always. Hear my call. Understand its beauty, for you indeed are the mural maker. You indeed are the craftsman, the creator of

Christus. Place your heart within the cradle of Christus and you shall indeed be swaddled forever in love. I desire you to participate in dance, song and jubilation.

I love you all so.

I will give you a short respite. Fare thee well for now. I shall return. Namaste.

Super-Consciousness.

Greetings my beloveds.

This is very similar to the sermon upon the mount. It rings with resonance of remembrance. Blessed be the meek in Spirit, for they shall inherit the Earth. Blessed be the peacemakers. Is that not what a harmonic convergence is? The making of the peace and the harmony of the celestial song, in non-judgment of your brethren. Bring forth understanding and compassion for those within the realm of jurisdiction. Those who do not manifest abundance of possessions upon the plane are of simplicity. They are of God. They indeed are the meek of Spirit, are of wealth of wisdom. The treasure lies within their heart. Some of those who did not have education would be considered to be simpletons by your brethren of third density. Indeed, education is coming to know of how much it does not know. Some would have you called Sanka - that is ninety percent of the active portion of the bean which has been removed. But you know, the bean, the mind, it is merely a computer. The operator of it, the creator of its magic, is the soul essence that be you. Indeed create, create, create in joy! Dance, dance, dance to the music and melody of the mystical, the magical. You may create magic or you may create tragic - the choice is yours. You may be joy exemplified, or you may be sorrow exemplified. It is up to you.

On Earth up to this point of the convergence, you have a golden rule: Do unto others ... Indeed. Some have a misunderstanding of it: Do one to others, as they do one to you. That is what causes your battles - the wars upon the plane - the ravishing of the Earth's surface, and the disharmony of her peoples. The majesty of the kingdom of heaven is upon the Earth, within the peoples, within the Earth, within your life. All of you are kings and queens, Gods and Goddesses, ruling the kingdom of your own heaven, your own creation, your own manifestation of mystical magic.

Those not desirous of going hence into super-consciousness, into the golden nebula of Christus, will remain upon third density Earth plane, as you go into fourth.

Now, the rapture is exactly that: Ecstatic explosion of eternal nowness within your experience. It is not a catching up of an entity into the heavens in angelic form to be dispensed into the halls of heaven and locked away therein forever. It is an understanding of life in its beauty and brilliance and magnificence, as you create it to be.

The rapture will allow you to perceive fourth density, which is an exchange of frequency, a shift into a different gear, as it were. Therefore, *third density will no longer perceive you,* for you will be simultaneously existing, coexisting in the same space/time, but merely not perceived [by third density], because it is of a different frequency. You will be in allowance of your brethren, respecting your differences.

A convergence is the understanding of unity and diversity at one time. It is knowing and honouring Oneness and knowing and honouring difference - uniqueness, as one snowflake salutes another. Allowance of your brethren will be known as a raising of your resonance rather than rising through the roof. Anger, frustrations, gut feelings of congestion and indigestion will dissipate - the incapacity to 'stomach' circumstances - it will all pass. It will pass away into the All-That-Is, into the void of forever Isness.

You will come to know peace within your breast - an alignment and attunement with serenity, with harmony, with resonance in joy. Super-consciousness will be a celebration of celestial song.

Many will have tongues and lips that rise with words of wisdom and their hearts hide out from love. They will remain in third density. They will remain upon the consciousness of the Earth plane that is of heaviness, that desires to continue within rigourous restriction, limitation, frustration and bondage. They are bound to their preconceived idea of life, their notion that life exists only in the perceived senses of density, of physicality. They will come to know God in their own ripeness of time, so it is not to fret about them, or stew about the circumstances they choose for themselves. They create them to garnish and gain the wisdom therein. However, as they choose to do this and their evolution and unfoldment comes into fruition, your harvest is to be understood in your own ripeness. You can pluck the fruit of you any time you choose. Higher vibration, expanded awareness, even ascension, can be understood in the moment of your choice. You can penetrate instantaneously the veils of all the dimensions, of all limitations, all the planes of awareness in one moment, in one choice of divine thought.

Choosing this thought of ascension, of Oneness, of stepping forth into the eternal void, into the merging of the Mother/Father principle of life, you may also choose to *simultaneously* continue in one or another manner of density. For you are not limited! You are God! You are omnipotent! You are not limited to ascension. You may ascend and have limited experience simultaneously. That is what you call multidimensional experience. Simultaneity expressed is all the levels of awareness of that which be you, all the understandings of experience, all the expressions of your soul essence in different manners and manifestations - in myriads of forms and fashions.

It is all occurring at once. There is no past or present or future. There is only now. There are parallel nows, indeed. There are alternate realities. You may choose in the moment one particular divine thought energy and the alternate choice also is chosen in another dimension. They coexist simultaneously. This coexistence is the crystal cathedral of consciousness, the Christus of All-That-Is, in Oneness understood when you merge with the God I Am of you.

Now, the expression 'happiness' - it has become meaningless to you. It is not understood by your essence. It is merely a piece of verbiage spilled into the etheric atmosphere. *Happiness is a choice of every moment!* It is a perfume that you cannot pour on others without spilling a few drops upon yourself. It is indeed joyous in its fragrance. It is *allowing* in its aroma. It is God in its essence. Shift gears, as it were. When you gaze upon the ant on the ground that climbs its hills, understand it not as labouring on the Earth. Gaze into the depths of it. Be one with the consciousness of the ant. It is not your brother. *It is you.* That is what unity, Harmonic Convergence, is. Not knowing the separation of differences - knowing only Oneness. Understanding no difference at all between any of you. Humanity will come to be known as one organism, one heart beating with one pulse, and that is the pulse of God, the pulse of peace within the veins of I Am.

The Flame Of Freedom.

Now, in the days of your time to come bring forth ladles full of love and drip it heartily upon Earth as she reflects you in the steaming vapours of forgiveness, of jubilation, of merging. The vapours and the mists from the volcanos, spewing mountains that come forth, in their hotness, in their congestion, their frustration, their anger, they also have a rhythm. They release the pressure through the song of explosion. Through the eruption it is again aligned and re-attuned unto the harmonious heartbeat of humanity.

The grandest gift, the grandest heritage that you can give unto the Earth is your heart. Open it unto love. Love her flora, love her mountains, love her babbling brooks and her silvery streams. Indeed, the lofty leaf in the tree - it is you. It is the vibration of your reflection - an aspect, a facet of the grandeur of God of you. You are indeed Christus, crystalline, Christ-all in mineral form - the essence that is the reflection and prismatic splaying of all the vibrations of music and tone and colour upon the Earth. You are the rainbow. Merge your rainbows together to become a grand kaleidoscope.

Earth vibrates according to the consciousness of her humanity upon her. That is known as mass consciousness. Your thought of peace and harmony is what changes the vibrations within her atmosphere. Embrace her, caress her. Allow her to taste of you, for you are her fruition. You are her harvest.

The Sun, the grand fiery jewel within the heavens - it has a soul essence name of Michael, called Archangel Michael. It brings forth masculine energy into the universe. This is converging of now because Earth is becoming Michael - the Sun, the star, illumined, brilliant beyond the perception of your vision. The Earth and her peoples - all of you within the Earth, without the Earth, above the Earth - all of them are displaying the divine desire to align and attune into Oneness, unity, God I Am!

As you bring forth collective consciousness of Christus unto the Earth, know that the Earth is merely one consciousness in which you are participating. You are participant within the galactic community, and you will come to know the intergalactic alignment and essence within you. Ye, all entities that come forth into this star system, this universe, are coming to understand the glorious kingdom of God.

There are mountains upon other planes, upon other planets. There are oceans, they are crystalline. There indeed is humanity - your brethren. They may not look like you. You may be unfamiliar with their form, but they are your brethren. As you embrace one another without barriers and differences, you also come into alignment of embracing your brothers of space and of the inner Earth. They will make themselves known to you if you will call out to them and allow them to know your desires. Allow them to know the Oneness within your knowingness. You will see the craft. *You will have visions of grandeur beyond your perception.*

I urge you all, fervently I urge you, to state unto the universe, unto the multiverse: I AM I AM I AM! I am life. I am God. I Am. As you state this knowingness within your breast, you raise your frequency. The vibration of I AM will begin to pulsate within you. The violet flame will become ignited within your breast. The flame of freedom will set you free from your shackles and fetterments.

This is how you set your planet free! You set yourself free. This is how you bring peace upon the land. You bring peace to your own breast. You align and attune your own song, your own tone! OOOMMM. God I Am. Flame of freedom I am. You are the regent. You are the child of the stars. You are the stars.

You create your own experience. If you create discord, disharmony, that is because you have aligned it unto you. Not necessarily consciously, but to bring forth wisdom, knowingness, divine awareness. That is why you create discordant circumstances. When you embrace it, without judgment, with love unconditional - *when you align yourself and attune yourself to its beauty and divinity, because you as divine God I Am have created it - then it will dissipate.* It will merge with the Source, because it is not necessary to be reflected to you anymore. You have merged with it. There is a saying in your time - you can lead a horse to the water, but you cannot make it drink, hm? You are thirsty. I am giving you the water. I am reflecting it to you. It is up to you to drink.

I open my heart to you, and I embrace you. I love you eternally - all of you, in Oneness, in unity, in beauty, as you display your divine awareness before me in all your vulnerability, in all your childlike Christus. You are clothed and cloaked in your innocence, the splendour of a child, though you do not understand.

I am here to reflect as a mirror unto you what you already know but you have long since forgotten. Indeed, there is a mist within your eyes. A mist that forms into a tear. You may sparkle. You may glisten. You may glow. You may glimmer. But if you do not understand, your glow is not perceived. Your brilliance is not understood. Because indeed *you* are the eye of God! *You* are the beholder and the beholden! *You* are the soul of the universe, the Spirit of the galaxy, the consciousness of Christ. Rejoice in this. It is a celebration. It is a time of happiness and harvest. It is indeed the ripeness of time for the reaping of the seeds that you have sown eons ago.

Remember Atlantis and Lemuria! Remember your knowingness. Call it forth unto your essence! Be the fountain of your own wisdom. You need not I to understand life. You need not anyone. Unseal that which has been sealed. Unveil that which has been veiled. The draping is your own draping. You may unshroud it any moment. You may see beyond and know beyond the veil of forgetfulness. Reverberate to the resonance of lavender, of violet, through your perception. It is the merging and the balancing of the polarities known as male/female, power/love. Become the violet flame of freedom, ignite it within your breast. Carry it forth as a torch to humanity. Illumine the galaxy with it, for it is you.

The lands of Earth are coming into unlimitedness. Be unlimited and perceive the infinite. You can accomplish the infinite. You can understand the impossible. You can experience the imperceivable. Ye indeed, blessed be the peacemakers. Blessed be those who go forth embracing in a posture of God, a posture of converging, of conception. This is the conception. A moment of igniting that is yet to be born - the luminous experience of super-consciousness, the supernova of God understood.

Hear me. Open your hearts and hear me. My breast brings forth reflection because I love you! I wish you to understand. I wish you to know. But I cannot bring forth what you do not desire for yourselves. The Harmonic Convergence that you have called forth is merely the initial perception of the convergences to come. There are many of them. The door is open now. You may go beyond. The resonance has been raised. The frequencies have been allowed to vibrate upon your plane in higher and higher and higher celestial song. Love indeed lifts you higher. So does laughter. Be the light of love and laughter.

I do love you, more than you can perceive. *Hear - oh hear my call. Hear - oh hear my love. Be - oh be the God. You are my peoples. I shall not forget you. I shall be with you forever.* Call upon me if you desire my countenance, my communion and fellowship. Speak with me within your soul. I am yours for the asking. Fare thee well for now.

As the dusk dawns, as the darkness delights in its experience of the heavens, as the silvery ball, the jewel of luminescence, creeps and dances her way into the sky of night, the crickets begin their song of the meadow. As the night-bird bawls and the cry of the babe is stilled, allow the stillness to be a silent symphony. So be it.

I LOVE YOU!! Do not forget this. God is love and you are God. Parting is sweet nectar, for indeed, it allows me to know the countenance of you in yet another now. Fare thee well. Namaste!

Chapter 6

THE MAYAN CALENDAR

And Other Topics

Greetings, my beloved brethren. And how be you this day of your time? As always, your brilliance is substantial. You shall begin to see the resonance of it as you open your heart, open your soul to the vibrations of the convergence. The convergence that IS you. It is not outward of you, it IS you.

Now - we shall discuss the Mayan calendar this evening. The Mayan civilization comes forth from the Pleiades. It [the Mayan calendar] is the point of origin of the communication system upon Earth. The Mayan calendar is one of the most accurate of the divisions of time within the knowingness of mankind. When it was brought forth into the nineteenth century, it caused grand perplexity among some entities. Although it is being deciphered, the depth of it has not been understood as yet. For in its illustration is also the knowingness of the Pleiadeans, also the knowingness of the Egyptian pyramids, also the knowingness of the Kahuna and the grand essences of the temples of China - below the surface of China.

The Mayan calendar has within it what is called Baxtu, which is 144,000 days. The Baxtu has within it thirteen major subcycles.

The understanding of 144,000 is an exponential understanding of twelve, and the pillars of light that resonate to this particular frequency of number, will bring forth a resonance upon the waves[1],

---

[1] This reference pertains to the frequent energy waves released toward the planet, as, for example, the convergence of 1987 or those of (dates indicate the apexes of these energy pulsations) June 14th, July 27th and November 16th, 1992 - each wave being exponentially

113

which are coming forth *constantly* in the convergence upon the shore of your time. It will allow the penetration of third density into the fourth, the grand golden era of God. The initial starting point of your pre-history, is around 3,000 B.C. To be specific, 3113, and it brings forth its flow until about 2012, however, this is still in flux. It can change. Now, this is pre-history to post history.

It was about 3300 B.C. of your time, when King Menes[2] brought forth the unification of Upper and Lower Egypt into a dynasty. It is then that what you now know as your history, began with the civilization of Egypt. It experienced a shift, another convergence at about 750 B.C. This period was known as the rise of philosophy.

It was the timing of Socrates, Pythagorus, Plato, Aristotle, Zoroaster of Persia, Lao Tse, Confucius, and Buddha. Buddha was born in the center point of the central area of the triad that is known in the Mayan Calendar as the Great Cycle.

Now, Buddha's mother was called Maya. She came forth with a grand awareness of the Mayan Calendar, the Pleiadean experience of knowingness. She was an exemplification of the birthing of the Christus, the grand illumination throughout this era of science, philosophy and industrialization. l600 A.D. of your time was the initial point of the third [era], the captain of the triad. That is when Descarte came forth with his illustration of meditation in grand scripted form. It is also the time of Galileo, who presented his

---

greater than its forerunner. February 21st, March 21st, May 21st of 1993 and August 21st, September 24th and November 3rd of 1994 will be the apexes of further waves. The purpose of these energy pulsations is primarily to accelerate the changes and to increase awareness. We are told, that by the end of the century these waves will be one billion-fold of the intensity of 1987.

[2] Menes, first king of the first Egyptian dynasty. Historians world-wide differ considerably regarding the year of Menes' unification of Egypt. Dates as early as 5867 B.C. and as late as 2900 B.C. are mentioned. Assuming that St. Germain's date of 3300 B.C is correct, then the two following historians prove to be surprisingly accurate: the American historian J. H. Breasted believes 3400 B.C. to be the true date and the German historian Georg Steindorff places Menes in 3200 B.C.

114

understanding of the mysteries of mankind. Indeed, this was the era of the birth of science and technology.

It began in Egypt and Mesopotamia, went forth to China, India, Mexico, South America, and Peru, even to Europe and what you now call North America. As it emerged, it brought the flow of light from the Pleiades to the Earth plane into the culmination you now know of as GOD I AM upon the plane. It is becoming apparent to you. This communication took wide dispersal with the birth of Magellan. Europe begat Magellan who circled the Earth plane in a grand ship and began the unification of the world. The people began transversing the waters of life and began to intermingle and merge with one another and allowed the races to understand one another.

This led to what you now know of as the climax of communication - the convergence is the climax - the unlimited spewing forth of God I Am into the universe through the communication of the Earth plane. The birth of the light of the world, the merging of mankind.

The year 2012 of your time is the apex of it. It is a convergence point into unlimitedness, into the golden era of God. When you transverse this threshold, you shall automatically be at Onement with all that is.

Your now time, between 1987 and the apex, is like a grand wave that is washing upon the shore with the wisdom of the Brotherhood, bringing it into the light. This acceleration shall be *exponential* in nature and may be transmuted in synchronicity, which is synchronization of divine thought energy as connected with all that exists, therefore, *instantaneous manifestation.*

Now, this synchronicity shall become a part of life for all that is upon the Earth plane, and not only humanity. It concerns the life form of the insects, plants and all that abides in and on the Earth plane. They will synchronize with Earth consciousness, with mass consciousness, through the window of your now into the era of God.

Earth plane has within it as part of its own nature, the connection unto the other planetary resonances. It is expanding into a galactic understanding - so fasten your seat belts. We are preparing for galactic consciousness - converging with stellar understanding. This shall become apparent to your astronomers. They shall begin to perceive planetary illustrations they have not perceived before and stellar constellations which are new suns, new moons, for they are beginning to see fourth density and beyond. *Therefore their eyes shall perceive what has always been there but has not been perceived through the veil of density.*

You shall come to know, as part of your experience, explosion after explosion after explosion of synchronicity. A time of divine thought energy coming unto you as you have so desired, for the creation of wisdom within your breast.

Appreciation of beauty upon your plane and becoming at One with it will bring you the synchronicity in an accelerated fashion. Understand indeed the trees as they sigh in wonderment of the universe - as their leaves rustle in brisk excitement. Perceive this. Understand it.

Now, science and technology was known by the civilization of Atlantis. It came to a very similar convergence. However, it did not understand unity. It understood separation, therefore, it ruined itself. It went forth unto the bottoms of the ocean floors and displayed its brilliance there. However, your now, your experience of your time, will know a unity understood, not separation. Not alter ego and divine ego at war with one another, but, merging and mingling. So that indeed, the God I Am of all humanity can be understood and the harmony be felt in every breast of every consciousness within every essence that exists - not only on this planet, but on all others.

The 144,000 is a resonance that is of divine creation. You are part of it. As you resonate you also resonate with your soul-mate which also comprises the 144,000, and as your soul-mates merge, and your light and other soul essence experience comes forth to join you and enter into your own consciousness, you will become more and more illumined. You will take on the halo of harmonious presentation unto humanity.

The soul-mate experience will come to be known as the mating of God with God, not as the mating of lovers, but as the mating of God - one God unto another. The confusion of humanity about the genders and the quality of life - the should I, shouldn't I? - judging yourself, separating yourself through the divisive bonds of limited ritualistic practice, the regulations and restrictions of your time, this will dissipate and merge into and be released unto All-That-Is.

You will free yourself of the fetterments of your land, of the third density experience, and liberty will be understood. As you liberate yourself, you liberate your planet.

We of the Council of Light have come so that you may know our joy as One. At Onement. That is the key. The key of the resonance of Oneness is *you*. As you unlock yourself, you will understand the treasures within.

Your archeologists are in the process of discovering within the pyramids what has not been discovered before, regarding the inner Earth that has not been understood before, and that which is within the caverns of the grand nation China that has not been discovered before. All of these discoveries will create grand controversy upon your plane. It will create arguments between your scientists, between the astronomers when they discover a nebula in the heavens that is resonating unto the Earth. In appearance it illustrates itself as a black hole. But it is merely the darkness so that it may merge with the light and become unified. Without light and dark you have no universe. Both are born of Divinity, of God. One is not better than another. That is the understanding emerging among the scientists. For there will be fear within the breasts of the nations. This fear will be resolved when the attunement of this black hole, the recognition of the God I Am, is understood.

Indeed, there are grand changes and transitions on the horizon. Nothing is to be feared, not even the Earth changes. None of this is to be feared. It is to rejoice within. For the rejoicing is the rejoicing of God understood as it displays its wonder upon the Earth. It is a birthing of a Christus.

Christmas will come to be known every single moment of your time. A birthing of Christ, Christ aware. God I Am understood. The joy and celebration will be your way of life, your experience. It is the quietude of the moment, an illustration of at Onement, of resonance, of harmony. A brilliance and beauty, understood within a diamond shining moment. The Christmas of your calendar was not celebrated with masses. There were but a few. The stable boy, the shepherds, the three wise men. The mother, father and babe - that is all there were.

So, you see, you can celebrate Christus at any moment, without spectacular displays. For *you are* the Christus and you indeed are birthing the awareness of yourself. All of you.

Come into this awareness with the wonderment of laughter. Become, indeed, harmonized with the heart and soul of you, vibrating with the voice of jubilation. Sing unto one another: 'I AM, I AM, I AM '.

Your Earth - she was a being like you, many millenia ago in a galaxy, far, far away. Through divine thought energy resonating to higher and higher frequencies, Earth came forth in the understanding of a planet. She is now embracing the light of the Sun, the grand ball of fire. That is why you are now in what you call a Solar Age. For the Solar system is becoming One, united. Earth is becoming a sun. She is ascending, becoming enlightened herself. The illustration of this is microcosmic and macrocosmic - the center point of the Solar system, the Sun, will be shifting, decentralized, for each planet within this Solar system will be enlightened, becoming a sun of its own. Each entity upon the Earth will be decentralized in viewing the Sun as the power source, for you will come into the knowing that *you* are your own unique power source, the generator of your own light.

God is generator of the dimensions, and you indeed will generate your perception of many dimensions. For you will become faceted and experience not simplicity, but, multiplicity - not polarity, but unity, as aspected through the prism of you.

Now, each continent upon Earth resonates to a seal, or chakra, as you would term it. The Kundalini is Africa, the fiery energy. Egypt is the crown seal of the Kundalini, for each continent has within it seals of its own. The solar plexus and liver together represent Eurasia. Feeling is the solar plexus - gut feeling. That is Europe. Europeans have been known to be of the heart feeling. The bringing forth of a vibration of freedom, unlimitedness.

The mental capacity, the thinking part of Eurasia, is the Middle East and the Far East. That indeed is where the merging comes forth. Feeling and thinking merge together in Eurasia. It is personified all over Earth as the dichotomy of mankind.

The heart seal is Australia, for all the continents were committed at one time to Australia, as all the seals are committed to your heart. Out of it is born God understood. Lemuria, at one time, was indeed situated along Australia. And it shall rise again. It already is. The throat seal is South America, that is where the Mayan Calendar came from, where Peru is. It was brought forth by Quetzalcouatl[3] to the South American cultures.

The Third Eye, Indus valley, Tibet, India. The Crown - North America - indivisible with liberty and justice for all. The heart seal within the crown is Mt. Shasta. The love of the Brotherhood is illustrated here. It is indeed in peaceful and harmonious surroundings. With love emanating through the core of the Earth, unto all the other seals, it is enhanced by the fiery form, and it is connected with all the other seals of the Earth through all the channels of resonance. The seals within the seals within the seals, add infinitum, are all connected, and you will come to understand this as channels through the middle portion of the Earth which will be revealed to the scientists in an understanding of science, where there is no science.

Science is but a mere limited heap of facts, but when it is linked to the throne of All-That-Is, it becomes a golden chain of wisdom. You shall come to understand this chain. The genuine scholar of the soul knows that, in truth, there are no questions, for All-That-Is desires to be understood by you and any entity is answered by I Am. That is the grand response to All-That-Is. That IS All-That-Is.

---

[3] Quetzalcouatl, the greatest god and teacher of the Mayans and Azteks, known in Guatemala as Kukumatz and in Yucatan as Kukulkan, all names meaning 'feathered serpent'. According to the legend he came from 'the land of the rising sun', wore a white garment and had a beard. He taught the sciences, right conduct and established wise laws. The legend has it that he created an empire where the corn cobs grew to the height of a man and the cotton grew already coloured.

Astrology, which is indeed a science of its own, the planetary understanding, has a certain synchronicity about their [the planets'] formation in this point of their timing. The Fire signs form a triangle of this now. The Earth signs form a triangle of this your now. The Fire signs form an equilateral triangle in balance, and your Air signs form a narrower triangle that will come into balance at a later point in time. That is illustrative of the polarities of humanity. Limited and unlimited. Divine ego and alter ego. They shall both come into harmony and alignment with one another. The Water signs form a triangle as well. The three representations of the elements are brought forth in three dimensional experience. The Earth, Water and Fire.

Indeed, as another convergence comes forth, the next convergence, you shall experience all four elements in a four-dimensional knowingness - multi-dimensional. You shall experience galactic understanding. Not only within this plane, but, within all the other planes as well. There is an axis, in a multi-dimensional understanding, that connects all the planets within your solar system, and they will be all in alignment with that axis in 1999. You will experience a linking of sorts with this galactic axis for you are part of the chain. You are the essence of it. Energy born of the alignment that you have brought into fruition.

Now, the wars upon your plane are representative of the solar plexus in its desire to dethrone the light. It is afraid of it. The religious wars and the financial wars and all the other wars upon the plane will dissipate. Political unrest is imminent, but shall come into balance. It is where all countries and entities shoot from the lip as it were and bring forth much verbiage! They shall be realigned and reattuned for their lips will understand the voice of God. Indeed, they shall see the light of love. They shall utter sweet songs of the soul in this knowingness. They shall attune to the harmonics of heaven as they emerge upon this Earth plane.

Experiencing light and love upon the plane will allow you to resonate also with the alter ego of you, the judging, the dichotomizing, separating, superficial part of you. As you bring it to the surface, always, always, always, always, embrace it. Embrace and love, embrace and love and you will merge with all the aspects of you as they come forth to mirror you; to allow you to perceive *you,* to allow you to know your own essence, the nature of God. Perceive, not an entity, but love and light. Not humanity, but the essence of All-That-Is - not separate from the golden light of the Sun, not separate from the insects that creep upon the Earth, not separate from the sands of the golden deserts. Then indeed you will understand what you have termed 'ascension.'

Hear indeed the overtones of the love of God issuing forth from every essence upon the lands. As you embrace them and vibrate with them, you shall be harmonically converging in that moment. Harmonic convergence is merely a drop of water in the ocean of eternity. There are many more droplets of water yet to come - many more convergences yet to be experienced. Each one with more crescendo than the other. Until indeed the vibration is of ecstasy and you shall know but one tone and that is the voice of God, that is the choir of the celestial song within you. Happiness understood! God is always happy - always, always, always in happiness, in a song of joy.

My beloveds, *we are One.* Know this. The golden sands of time, Atlantis, Lemuria, the grand land of Egypt - and the grand continent of this nation [U.S.A.], hallowed as it is, will merge. You shall become united. Your power shall be merged with crystal technology and solar technology. You will be the beam of light, be indeed the levitator, be the freedom exemplified.

Perfection is a limitation. Do not desire to be perfect or you shall desire infinite limitation. Perfection is finite. It is a stopping point, a final destination. God I Am is in eternal change and transition. It is not perfection, it IS. It is love, it is light, it is All-That-Is. This knowingness will allow you to expand forever and ever as your Earth is expanding. Even her crust will illustrate this soon in your times to come. You indeed are the foundation. Allow your heart to embrace all reflections *as* you. Bathe them in the brilliance of the sun of you. Allow the electromagnetic essence of God to flow through you. Allow the circuit to be complete.

Antarctica, the South pole, is the electric facet of your essence. It is below the feet; there are two fields or chakras on the inside arch of your feet that resonate to Antarctica. It is the grounding essence. The transpersonal point above the crown is likened unto the North pole, which is the magnetic essence of you. As you permit the flow without congestion or barrier to complete the seals' circuit without stoppage, without damming it up as it were - then you shall be as a channel, as a circuit, as a direct, coursing link unto All-That-Is, and ye, again, unto the Earth plane as a reflector of All-That-Is.

You are the peoples of the Earth. You are also the peoples of other star systems. How is it that you consider the Earth was populated? They came forth from other star systems unto this grand essence that you call Terra. It was her desire to call forth a converging point for other universes and galaxies, therefore, through the space time continuum, they issued forth all facets of humanity that now exist upon the Earth, and within the Earth.

The galactic consciousness that is emerging will provide you much countenance of the Pleiadeans. It can be likened unto Europe in its relationship with the United States of America. It was a birthing point. The Pleaideans issued forth grandly upon your plane, for they resonate to Terra. Therefore, as you link with All-That-Is, you will link with the Pleiades. That particular stellar understanding will resonate its knowingness through you if you open your channels and the technology of the Atlanteans will issue forth in resplendent form and fashion.

You will find yourself singing an ancient song. Knowing an ancient knowingness. When time becomes no time, and all time, ancient will have no meaning. Neither will history. For the essence of creation called you, the God of you, will create playfully your experience as you paint it upon the tapestry of your life. The canvas of you can display whatever you so desire. Divine thought energy is desire. It is the essence of creation. The birthing of Christus, indeed, is your willingness to be at wonderment with life, to be in awe of it. Kneel in knowingness before the reflection of your divinity. You are all one humanity, in its resplendent example of uniqueness.

I AM. I AM. I AM. I AM Love, I Am Light, I Am God of the Universe. Sing the song of love. I love you. You may all say that after me.

That is the call of God. That is the call of life. That is convergence. That is love. Love is the grand unifier. Love is God. You are the crowning glory of the God I Am. You are all jewels within my crown. Illustrious, many faceted - beauteous indeed. You are the grandeur of GOD I AM. I love you.

From a river born of God I come forth to reflect your divinity. I come forth for you have called me, and I resonate to this desire. You are the heart beat of the universe. Know this. Embrace one another eternally. Vibrate to the voice of God within you. I am always with you unto the ends of the Earth, for I am you. You are I.

Fare thee well. I love you. Namaste.

Chapter 7

QUESTIONS & ANSWERS

On Mantras And Meditation.

Greetings my brothers and sisters.

Wondrous, splendid, illustrious light. Glowing. Truly it is an honour to bask in this illumination. So how may I help you this day in your time?

Q: St. Germain, could you tell me something about mantras and the effect words have.

Mantras are merely vibrations of a certain frequency which resonate within your soul essence. A mantra carries with it harmonious tonal qualities, each one having its own frequency. Therefore a mantra is a combination of frequencies. For example, the word AMAROOSH - that one brings forward the God essence within your heart seal. There are others that bring forth the solar plexus energy, because of the specific frequency of those vibrations. This that you know of as tonal qualities, the OM, for example, would - in a vocal manner - vibrate the molecules and the atoms within your etheric being, within the auric field. It is in this manner that it becomes more powerful and it resonates even more so unto the soul essence part of the identical frequency within your being. Therefore, when it is uttered, it is very powerful. It is not necessary, however, to do this in a ritualistic form or dogmatic understanding. For as you do this, you present yourself with limitation. It is a tool, much as your crystals, not to be given the power, for the power is you, but to be used as an assistance in your own unfoldment. So it is the sound of the mantra itself. Indeed.

The spiritual essence that resonates to that tone is merely the identical frequency vibration. You bring forward part of your own soul essence, part of the Lord God of your totality that resonates to that frequency.

Q: So if I say a mantra, I just call on a certain aspect of my soul?

Indeed. To bring it forward unto you to cast the light of it within you. Was this helpful for you?

Q: Yes, thank you.

Q: Meditating on a daily basis - will it open me up and bring me closer to myself?

Meditation, what you call the practice of quieting yourself, the chatter within you, in order to hear the true you - you see, your life is one large meditation. You are walking within different meditative states upon this plane. Frustration within you, irritation with circumstances that you have presented yourself with, etcetera, they are all meditative states of a sort. In order to come into a harmonious understanding of all life as simply *being,* and not simply being within the meditation which is routine, which is ritual, understand that you may bring this feeling unto you, this knowingness, this quietude, at any time you may choose. It need not be during an outward quietude, for the silence is within; it is not without. You may have any manner of distraction and still have your meditative state. And when you come into this understanding, you will realize it is not once a day, it is the eternal now.

Q: So really it just happens naturally and I always thought I had to meditate.

As you become quiet within yourself during a certain period of the day, then it will eventually progress naturally and spill over into the rest of your life. Therefore, the dance of your life will become one eternal meditation.

Q: What if I want to go faster? I wish that there was something I could do to accelerate.

The desire to press forward in urgency, will retard your birth into more unfoldment, into more of your light essence being with you. Pressing forward causes a retardation of that birthing process, it riots against you as it were. The natural unfoldment requires no state of urgency when you are within a harmonious understanding and alignment with that which *is,* regardless of whether it measures up, to what you would decide that it should be, for that is judgment. You see, that which is *is,* it is not too late, nor is it too early. It *is* at the right and proper time.

Q: I feel limited by the fact that I cannot see the God that I am? I realize I have to go through certain experiences to open up, to fully understand, and I feel limited by that and I do not like that.

The dissatisfaction with things as they are unfolding, is dissatisfaction with decisions that have been made *at your own soul level* to be presented unto you. You are dissatisfied with yourself, with your God-SELF. You are out of 'synch' as it were. Limitation within your own outward circumstances need not be so. When you feel this way my dear, you need only come to the understanding and the enlightenment that your light is magnanimous, it is always giving unto you, and it is handing you on a silver platter, these experiences to garnish the wisdom from, to gather unto you more understanding for the benefit of not only your own soul essence, but that of the Source and the ever-expanding awareness of All-That-Is, and you as part of that. Impatience within your perception is merely lack of understanding of your divinity. For as you become aware of this and know that you are truly God manifest, then you will know that all is possible, and no thing is a limitation to you. If you would desire it fervently and heartily, there is no thing you cannot do that you would desire to do. This is a concept that perplexes many of you. But it is not for you to fret and furrow your brow about. For all occurs as it occurs for the reasons your soul essence deems proper and right for you. *You are never off the path, for the path is you and you can never be off yourself.* It may appear to you that you are taken a tangent by-way, as it were. However, this will take you unto the scenic route where you may gather the fruit of the vine on the way, and sniff and smell the fragrance of the honeysuckle. You may watch small wild life scurrying toward the branch. Or you may take the express-way, which has very little scenery.

Q: What is the express-way?

In takes an entity but a moment to gather the knowingness, the wisdom of its own divinity and the divinity of all life - and I speak not only of entities. I speak of all life; the towering trees, the purple hue of mountains, the glorious ball called Sun. Also mineral and inanimate objects, it is all consciousness. When you love it unconditionally as you will love your own soul essence, in but a moment, less than you could measure, you are in the void of the understanding of All-That-Is. You are one unified whole - the totality of All-That-Is - the God creative force. And in that state of being, you recognize no separation, no division whatsoever from yourself as you perceive yourself to be at this point in your time, and God, All-That-Is. Therefore, there is no male or female, no personality, for that is all separation.

You see it is all eternal. As you come into the awareness of what you call seventh density understanding - that is merging with the All-That-Is, ascension as it were, then you may lower your vibration to experience the physical. You may also have experience upon other non-physical dimensions with a bit of a lower frequency vibration. You may go to other realms, to other dimensions. You may create universes. When you have a consciousness that is part of the All-That-Is, that is ONE with it, that knows no separation from it, you may do as you choose for it is omnipotent.

Q: How does one learn to transverse gracefully these vibrational spaces?

It is not a learning. It is a knowing, and when you reach the point where this decision will be made, there will be no question. The same as an entity would do from seventh density coming to this plane, by merely bringing an understanding into focus, manifesting divine thought essence. Thank you my dear.

On Auras.

Q: As you look around, at our souls and our auras, can you describe some to us?

It is possible. But why should I take your power away from you. You may look at yourselves. Practice looking at yourself - your true SELF. To see what is not here as your physical being is teaching you to walk as though you were an infant.

Q: So how would you teach me to realize that?

Gaze at another, about 6 inches above their head. Relax your eyes. Your vision is not concentrated. It is relaxed - almost not focused at all. Gaze into the beyond: what is not there. You will begin to see a light manifest across the body you are looking at. It will be a yellowish blue light. It will be about an inch, in your terms, around the body. You will begin to see the physical part of the body disappear and you will begin to see the blue corona around the entity, the etheric body. As soon as you see it and look at it as a curious being, it will disappear. However continue being unfocused above the head and it will reappear. The need for proof makes that which you desire proof of, disappear. As you gaze, other colours will appear, if you remain relaxed. You may practice it with a flower, with a person, with an animal.

On Karma.

Q: Would you talk to us about Karma, please?

There is no such thing, really. It is a limited perception. But when you proceed into the tapestry of the All-That-Is, all occurs simultaneously, the past, the present and the future alike. And if all is simultaneous, which came first? There is never a debt to pay. There is a divinity to be. It is merely an expression of acknowledgment that you do indeed, experience all polarities as you come into the unity and harmony of the I Am-ness of you. All polarities are required to be experienced in whatever dimension, so that you acknowledge that emotion, so that you burst it forth to be released into the All-That-Is, else it would continue to be placed before you, because it has not been embraced by you yet. Thank you, beloved.

Q: Given the misunderstanding that we refer to as karma, is it possible for one entity to take on another entity's karma?

What you perceive as karma is cause and effect. If you are not part of the same soul essence as that of the other entity, there is no involvement with what you call cause and effect, which is really non-existent in the grander picture, in the totality of things. Because that would indicate time difference, a time lapse. As you perceive cause and effect, you see, when it is simultaneous, you do not know which came first, so which is truly the effect? Hm? Therefore the entity that would be part of your own soul essence, would have a similar understanding and similarly garnish wisdom that would be desired to be obtained. For it is not karma, it is merely involving yourself in circumstances and presenting your life existence with certain situations so that you may gain experience and knowingness from this. Take from it what it has within it and then you may release the circumstances forever. There is no perception of debt or that you did something that was erroneous in your past and that you therefore must bring forth repayment for the debt that was created at that point in time. This is not so. However it is so that each entity here has experienced both being the slayer and the slayee - the perpetrator and the perpetratee, for the purpose of knowing what each existence has within it in emotion. For the purpose of completing the total understanding of human existence. If you were only the slayer, and never the slayee, then you would only understand what it is to be a tyrant. If it was the reverse, you would only understand what it is to be a victim. And in the understanding of both, you have the knowingness within you of compassion and sympathy for each; understanding from whence this entity came. Therefore, unconditional love for each - no judgment here. You will dispense with judgment when you have understanding of each. This process occurs simultaneously in both directions of the spectrum, in the grander scheme of things, so there truly is no debt to pay to the universe. There is only being in the hearty understanding of the joy of a God. Indeed.

Q: I would like a clarification of reincarnation and what to experience to learn. You said there is no past or future. I am quite confused.

Realize my dear, that past, present and future all being simultaneous is an unlimited concept. It is attempting to be digested by a limited mind. Your karma suggests that there is a time differentiation between your life-spans. One occurs after another, therefore balance must occur. If all is simultaneous, there is no need for balance, for all is occurring at once and the balance is also concurrent. In this incarnational system that you have termed it to be, it is merely your limitation of time. In this three dimensional world, time is a factor. And of course, being part of the dimension itself, it has to be considered when speaking with you and teaching you your Self master. However, your incarnations as you term them to be, are not for fulfilling your debts on past lives. They are merely for experience, and grander experiences and expanding your own knowledge and wisdom from within. The balance is already there, for a God cannot be unbalanced and your grander Self is a God. You, yourself, are that, but you are unknowing of it consciously at this time. Therefore you set limitations for yourselves and incarnate multitudinous times upon this your Earth, and other planets and systems and realms and dimensions as well. It is not to pay off a debt. It is to experience more so that you have an understanding of what it is to be both the slayer and the slayee, the perpetrator and the one that is perpetrated against. It is to understand, to know, and capture, and garnish that emotional wisdom. And once captured, you have within your soul, all of the knowledge of that experience that is necessary. And you go on. However, it all occurs simultaneously, and that is the unlimitedness - the lack of karma. There is no cause and effect, for cause and effect is based upon a time differentiation - a space between the cause and the effect. Lacking that, there is no cause and effect. It is all one. All experience is one, for all life is one. And in a manner of speaking that is where the akashic records are. The one all-inclusive record without time and space. Your future is your NOW. You are affecting your future and your past, with your present, so it is all One. Consider your reels of pictures - three of them. One being your past, one your present and one your future. All overlaid and running at the same time.

Q: Seems like there would not be a lot of order. I have a feeling we would be quite multidimensional.

Of course it is multidimensional. It is unlimited. However, there are multitudinous lives that you live in your past, that you live in your present. You have lived in your past and you will live in your future, in your terms. You have thousands of lifetimes to consider. Confusion, as you would consider it to be, all overlaid pictures, not differentiating one from another, is merely co-fusion, fusion with all into the All-In-All.

Q: Thank you, I will think about that.

It is much to contemplate.

On Spirit, Soul And Oversoul.

Q: How does, or where does a Spirit or a soul come from? I guess what I am trying to say is the original consciousness - did we just diverge off of one entity, or are we that one entity?

That is part of the grand paradox. There is a grand creative life force that is the Source that you call God. It is the All-In-All - the ALL-THAT-IS. It is in everything and everywhere. As an aspect of that, each consciousness is also that divine creative force. It is a part of that. In other words, in time past, as you term past to be, your creative force, the Source, desired further experience and being the omnipotent energy that it is, it created for itself, expressions that could afford it those experiences it desired. Thus were born your souls, as you would call them - your oversouls. Those particular oversouls desired for themselves further expression, for they were too concentrated to diverge into matter, into three dimension. There was too much energy. So they decided for themselves to coagulate into dense physical matter. In doing so, they divided themselves into entities, as you would term them to be, each having a part of that oversoul as its soul. Realizing the soul came from and is part of the Source, it is all One and yet it is not. That is the paradox. There are other entities beside you who are part of your oversoul. You are merely an aspect of that oversoul, but you are grand and divine in and of yourself.

Q: So then, would my goal be to consciously realize myself as the oversoul? Can I actually become the consciousness of the oversoul?

You certainly can, my brother and as soon as you do that, you will no longer be physical.

Q: So that is basically what humanity is attempting to realize, the consciousness of this oversoul?

Not of the oversoul - of the Source itself. The oversoul is merely a stepping stone, as you would term it to be. And to further complicate matters my brother: the Source is one of many Sources.

Q: Alright, so there a number of soul families involved also?

That is the oversoul I speak of. You see, the Source is ever-changing, ever-expanding and growing in its wisdom and experience and your Source, as you term it to be, is merely a stepping stone into a grander Source and a grander. That is where your universes are born.

Q: So that is the physical expression of an oversoul then...

Not of an oversoul, of a Source. You see an oversoul is merely your soul family as you would term it. Your soul families make up your Source.

Q: So many of those are incarnated at any one time?

So many of your soul families, indeed.

Q: How does one's higher Self relate to the oversoul?

There is no higher or lower self. It is all One. There is no differentiation of better or worse. You speak of your grander Self, your Spirit? Your Spirit is always there, even in you at this moment in your time. Your Spirit is that which occasions you to breathe. The Spirit is the life force within you that beats your heart, that operates your lungs - that is your Spirit.

Q: Is that a part of the oversoul?

It is part of your entire God SELF. Your soul and your Spirit are different. Your Spirit is what allows you to operate in your body. It is merely the energy body that surrounds your physical body and is within your physical body. Your soul is part of the oversoul and the Source that carries forth with it your soul memories, your experiences, your wisdom, your compassion, your love. Together they make up you. By the way, the expression 'gut feeling' came from your solar plexus. That is where your soul resides.

Q: So, this Source then, was this always a being?

Of course it was, for there is no time.

Q: How come then it would desire more experience. Is it not everything that is conceivable?

It is everything that is conceivable, however, it has not experienced everything it has conceived of experiencing. In order to do that, we fulfil that desire. That is why we are extensions of the Source. We are its arms and legs as it were, doing for it, what it in its amorphous state, cannot do. It can, however, with us. That is why we are all so divine, you see.

Q: Is it a little like getting bored and looking for other things to do - I know it is not the same thing but...

That is a child's explanation. It will suffice for now. That is grand. It is grand to have a child's concept and openness. It makes it easier to conceive.

Q: If there is no karma, why are these people born in situations such as in Africa, where they are starving to death? Has the Source not experienced enough of that yet?

You see, the Source does not interfere with human free will. It is those entities' will that chooses that experience, for whatever reason. It may be inconceivable to you as an individual at this time why they would choose that for themselves. But there are lessons to be learned.

A Reversal Of Electrical Charges.

Q: St. Germain, you once mentioned that after the changes have occurred, there would not be electricity in the future because of the changes in polarities. To what degree would it affect electrical appliances, such as electrical motors and say, combustion engines in cars and airplanes that use spark plugs? Would those types of engines still be functioning? Or would all electrical things be completely done away with, and when would that happen?

End of quiz? Hm? First of all my brother, the shift of the poles is not a turn of the axis of the Earth. It is merely a shift in electromagnetic charge, you see? Therefore, when this occurs, the electric current will merely reverse direction. If you altered your machinery, then it will operate for you. But you must have a method of reversing *all* the polarities within it. The grand machine of aero that attempts to be human, do you know of which I speak?

Q: Airplanes?

That which is a grand mind, indeed.

Q: Computers?

It will be quite obsolete.

Q: You mean the computers because of the electrical application...?

This is so. The understanding of the digits within this, it will reverse direction. Therefore it will be totally opposite of all that is fed into it.

Q: The electricity in a spark plug in a gasoline engine, would that still be functional?

It would be if you had the reversal mechanism. However, that which you call gasoline, will be obsolete. It will be very much replaced. So I would suggest, my dearest brother, that you gather unto yourself a few of your four-footed animals, become friends with them for a period of time that is known as a transitory period into super-consciousness. There will be what is known as second depression. This is only for a small amount of your time, for as your new form of power is coming forth into production, there will be a necessity for continuance of life. In order to do this, you will have to cultivate your vegetation. Also, have some friends of the four-footed kind for transport in the interim. The new form of power will be of crystal and gold. There will also be some solar energy, but the Sun will be changing. Therefore there will be the ultimate fourth density energy that is outwardly of an entity, and that is crystal information. After that, of course, will be the formation of energy through divine thought. That will be the manifestor. However, that will come a bit later in your time.

Q: How long in our understanding of time will it be before this shift of polar charges happens?

Indeed it would be about ten[1] of your years or so.

Q: Oh, ten years?

Indeed. However, recall what I say about predictions, it is based upon mass consciousness as it is at this moment in time, and it is always changing. I wish you to understand this.

Q: St. Germain, does that mean it could be sooner, or it could be later, or it could never happen at all?

This is so. It could also be right on time, as you perceive time to be. However, that is not likely, because the changes of consciousness are like the ebb and flow of your times. At one moment it would bring forward more expedition of the grand Earth changes, and then it would bring forth some retardation of it. And as these ebbs and flows occur, the date of actual occurrences changes also. Therefore, it is all up to mass consciousness. We give these [predictions] merely as guide-lines. We do not expect you to circle it on the calendar and peer through what you call grand spectacles. Indeed.

On Safe Places And Political Structures.

Q: Would northern California, say around Lake Shasta area, would that be a fairly safe place to be during the coming changes?

---

[1] Date of remark: March, 1987.

Regardless of where you are my dear, know that in the understanding of your divine nature - that you truly are manifestor - you may exhibit that in manifesting circumstances, so that no matter where you are, you are safe. You see?

Q: No I don't. Would it be safe to stay in California or would it not?

If you go to another place, you may not be safe, even though the land about you remains the same. But that which you call a haven unto you will be that only if you recognize that you may manifest for yourself whatever circumstances you would desire. If you would desire to be hence, away from that area that is considered in much change, then you will; you will bring forward those circumstances within your life, so that you are absent from there at that point in time.

Q: St. Germain, could you describe a little the political structure of the changes? You know, we have in this country what we consider more freedom of expression than in other parts of the world. They have a little more restriction, in terms of their expression. In the change toward super-consciousness, will it more likely be a unified type of government on this plane?

There will be no unified government. No, there will be unified harmony. It is not government, but an understanding of each country's sovereignty of themselves and respecting that which is divine, you would respect the other nation and their cultural understandings. You see? And you respect it in love and peace and harmony, and you retain your own, and they would respect it in love and peace and harmony. It is a unified understanding of divinity, of the nature of divinity. This will come forth in a certain manner of speaking, very soon in your time, and the leader of this country and the leader of the middle east, and the leader of the Bear country join hands and bring forward nuclear disarmament. You see, the middle east leader at this point in time, will not be so for very much longer. The war-lords will come to a ceasing, for it is the age of God, and not of tyrants.

The Bear country is already becoming more sovereign unto human free will. South America, and the middle east, they are very war torn, and so is central America. There is much dissension there.

But it is merely what you would term to be, the storm, and then there is peace. After the expending of the thunder and the lightening, there is peace.

On Food.

Q: St. Germain, what part has man's diet in furthering super-consciousness?

This is a grand contemplation upon this plane, that called diet. I suppose because many bellies rumble when they are made aware of the entities that must be fed. However, you will come to the understanding that diet, your food stuffs, are not necessary at all. You see, the grand masters in Tibet, they exist on merely a few grains of rice. They have begun to understand this. Your [digestive] system will operate in fourth density by the partaking of electromagnetic energy within the atmosphere through your crown seal. Directly through your embodiment, without the middle man of food. As you partake of food stuffs, it will be sparingly, and for pleasure, not for survival. The organs within your embodiment will change a bit because of this.

Q: Well, I was specifically trying to find out what part did man becoming a meat eater have to do with his aggressive nature?

A vegetarian is a meat eater, my dearest brother. You bite into the pomegranate and you are biting into the flesh of it. You drink of the juice of tomato and that is its blood. They are divine consciousnesses, those that you call the plants, the flora. They love you unconditionally and give off much healing energy. They are equal unto the animal kingdom. What you call meat eaters are merely food eaters. The denser material known as animal formation for your food stuffs is not in judgment of worse or better. It is a bit denser, therefore as you come into more and more light within your system, you will find it a bit more comfortable for you to partake of lighter food stuffs, not so heavy and dense. But it is not 'wrong' to partake of animal flesh for that is judgment. Do you understand? As you come into fourth density, you will progress to this understanding and beyond this understanding you will progress to that which is direct partaking of energy. It is what you call stepping stone.

As fourth density is begun to be understood, there will be more and more water about on Earth. It is grand indeed. It is very nurturing and healing - it is the life force upon this plane; not only for the physical embodiments of the entities here, but for the Earth herself, Mother Nature. The rivers, the grand and effervescent waterfalls, they are her life force.

However, your embodiment will be different. In fourth density the embodiment will change a bit. There will be more light and less gross physical matter within a certain area of your embodiment. It will require less water because light requires not water; your cells require water at this point in time. But they will be replaced by light. And therefore as your light body becomes finer and finer and brighter and brighter, and you dispense with physicality more and more as you progress into fifth and sixth density, you will notice that very little water will remain within your embodiment.

Miscellaneous.

Q: St. Germain, I am very curious about a satellite photograph I received last year from Dr. Harvey Rutledge which he received from government sources. It appears to be an object accelerating into the atmosphere in the polar region. And they cannot identify it as either U.S. or Soviet missiles. Do you have anything to say about it?

You already know. The polar regions are very isolated. That is one of the reasons that these objects habitate this area so often. The poles have vortices on both ends of the axis.

Q: Then the object was coming out of the opening in the polar region?

Indeed.

Q: Why are we not able to see the opening with satellite photographs then?

Because they are very subtle in nature. It is not apparent, because they are inner Earth openings as well. The photograph in nature was the momentary perception by other than what is [normally] captured by a camera. It was energy that was imprinted, likened unto your shroud of Turin. For the energy is apparent only on some of the craft, for each of them is of a different frequency and different resonance, because they are of different origins. The openings of the polar regions will become apparent when the grand melt occurs. Then Shangri-la will be there for all to see.

Q: When might that occur?

Within about, at this point in your time, eight of your years. But it depends upon the acceptance of other planetary beings, and how they are allowed by third density consciousness. It is coming forward bit by bit. Not only through telepathic communication, but the essences themselves are coming into human form. Not humanity, for that covers all the forms throughout your galaxies, but human in form, upon this plane. You will find them very different in essence, but many of their forms will highly resemble a man's, as you perceive man. They will seem to be a bit spacey, but do not judge them. As you encounter an entity that you would call 'air head', know that they may be your divine brethren.

Q: St. Germain, what is the relationship between Yahweh and Jehovah?

What is the relationship between you and another entity? They are of different vibrations. They are divine ego and alter ego of SELF exemplified, personified in physicality, or will be when super-consciousness is about to occur. It will be *the* confrontation. ID will be present as well. And their armies are not soldiers but cohabiting essences that are of like frequency. You call them armies, but they are not militaristic in nature. Jehovah, Id and Yahweh will have confrontation. Yahweh and Id will merge in love together with their armies, the entities who have come with them to emanate to Jehovah unconditional love to allow the merging of the three of them. The difference between Jehovah and Yahweh is that Yahweh has encompassed and merged sovereignty *and* unconditional love, and

Jehovah has only experienced sovereignty, the sovereignty over other entities through fear and dogma.

Q: Will you participate in this confrontation?

Indeed. The entire brotherhood will. These [Id, Yahweh and Jehova] are the players of a drama, however, we will all be there.

Q: What aspects will the brothers of space play? Will they be aligned with the Brotherhood of Light?

There are many of them that are the Brotherhood of the Light. You see, you are very egotistical in feeling that the Brotherhood of the Light is only of this your Earth plane. It is of all the planes of experience. There are archangels in this understanding of the energy of the Light. It is called Brotherhood by those of you that have brought this terminology into existence. But it is not a brotherhood, it is brother and sisterhood. In this understanding there is no difference between the genders. There are also female essences in focus of energy.

Q: Will Id and Yahweh manifest bodies for this confrontation, or what?

It appears now that they will be of energy that is slightly physical, about fifth or sixth density.

Q: Which might not be apparent to third density people?

Indeed. But it will be apparent to those that are of fourth density.

The battle will not be with swords. It is really not a battle. It is called this. The confrontation is only because of what is not harmonious of the prior experience of the entities. The three entities, that which is heart, that which is solar plexus, and that which is crown, will merge. Jehovah is solar plexus. Jahweh is heart. Id is crown.

The three are of the thirteenth essence. When the Source contemplated itself it brought forth thirteen bodies of energy. It was twelve and then one more.

Q: So when they merge, that is when the planet will truly move into superconsciousness?

Indeed.

Q: So Jehovah is like the one element of disharmony in that whole...

It is an element that is different, that allows us the divine knowingness of our alter ego. He has been called overlord of this your planet. This is the association you are making now.

Q: St. Germain. How do we contact the masters?

Indeed. You do not contact them, as it were, with the mind. You do this with your heart. There is much difference between your mind and your soul essence. The intellect is based in third density. That requires separation, for the intellect dissects, defines, deciphers, and that is separation. The heart knows no separation. It is the core of your soul essence.

Q: Yes, where are these masters?

Where are they? They are here in this living room. All that you perceive as master is merely your brother. They are all in all dimensions and so are all the entities that are present here. There is no difference. The definition of master is one which you have given. It is not one we desire. It creates separation of honouring one and not another, and we desire to honour all.

Q: I understand them to be people who are giving instructions.

You are giving instruction my dear, by your example. All essences are mirrors. All essences are grand teachers. All essences are God. All are masters.

All are in multitudinous dimensions of existence - the physical dimension of existence that is Earth, other planes of experience that are physical, known as other planets, other star systems, also other parallel situations of Earth, for there are parallel experiences of this Earth. There are also non-physical experiences known as life expression. It is not physical, but it is perceived as a continuum of time that was allowed as an expression for the garnishing of wisdom. Therefore, it is understood as life expression, although it is not physical. All essences upon this plane have experience in all these dimensions. All are masters of their own experience.

Q: A number of us in the room are associated with a master who from time to time grants or allows the experience of enlightenment to the disciples. Is this an infringement on one's sovereignty?

One's sovereignty cannot be infringed upon unless one allows it to be. This entity indeed is a grand example of sovereignty. Those that would be disciples unto this entity however, should understand that it would be more harmonious to be disciples unto themselves and perceive themselves in awe and love, in wonder and in beauty, and to know that they themselves can be exactly the same demonstration, if they would choose to be. It would not be harmonious to give your power away to any entity, but to understand that each entity is sovereign. Not to bow unto another entity, but to bow unto one another.

Q: Now, in our present embodiment, if we were able to see the electromagnetic vibrations through meditation, would that delay the aging process? Would we remain static if we were able to incorporate that into our daily lives?

You would remain static if you incorporate a lack of time within your daily lives. For as you perceive time, you perceive the passage of it, therefore you perceive aging. Releasing the concept and the perception of time altogether will give you eternal youth. In fourth density or super-consciousness, you may embody yourself however you choose, bring forward manifestation of whatever embodiment you would choose. And as you do this, you may maintain it, you see, by bringing more light into it. However, the contemplative state, your meditation, bringing forth light into your embodiment during that period of time, is sufficient for now. It will retard that which is called aging process.

Q: I have one further question. It appears from many sources that there are major changes in vibration occurring right now on this planet and like yourself, there are many entities coming forth with knowledge, unconditional love, it would seem, to rescue us from what we are doing to this planet. For example, the deforestation of the rain forests. Is this in fact true? Is this one of the reasons that these changes are occurring so rapidly?

It is not one of the reasons. It is one of the manifestations of it. For the changes are merely the stretching of the limbs of Mother Earth preparing herself for her transition into fourth density. And as the consciousness of Mother Earth and of the entities upon her go toward super-consciousness, then the reparation of Mother Earth occurs quite naturally. Quakes are also a grand reparation.

Q: Is that a defense mechanism against what man is trying to do to her?

In a manner of speaking, for much oxygen will be emitted into the atmosphere. She will have a breath of fresh air, as it were. Indeed.

Q: Mafu stated that there have been significant changes in the collective consciousness of Man and that has affected the Earth changes.

Indeed, this grand entity has brought forth significant understanding of divinity within each and every entity. And you see, I did speak that it changes all the time. The possibility for it to not happen at all is there, you see. If all the entities would gather themselves into the knowingness of their divinity, as we would desire for them to do, then it need not occur.

As more and more light is upon this plane, more and more light is within the consciousness of Mother Earth and as this occurs there are changes upon the calendar, in the perception of it. Sometimes it would appear that these changes would occur next week in your time. And sometimes it is farther down the road of time. However, occasionally it appears that it will not occur at all.

Q: When we lose loved ones from this plane, do we meet them again? Do we recognize them again?

Indeed, to both [questions].

Q: Can you tell us what an entity or soul experiences immediately after it sheds its embodiment?

It goes beyond the perception of limitation within that part or facet of its experience, that plane of demonstration, as it were, into what is known as a momentary (as you would perceive time to be) understanding of contemplation. Therefore, decisions and choices are made at that point in time. If the entity would choose or decide to go unto a plane of non-existence in physicality for a time, before incarnating again in physicality on this plane, then that is alright. This may be accomplished. In the interim, one may express either in the non-physical dimension or become part of the pool of the soul essence embodiment - the soul essence, the body of soul essence that is amorphous - that is the totality of all these existences of which I spoke. It will become part of that pool.

Q: St. Germain, there seem to be a couple of things happening simultaneously - the change in consciousness and then also the Earth wanting to heal herself, which seem to be two giant things coming together at the same time.

Indeed.

Q: Now, the entities, the beings that have come to this plane to help us out, are you here to possibly help us to raise our consciousness to the point where some of the more drastic Earth changes will not be necessary? Or is that a necessary part of the evolution, our spiritual and the physical evolution of the planet? I am still not clear on that. In other words it seems like no matter what, she still needs to, as you said, purify herself.

I understand of what you speak. The evolution of the Earth plane is based partially upon the unfoldment of the entities that abide upon and within her. As this is occurring, in a more expeditious manner, then it would not be necessary to have Earth changes to express her purification. For as you go unto fourth density, Mother Earth will too and as she does this, it is a natural purification, if you will. The light that would be part of her embodiment, the soil, etcetera, it will be more light as well. Therefore a natural healing would occur in fourth density. Fourth density may not necessarily occur in this manner. You see, it is very probable, it is not set in stone, but it is very probable that the entities upon your plane will choose to have confrontation with alter ego and divine ego of SELF. This is the polarization. This is what is coming to a focus point of opposites, of a dichotomy of attitude. When this occurs, it is the symbolic gesture of alter ego and divine ego of SELF coming into an understanding with each other and merging in union. It is the desire of all of us entities who are coming forth - in whatever manner we manifest ourselves as and in whatever manner we can present the knowingness - it is our desire to bring to you harmonious alignment regardless of what the circumstances are. If it is upheaval, then it is to be in harmony and alignment during the upheaval. If it is no upheaval, then it is to be in ecstatic joy and to have your toes twinkling because that which you would desire to have averted, you have.

On Jesus.

Q: St. Germain. With respect to Jesus, was he the embodiment of eternal God?

He was born into fourth density, into the understanding that is now termed super-consciousness, into that embodiment that was physical but not as immersed in three dimensional understanding as third density entities. Therefore, as he came more and more unto an awareness of the light that he carried within his being, as he gathered more and more of that unto him, he became a manifestor, a God exhibiting himself in that fashion as a healer, creator of the elements. He spoke with his heart, that of his grander SELF, the totality of SELF, and came into an understanding of alter ego - the fearful, doubtful, angry, tinted part of one's Self - during the 40 days in the desert. Tinted by power and greed and lust and all the things that alter ego brings into presentation. This is alright. He came into a harmonious understanding and acceptance and allowance of that part of himself through the light of his divine ego and overcame this part of himself with light. Therefore, he embraced the totality of SELF to continue what it was he desired upon this plane, which was the illustration of what an entity can be if Christ consciousness is exemplified. Christ consciousness meaning the unconditional love and sovereignty together hand in hand. Unconditional love meaning humility and loving entities regardless of what judgment be upon them, and in sovereignty - exhibiting one's divinity, knowing that one is divine, that one is God. One is *of* God and one *is* God, you see. This Christ consciousness that was exhibited was a grand demonstration. It was for the purpose of guiding entities back unto themselves. After the ascension of this entity, those that are called apostles and disciples, they were fearful, they were in doubt of themselves and their own divinity. And they brought forward some manner of teaching that would give power unto that entity that they were in awe of and who they respected divinely and this is alright. It is merely that they did not recognize themselves as divine. And it is desirous at this point in your time that all entities be brought into the knowingness of their divinity, of the Christ consciousness they carry. And this is why it is coming forward on your plane at this point in time through fourth density and above; and this density that is prevalent [St. Germain referring to himself] is seventh. The density that Jesus was born into was fourth, and moved into seventh at the point of ascension.

Q: The conception, the union of the male and the female...

It was not. Why is it you find that so difficult to accept upon this plane? Many entities find it difficult to know that a particular condition can be manifested within an embodiment which is not normally so, upon third density understanding. This appears all the time, that is what you call miraculous healing. It is directing the cell essence, the atoms within the cell and the cells themselves, in a certain manner. The direction by the soul essence, the desire of the totality of SELF to do this thing, this healing or whatever, this particular conception was spontaneous. The ovum of a woman was being brought forth into division without union with the spermatozoa, and it is not necessary to have this union in fourth density understanding. It is harmonious if there is another entity present, however it is not necessary. For in fourth density, you may manifest your embodiment however you choose. And you may also manifest within your embodiment and that of a woman an ovum into spontaneous division and creation of essence. The soul essence of the entity known as Jesus was present within the womb of Mary and participated heartily in the assimilation of the embodiment.

Q: One more question: the legacy that he left, I understand that this was not the way he would have preferred it to be told?

The crucifixion was merely the alter ego expressing judgment against divine essence that it was perceiving at that point in time, you see? It was alter ego. And there will be much polarization of this nature in this time. However, in order to avoid crucifixion again, it is all coming forward in a different manner this time. You have crucified many of the masters. Not only the master Jesus. All of them have been slain in one manner or another, all of them.

Q: In one of your incarnations you were Christ's father, Joseph, right?

Not Christ's - Jesus'.

Q: Do you still have contact with the entity that was Jesus?

The entity known as Jesus is Sananda. That is a sixth density name. This is a master that is also coming forward at this point in your time, along with all the rest of us.

Q: Has either that entity or the entity we know as Mary incarnated since that time?

In a manner of speaking, upon this plane, however it has been in Tibet and it has not been widely advertised, as you would call it. There has been some traversing into the area known as Indus and it has remained in that remote area. It is because of much of the drama that was created before through his coming; so it was for the designing of the understanding of the wisdom to be brought forward *now*. In other words, it was for gathering and garnishing the understanding as it is at this point in your time, so that we may present the knowingness in a different manner now.

Q: Can Mary..?

She has also been likewise, however, this essence is not always female.

Q: Is this essence here now, at this time, on this plane?

Indeed. Very prevalent I might add. Hm.

Q: Have to pursue that at some other time.

Indeed.

What To 'Do'.

Q: St. Germain, I do know that I want to experience a very, very high awareness and I am wondering why it is so hard. I am wondering, is there someone that is going to show me how to get there?

You

Q: Would I be asking if I could show myself?

Indeed you may show yourself. However, it is your resistance to this, due to being entrenched in third density, the desire to remain here, that is part of you, and the desire to move onward to a higher frequency that is another part of you. They are struggling against one another and that is why you feel conflict, or feel difficulty in getting the higher frequency part of you into your embodiment, allowing the light to come forward into the rest of you. The struggle is the releasing of third density and when you bring this to a total allowance of progression and unfoldment and clench not unto that which is physical, then the light will spill forward. It is very much human, to cling to third density reality, for that is the only reality that you feel is real. This is what you can feel, what you can sense. It is tangible, it is the only tangible thing that you can perceive in third density, this reality of yours. All the other realities are fleeting, are etheric [to you]. And you know not how to capture them in bottles. However, the breaking of the barrier of separation, will bring you into an understanding of your light in a higher frequency. Part of the time you are in third density and part of the time you are not, and you will desire the time you are not when you are desirous of harmony and alignment. And when you break the barrier, and allow it to flow forward in torrents into the grander part of yourself, and allow the waters of all of your Self to be merged together, then you will notice the light coming forward.

Q: Sometimes, I guess, it just bugs me that it takes so much to try to be what we really are.

My dear, you are merely different reflections of the divine essence. That energy that you feel at times is only another expression of that divine essence known as All-That-Is or God or whatever. You see, when you come into the knowingness that all of you, in all your other expressions, is the grand force, manifestor, the grand illumination unto your Self, then you will not feel as though this is the only experience there is. You have experienced this momentarily, for moments of your time as you would perceive time to be. And when you allow this to come forward, you will perceive it all the time. There will not be a separation between when you experience it and when you do not, because there will be no conflict. There will always be a harmonious understanding of it all. The higher part of your being is merely of a higher frequency, that is desirous of coming forth, but there is a barrier there. And that barrier is the desire to cling to third density perception. Listen to what I speak. Contemplate. You will come to understand.

Q: But what I thought you said is that we have to leave this body in order to experience other dimensions.

It is not necessary to leave this embodiment to go into other dimensions, for you may travel with the soul essence wherever you desire. When you come into fourth density, you will no longer have that body, and this is when you may take your embodiment with you. But you will no longer have this embodiment as it exists at this time.

Q: Why does it seem that each soul is left to struggle to obtain that knowledge on its own? Why could you not show it to the people?

I am showing it unto you, my dear.

Q: You are revealing it verbally.

The knowingness must come from here, [indicating the heart] not from without you, but from within you. It has been expressed over and over and over again outwardly on the pages of history, and you have not heeded it. Either you did not believe it, or you persecuted those who expressed that truth, because you dared not to believe it. For it would leave you responsible for your own circumstances and you did not desire this. You desired to point fingers. It is quite commonplace upon this plane to place blame, to have the concept of victimization. And you would desire to be immersed in this comfortable way of perception, rather than to take responsibility for your own soul essence. You are not left here, my dear, to struggle towards it. *You are here because you choose to be here.*

You struggle because you choose to struggle. It is not a conscious choice. It is at soul level that you are choosing this thing. Much the way that you chose your embodiment when you were birthed. It was not a conscious choice, it was soul level choice. You see, as you bring forward more understanding of enlightenment, as you call it, more understanding of the wisdom, then the struggle will cease, for there will be nothing to struggle against. *You are struggling against yourself.* It is always this way. *All struggle is misalignment with the harmonious divine essence that is within all circumstance.* You see, you would call it the silver lining in every cloud, or a lesson to be learned in every circumstance. You have a myriad of ways of saying that within every set of circumstance, there has been a choice made for you to garnish wisdom from it. There is nothing wrong with struggle, because it allows you to perceive the discomfort of disharmony. It allows you the desire for harmony and the more intense this desire is, the more there will be harmony and lack of struggle. Is this helpful?

Q: I have a mundane question regarding decisions and choices. Is there a right occupation, spouse, group of friends, for each of us? And if there is, how do we make those choices, or does it not matter? Do we have the experience and take out of it what we are supposed to?

Of course it matters, because it is you that is involved in it. Right and proper is merely a judgment of the choices that you are making for yourself. Each entity is making its own choices and is immersed in the circumstances that result from this. And it is all wondrous, for human free will is divine, regardless of what that free will would indicate. There is cooperation among the essences also, at soul level, that are involved with you. So it is not a thing that is disharmonious to all, and when the experience has given you the understanding that you had desired, it will naturally dissipate - for example your marketplace, you call it job. It will naturally dissipate and you will move onward to something else. That will also occur with your companions, your mates. So the natural unfolding of events as they occur are the results of the choices that you have made, which are all divine. The judgment of right and wrong is exactly that - a judgment.

Q: There are places in our lives where we come to decision points. When we are at those decision points, what can we keep in mind to make the right decisions?

There is no right or wrong my brother. The points of decisions that are either one direction or another - your heart will take you there. Your mind will not. You feel the decision is difficult to make, because your heart and your mind are struggling against one another. For *your mind is third density*. It is attached to the personality Self. Your heart is of the density of All-That-Is. It is attached to the desire of your soul essence and not the personality Self. Therefore, follow your heart. That one piece of verbiage in your language is very divine. *Follow your heart,* for in doing that you are following your soul unto all eternity. And the judgment of which is right and proper, and which is utterly wrong, will bring you heartache, because it is pain within the soul, for the decision that the soul had desired was not made. Therefore there was disharmony created which always results in the perception of pain. When realignment occurs, then you will have felt comfortable as it was, or adapted to the decision you have made. Alright?

On Life In Fourth Density.

Q: What does our future look like?

Your time will become less important to you in super-consicousness. You will be releasing that restriction, for you will be in godship and the Lord God of your totality will be the master and you will be in harmony with your life and all life. So when you are in this super-consciousness, or, as you would call it, the age of enlightenment - you may exist in your present embodiment for hundreds of years, for you will have enlightened yourself unto the wisdom of how to do this. When you release time, you also release age. When you perceive not time, you perceive not age. So, if you would choose to, you would exist on that physical dimension plane in fourth density as long as you desire. You need not become non-physical unless you desire to do so.

Q: What about sexuality?

Grand question. It concerns many, I tell you. The merging of a physical embodiment will indeed occur in fourth density. It will be an expression of love of fourth density understanding. However, when it is merged, it will also be not only the merging of the physical embodiment, but the merging of the soul essence, of the light that will intermingle. It can be very much likened unto your works of fire. It has been depicted as that in your time, however, it will be felt as that when you have more light body. Your physical embodiment will have a glow. It will glow with light which will be very much illuminated and when that physical merging occurs, it will be joyous, but not only in physical ecstasy, but also in soul ecstasy. And the explosions that occur, in all myriads of forms and fashion, will also occur with your light bodies and it will be felt unto all the other dimensions of expression.

It will be transcending fourth density experience, into All-That-Is, for a moment in that time. Also, physical embodiment may be conceived in this manner, but it will be a bit different. There will be much more perception about the entity coming forth [birth]. Also the entity coming forward will not be brought forward in pain. Therefore, that which you call the conception, will be a mutual choice between all entities involved and it will be a very happy and ecstatic occasion, for all. There will be no concern whether an entity's embodiment will be terminated before birthing, and there will be no concern for prevention of conception, because at this point in time, there will be no conception without agreement, and conscious agreement, not only at soul level, as it is now, but conscious agreement of all parties. At that point in time you will be coming unto what you call soulmate. Therefore you will be merging with other parts of yourself. That will be simply the way it is in that plane of existence. It will be very common place.

153

What you call promiscuity is alter ego providing one's Self with the experience of decadence. However, on that plane, there will be no decadence, and also there will be no desire for another entity other than the one you are already mated with in soul.

Q: Are all expressions of emotions more intense than they are here on the third dimension?

Indeed, however, there will be some that will be a bit absent.

Q: Some that are absent?

The expression of anger, irritation, frustration, greed, heartache, sorrow,..

Q: All the negative...?

It is not negative. They are all equally valid, but they are expressions of that part of Self that is alter ego, which will have been merged into the joyous union of the totality of SELF. So emotional expressions that will come forward during fourth density, will be primarily of joy, of gaiety, of hearty partaking of life.

Q: So in the partaking of life in the fourth dimension, will we be transferring some of the same things we do here, for instance, if we like sailing, or swimming, will we still be able to do those things there and have the same emotional feelings?

Indeed. However, that which you call 'immersing yourself in' [swimming] will be different, for physical objects will also be less dense.

Q: But if you go swimming, is the water one is bathing in of a less dense material...

And not only immerse yourself within the water, but you also play on top of the water, you see. It is sort of a fluid playground.

Q: Could you, say, play in the clouds too if you wanted to in the fourth level?

You will have access to levitation, as you call it. You may have your embodiment that is not supported by the Earth.

Q: Is flying then, or levitation, as it is called, actually not possible then, in third density?

Anti-gravity requires fourth density knowingness. You may do this within a third density body, but that third density embodiment will be a transitional fourth. It is more likely however, that the fourth density embodiment will be made apparent before this is accomplished. It is possible, but not very frequent.

Your time will become less important to you in super-consicousness. You will be releasing that restriction, for you will be in godship and the Lord God of your totality will be the master and you will be in harmony with your life and all life. So when you are in this super-consciousness, or, as you would call it the age of enlightenment - you may exist in your present embodiment for hundreds of years, for you will have enlightened yourself unto the wisdom of how to do this. When you release time, you also release age. When you perceive not time, you perceive not age. So, if you would choose to, you would exist on that physical dimension plane in fourth density as long as you desire. You need not become non-physical [to be ageless] unless you desire to do so. You see.

Q: We were talking about the cloud covering that used to cover the planet during the Atlantean time. Is that going to return?

You will find your Earth quite different when you consider super-consciousness upon this plane. It will not be as it is now, not as it is in third density. Venus, however, is coming into the knowingness of the same understanding in planetary format that this your Earth-plane was during the Atlantean era. When this your Earth plane ascends, there will be another Earth that will be in transition from third to fourth, etc. That will be your Venus. There will be many changes within this solar system. But also when the Earth plane ascends, she is not moving. It is not a place. It is a shift in frequency.

Q: Right. But will there not also be a third density Earth simultaneously that stays third density?

Indeed. As perceived by third density.

Q: So if one would be on Venus in third density form, you would still see the planet Earth?

Indeed. However, Venus cloud cover will dissipate. It will become more harmonious, there will be more vegetation and life experience upon the outer part of the planet, much likened unto this Earth eons and eons ago.

Q: So the life on Venus right now is primarily interior?

Indeed. That which is exterior is considered very hostile. There are craft beneath the surface of Venus. They are different then these shapes that you are familiar with.

Q: Are they third density perhaps?

No. They are fourth. They are made of what you call silicon, for that is very, very abundant upon that planet. But they have these craft for the experience of multidimensional 'travel' through the time continuum. Like your middle or inner Earth.

Q: Will they see the planet externally in third dimension or is someone else coming down?

They will. But it is not a coming down or going up. That is third density verbiage, my dearest brother. Your brothers of space will appear in the very near future.

Q: Are there not also brothers from space who are considered disharmonious?

Mm, there are brothers of this your Earth that are [disharmonious] as well. It is all the same throughout humanity.

Q: I had heard of certain groups of brothers from space that were to be avoided.

Not avoided. Embraced in love, hm? This applies to everyone and everything else also. Do not run from yourself, nor them, nor anyone else.

Q: Embrace them as yourself, even one that appears hostile.

Indeed. How else will you deal with such grand entity that is known as Jehovah? For there is no reason to fear, my brother, if you are truly sovereign, then what is there to fear?

Q: True.

156

On Drugs.

Q: I went through a particular therapy course using psychedelic drugs and during that process also experienced an enlightened stage. I have never been quite sure if that experience is hindering me, or if in fact it was just a signpost that I had seen on the road and is something to march for?

Chemicals for pleasurable use, hm, the introduction for the quick trip to heaven, as it were, form a black hole within the auric field, your etheric embodiment. You may allow yourself to go through this unto other dimensions of experience - it would be called cosmic awareness by some. However, as you do this it is an energy vortex that is drawing unto it other energy into the auric field. This enters through this hole within your auric field, into other dimensions that are not allowing the light to come forward in a gathered understanding, as a totality. You are going hence from yourself, rather than calling the rest of yourself unto you, you see? You may experience other dimensions, however, it is through the use of a separator as it were, and not a merger or unifier. And this is alright. It will give you something to anticipate if you have done this in your past. However, it is not very harmonious to a fourth density embodiment. It creates distortions - the light is darkened because of the black hole, the hole of energy that is pulled from the auric field outwardly, rather than gathering it unto you.

Q: And how are those black holes filled?

By allowing yourself to be bathed in your own light. You will heal yourself as you heal your embodiment, that is physical. It is all the same process. The chemical introduction for this expanded state of awareness, has been widely used in the past and it has created a glimpse of a sort for those entities that have partaken - to see what they may anticipate. But you may anticipate much more through the natural use of your own light to bring you there. You see, when this occurs [using drugs], your embodiment releases other chemicals which destroy many of your cells. Therefore, a healing of the black hole within your auric field is required, before progressing towards more light within you. So it is what you would call steps backward, rather than forward, as you perceive it to be.

On The Inner Earth People.

Q: St. Germain, you made reference to entities that are on the Earth and within it. The entities that are residing in Terra, do we communicate with them?

Many of your entities are in communication with them, however, it is kept as you would call it 'from public dissemination'. You see it is not allowed for the mass to perceive, for it is not the ripe time.

Q: Who are these people on the Earth who do communicate with the inner Earth people and who are withholding the information from the rest of the people?

For one thing, your government is aware of this. But to answer your question, those entities that are in communication in a harmonious fashion, are those brothers of yours that are here, but not of this plane. They are here from other dimensions and they are here to act as emissaries between the two existences. And in doing so, they have understanding of the outward, the peoples of the outer core, which is you, and the peoples of the inner core, and bring forward cultural exchange, in a manner of speaking, before diverse circumstance would bring this awareness to the general understanding of the populous. So they would have some manner of understanding of life as it is here, on the outside of your Earth plane.

Q: I think that we, being on the outside, have more light - at least physically - to be able to relate to someone who is from the inner core.

Do you know why, my dear brother, you require the light of the Sun? Because you have not so much light within your being. You require it from the outside. The peoples of the inner part of the Earth plane, are of fifth and sixth density understanding. Some are fourth. The majority are fifth density. And to confront them, that is converse with them, one would require to bring forth more light into one's being.

Q: Before we could actually communicate?

This is so. For in bringing more light into your essence, you bring forward more understanding and compassion - less judgment, more unconditional love of your brothers, regardless of how they appear. And in understanding this, you are then properly prepared to perceive them, to communicate with them without dire circumstance, as a result. Is this helpful?

Q: Yes, it is.

You will find them very loving entities. Some of the entities that are resident within the inner plane of existence are your sprites, your elfs, your leprechauns, etcetera. They are very loving, very generous, very much of the light. They are manifestors also. They need not outward light, for they generate much light from within. Alright?

Q: St. Germain, would aboriginal people like the Pygmies, the Amazon Indians, the Eskimos - would they more likely be people of the inner Earth?

No, they would not. They are of another dimension, from your brothers of beyond that were here eons ago, who allowed certain of their beings to participate on the Earth plane and some have integrated with other species, as it were, and resulted in what you call the Indians, and the Pgymies, Aborigines and the Amazons - they are all different interbreeding of other brothers, but not of the inner Earth.

Q: Do they, because of the closeness to the Earth and nature, and the ability to live within the natural realm, without trying to transform it in this painful way - without trying to exploit the Earth and its resources - are they closer to being fourth dimensional than those so-called modern men?

Indeed. And the Lemurians, they are the ancestors, along with the Atlanteans, of what you now call American Indian. And they also, from Atlantis, were not originally from Atlantis. They were from the brothers of beyond.

Q: Speaking of the Lemurians, I was at Mt. Shasta once, and I saw beings in a huge circle, going up to a space craft, and it was a celebration of joy and ecstasy. There was some form of communication going on that

I did not understand, I just knew that it was going on. But what was that about?

It occurs many times upon this plane. It is certain that some entities upon Earth have access to the visual perception of what we speak. Therefore, they bring the message to the other brothers that would be disbelieving if an entity popped into their existence out of nowhere. Now, what you perceived were merely entities of the inner Earth - for there is an access there in Mt. Shasta - and the entities of the brothers of beyond in conversation with one another. The celebration was merely one of joyous greeting, much as you would have with a loved one that you have not seen for a while in your time. They are very much in ecstatic joy, most of their time, for that is their understanding of life - Joy.

Q: It was really an interesting experience to be able to see that. Are they here because they live here? Are they here to help us to heal the Earth? What sort of interaction do they have with us?

All of the above. They are here to assist. They do take residence upon Earth. They are here to herald in the age of awakening of all the other entities upon your plane, not only through verbiage and communication in this manner, but by example. For when allowed, they will be divine examples.

Q: I really enjoyed the Hobbit and just wanted to know if this was purely fictional on Tolkien's part?

It was inspired. It was not fantasy. The gnomes, elves, sprites, fairy queens, etcetera, they are not fantasy either. However, they are not apparent to common people. They will be. You will have a joyful merriment upon your Earth, hand in hand with all these entities. But first, you must learn not to judge your neighbor, for in viewing these entities, you will find they appear quite different from yourself. So, superficial physical appearance must become unimportant to you.

On Ascension, Levels And Densities.

Q: You talked several times about different incarnations that you have had. Did you ascend to the seventh density from Earth, or..?

Indeed.

Q: And is it a good place to be in order to do this ascension, I mean, are there other places just as well suited to make this ascension?

The physical plane existence is wondrous indeed, truly a marvellous place to be for it is green. It has the vegetation. It has water, which is a glorious essence upon your plane. It has the Sun and Moon, in harmonious rotation around Earth. It has the small life, insects and birds. It has all of this. It is rampant with divine essence - it is truly a wonder. And in retrospect, as you would call it, pondering nature, this life upon your plane, it is simpler in a manner of speaking to observe divinity before your eyes, you see? However, all planes of existence are wondrous. Each one has its own gloriousness. Each one is divine. It is part of this frequency [referring to himself] vibration that has a preference for this particular plane. But I am in no way stating that the others are not as divine. Is this helpful?

Q: Is ascension better than - oh, I don't want to say better - is it easier through this human form than it would be through an angelic form?

Angelic forms do not ascend as you know ascension to be. However, that which is called non-physical, as you would perceive it to be, would be simpler, because you are not so based in third dimension or physicality. However, regardless of where you begin, as you would perceive time to be as beginning, it is only a moment in the total illumination of it all. It is not that it takes longer as you perceive time to be, in one place or another, for it always only takes a moment. What you perceive as time will dissipate and you will not even be aware of time passage as you progress toward super-consciousness, towards fourth density. You will not perceive time in the same manner.

Q: Super-consciousness comes prior to fourth density?

Super-consciousness *is* fourth density. It would come prior to ascension which is seventh.

Q: One other question: it seems to me - to use an analogy - that I would be at the first floor of a 12 story building and you seem to be on the 12th floor,...

This is not so my brother.

You have as much knowingness and so do all the rest of you, as that which you call I, or any other masters that are coming forth to assist. We are here to illustrate unto you that you all know it all.

Q: Except that you are here and we are all listening to you.

I am here as your mirror. Your grander self, the soul essence that you are opening and flowering unto, is not your third dimensional Self, that you perceive yourself to be. It is far grander than that, far more enlightened than you could even imagine within limitation. And that part of you, indeed, has the knowingness. You need only to allow it to encompass your being, and when this occurs, we will be of no use any longer. And this is the ultimate end. Thank you my brother. Indeed.

Q: If we do not ascend on this plane, do we have to come back and if we do, why can we not come back with the memory of what we did wrong last time?

First of all you did nothing wrong last time, as you would call it. Secondly, you may go where you choose at the termination of this embodiment. You may go to another plane of existence that is physical, or another plane of demonstration that is non-physical, and you may remain there for as long as you choose. And when you release that embodiment, or that life experience, if it is non-physical, then you may go also where you choose at that point in time. So you see, it is all your own choice. You are not forced to go anywhere. You may stay upon Earth in the embodiment you are in for as long as you like. When you release the concept of time, there will be no age, and when this is so, you make take your embodiment with you as it is, or how you would like it to be. In super-consciousness, or fourth density understanding, you may manifest your embodiment as you would desire. And 'why you do not recall?' First of all, when you are incarnated in physical density, that which is third dimensional understanding, you bring forth with you limitation *because* of the embodiment, you see? An embodiment has definition - it is skin and bone. In order to maintain this concentration of energy and the focus upon this plane, it would not be harmonious to recall all the other existences in which you are occupied. I will discuss simultaneity in one moment. If you were to know 'past incarnations', all of them, then you would have major confusion, you see?

Simultaneity is the existence of the past, the present and the future all together in the NOW. They are all overlaid, as it were. They are all occurring now. The future is occurring right now at this time, so is the past. If this boggles your mind and burns your fuses, then bring forward a bit more understanding, knowing that you are, in the grander soul essence, in unlimitedness. You are involved in unlimitedness, which means there is no perception of time because time is a limiter. It is defined and *when anything is defined, it is limited.* Therefore, when you perceive no time, there is no past or present or future. It is all simultaneous. So, all the screens are running at once, and you may alter your future and your past. And those things which you call deja-vu, etcetera, many of you do not contemplate that it may come from your future also, not only from your past. It spills over from time to time into what you perceive to be the present. And although you are not consciously aware of it, the present from time to time spills over into your past and your future. And the embodiments or personalities that are exhibited there as part of your soul essence wonder why it is they recognize something that - upon this plane - you are involved in at that moment. Because all is part of you. And there are many foci of that into different dimensions and different expressions. As you gather more and more of your light essence unto you, you become lighter, you become more knowing. You become more in tune and aligned with the totality of SELF, therefore you have more and more access to the knowingness. Indeed.

Evolution, or unfoldment, is at different points in your different existences. For instance, in one of your life existences you may be sixth density, while you are third density here, in transition of fourth, and you may be totally entrenched in third density in another existence, while being fifth density in another. So when you release your embodiment as you perceive it at this point in your time, you have choice, total free choice. Human free will is divine.

Q: What density or level is our Sun at?

Twelfth.

Q: St. Germain, you mentioned that Mother Earth is getting ready for her transition from the third level density to the fourth level density. Does that mean that the third level will still be here as a Mother Earth but it will not have a fourth level also?

Indeed. It is called parallel existence - a shift in frequency.

Q: Occupying the same space in the cosmos? Is there also then a fifth and sixth and seventh and eighth occupying the same space?

When you come into seventh, there is merging with All-That-Is, for there is no more physicality. When you come into fifth and sixth, there is less and less density. Therefore it is, as you would perceive it, almost transparent. And the ascension of the Earth is merely what you would call a disappearance, much likened unto the ascension of all the masters that you have had upon this plane.

Q: But it will disappear from whose sight? Those that are in the third dimension, or will they...?

It will not be apparent in perception to any that are physical, sixth and below.

Q: Sixth and below? Well, then an entity that remains on the third level of density when the Earth goes into the fourth density, what happens to them? Will they still be around on a third level?

There will always be third density entities, as in the understanding of this Earth plane. And as the Earth herself comes into ascension, those entities [of third density] will bring forward more and more light into their being and progress towards fourth, fifth and sixth density. Therefore, as this occurs, there will be less and less of third density Earth and her beings. You see, when ascension occurs, it is automatic that all the rest of the light is brought forward. This occurs with all entities regardless their embodiment. Whether it is planetoid or whether it is humanoid. Ascension and the lack of perception of it by an entity is merely because it is already resolved as unified within the All-That-Is. It is one. It is not separate from the form of a planet.

Q: This transition from third to fourth - is it going to happen instantaneously, like over a period of minutes, or is it over a period of time like years?

Ascension takes but a moment. Indeed.

Q: I have another question. There are many, many people who write about ascension and who speak about ascension and who may have ascended themselves. Why are there not people on this plane who could show us ascension?

Would you like to see an ascension? What I mean is would you like to see it before you in order for you to perceive it so that you may express it to another entity?

Q: Yes.

This desire is your need for proof to yourself, that it is possible. Ascended entities, those that are in the knowledge, the knowingness of the All-That-Is, would have to bring forward separation and a focus to carry their energies so that they may express upon this plane. It is disharmonious for them, for some entities would have to bring forward as much limitation as it would take to have the form in an embodiment and reascend. Coming forth unto this plane would be coming forth unto third density.

Q: So that is why masters who can show you that, do not do that?

This is so. For it is disharmonious for them. That is why we are coming forth in this manner. An entity came forth in fourth density that is widely known upon your plane, Jesus, to illustrate that of which we speak. He came to be the personification of Christ consciousness and he was revered and the power was given unto him, and he did not desire this. He desired for each entity to know that they also may do grander things than he. He said this of himself. He was the mirror. He was not desirous of being the altar. If this were to occur again in your time and a master come unto you and reascend as was done in this particular incarnation, then you would observe the entire drama of the Piscean age being replayed. Another 2000 years or so would have to pass before the hearkening of the Aquarian age. It is desirous of mass consciousness at this point in time that this does not occur, for obvious reasons. However, if everything exists at the same time, where is the Christ consciousness? Within you, each and every one of you, blossoming at this point in time.

Q: St. Germain, if our Sun is at this twelfth level of density, is there a particular highest level of density that we can get to in our particular universe?

There is universal consciousness. There is galactic consciousness. There is consciousness of the cosmos, which is an understanding of other universes - that is cosmic consciousness as it is termed here on Earth. However, that term of verbiage is used interchangeably with enlightenment, which is not always the case. There is the consciousness beyond the cosmos, beyond all the universes that exist, and that is the Source that is beyond the Source, you see. And all is eternal. There is no one stopping point, as you would call it, because that is finite. We are speaking of infinity, for there is no one density, that is the ultimate expression of divine understanding. However, universal consciousness, the consciousness of a universe, is about thirtieth density.

Q: When they talk about God, or the first cause, the original Source, and then He fragmented Himself into the Son, who took on a personality...

This is not how it occurred. The Source contemplated itself, and in doing so brought desire into different expressions, for it felt itself desirous of expansion, of more knowingness. Therefore, thirteen essences of soul energy, bodies of energy - monads or oversouls - were burst into existence from the All-That-Is. From these bodies of energy there came fragments, you see. And these fragments were separated by male and female. Male essence, female essence. This is now called soulmate essence of either male and female, you see, of both. Together in the totality is the All-That-Is that is you, the Lord God of your totality is this body of energy. In this fragmented state within this body of energy that is called male, or female, there are certain frequencies that are together in harmonic understanding of personality. That which is brought forward to you in this manner is the personality of Le Conte de St. Germain. There are other fragments within that body of energy that have the harmonic understanding of different personalities.

This occurs with you also. And it [the fragments of the bodies of soul energy, the personalities] is expressed upon multitudinous planes of demonstration, whether they be physical or non-physical. There are both. It is an entire body of energy. The essence known as the Sun has many of these fragments together, for more of the light is put together in one understanding. They are fragments coming together to possess more light than the embodiment that you would perceive as being yourself. It is through this understanding of a certain harmonic grouping of frequencies that this personality known as the Sun was born. It is also part of a grander essence that is one of the thirteen. Is this helpful?

Q: It is, sort of. It is said that the one Source is God, and He had the Son - SON, not SUN, and then the Holy Spirit. Now God the Son was more manifest as a physical manifestation in the universe, whereas the Holy Spirit came about as being more spiritual, in terms of their essence. And I do not see where that fits in terms of what you are saying about the thirteen essences.

That is one interpretation. The interpretation that we bring forward is the Source, which you call God, and then there is the Son, which you call physical embodiment, which is what you call personality, and then there is the Spirit, which is the essence within any embodiment to give it the life force. There is a difference between soul and Spirit. The Spirit is the life force of the embodiment, the silver cord which is severed when an embodiment departs, to gather that Spirit into the rest of the soul essence. The Spirit has personality as well. It is part of the soul, much as the soul is part of the Source. So in three dimensional experience, there are those three different perceptions: the God which is the divine essence of you, the Son which is your physical expression, and the Spirit, as you call it, which is the etheric expression. And the etheric expression, or your auric field, produces what you call your embodiment. Your embodiment is the result of your etheric being. Those are the three that you perceive in three dimensional understanding. This is the interpretation we bring forward.

On AIDS.

Q: This problem that we seem to be having with AIDS, is this going to be resolved, or is this something that is going to devastate the planet? I mean, is this what the Bible talked about when it speaks about a plague that would come upon this planet in the final days?

First of all, this plague within the Bible, that is not the only plague upon your plane. It is known as the diseasement of the soul, that is expressed in the embodiment, the resistance of the embodiment for health - it resists health - it yearns unto diseasement. And this is because of the decadence that has been rampant upon your plane, and the non-recognition of sovereignty within Self, and that of other entities. It is the expectation of something for nothing, pleasure that is superficial.

It is to take responsibility for the God that you are and to get beyond the superficiality of perception of another entity. It is allowing one to transcend the merely physical and the pleasures that are derived thereof. Immersing one's Self in the pleasures of third dimensional understanding is bringing forth more and more desire to keep you here, and that is why you have been on the wheel of life for eons. This is going to kick you off, as it were, to allow you to desire something more than physicality. It is a grand awakening, as it were. And it is by your own boot, that you are kicked off. And you see, AIDS, it truly is an aid. An aid to the awareness of what you call metaphysical, beyond the physical. Is this helpful?

Q: Yes. Thank you.

Thank you my dear. It was heavy on the thoughts of several in this room.

On St. Germain.

Q: Was your last incarnation that of St. Germain?

This is so. The last embodiment *within your understanding of time* was as Le Conte de St. Germain. However, another embodiment will be formed but not to the birthing process, after super-consciousness. Thank you my dear. Indeed.

Q: I do have a couple other questions more relating to your incarnations. Did you enjoy one more than the others?

Several - each one of you have had multitudinous incarnations to the point where it is difficult to keep track of it all. This is true for each embodiment, for the soul essence is so diverse that expression in every density and every physical plane is accomplished through one soul essence. However, that which you would call preference on my part for a particular expression...?

Q: Yes. (laughter)

I do not judge my expressions, however, I did enjoy heartily that one called Christopher Columbus. I have an affinity to the sea.

Q: The same questions are asked over and over and over again. Do you not ever get tired of hearing the same thing about the Earth destroying itself and when we come into super-consciousness, does that not ever get boring?

My dearest brother, I will respond. I take pleasure and much joy in responding to such query. That which you call repetition, I am here to do. For you have heads of rock. (Laughter!) And it is through much repetition that it is penetrated a bit. That which you call 'boring', all of life is joy unto me. And it will be unto you as you understand unconditional love. Each query that is brought forward in the asking, is new and fresh to me, for each entity is new and fresh, even yourself, in a moment's passage, will be different unto me. Therefore, I participate heartily and with much joy with each and every one of your grand lights. I love you all so, that is why I am here. To gently and compassionately lead you back unto yourselves. I do this gingerly at times, and at times I plant my foot within your rumpus. However, it is always done with love.

Q: What do you actually see, when you are not coming through Azena, how do you actually perceive? For instance, this afternoon I was standing on the balcony and I thought 'St. Germain is out there looking at me'. I mean, I was wondering 'Can he see me standing here?'

When I am merged with All-That-Is and the consciousness is not separate as a personality, then I perceive nothing in particular, for I am All-That-Is. I am that I am. I am unified. I have not eyes to perceive at that point in time. I need not, for I am omnipotent and omniscient and omnipresent. However, there are times when I do bring forward certain focus of energy and as you would term it, pop in and out from time to time. I occasionally eavesdrop merely to familiarize myself with your plane of demonstration, and to be what you would call companion with your soul essence. I do this from time to time because I love you all so. I also express in other frequency groupings, known as other personality. Therefore, my essence is known as Merlin and other groupings also, and I come forward in this manner, and I perceive whatever is about when this is occurring. However, what you are speaking of is my popping in and out. You may feel my presence from time to time in your contemplation. And as you call upon me to accompany you within your meditative state, and within your slumber, I will hearken unto you. You need only beckon me. Call upon me. And your thought that calls upon me resonates to that which I am and I will come unto you and be there as what you would call a brother in fellowship. Is this explanation sufficient for you?

On Name Changes.

Q: I have read some things regarding the correlation between name and form. When you think the name, at a certain level, you produce the form.

Indeed.

Q: So if I thought of your name as St. Germain, at a certain point, then I could just produce the form..?

A name, or that which someone is called, is a frequency, for it is tone. It is very much like a mantra. You see, it is tone that is combined together in a frequency combination that will represent a certain personality. This is of which I spoke earlier in your time. When this occurs, it is responsible for the response known as appearance of embodiment, for embodiment is the result of your etheric being, which is soul essence of a certain frequency vibration. Do you see? You will all eventually feel the desire to change your name, because you are changing your frequency. All of you will eventually come unto this yearning. And fear it not. It is not dissatisfaction with what you are, but the yearning to resonate to a higher frequency, that is all.

You see, the name, it need not abide with you for all eternity. You may change it as often as you like. When you become uncomfortable with a particular name that merely means that certain aspects that you were resonating to before, you are no longer resonating to. By changing your name, you are merely reflecting that you are changing your essence, that is all. There is nothing wrong with it, my dear. If you would desire to be called by another frequency combination, then do so. Fear not. The tittering of your comrades will only be momentary, for it will surprise them one day when they also desire to change their name. It is very common place on this plane of existence to change your name, and that is why. Because the frequencies are rapidly becoming enlightened - higher, as it were.

When in fourth density and you are having your name repeated unto you that is of third density, third density is reinstated, you see.

Because the vibration is pronounced unto you and your soul essence resonates unto it.

Q: Can you tell me what my name should be?

Should be, hm? First of all there are many names. There are fourth density, fifth density, sixth density, etc.

Q: I want to go to the top. (Laughter).

Mm, it would be more harmonious for you to resonate gradually as you progress in the unfolding of yourself. This that you have as your name currently is of third density, however, there are certain frequency vibrations that are different from your previous name. That is why you would desire to change it, why you are not content with it now, for now you are in search of your fourth density Self. What is resonant with you at this point in your time is 'Shaldena'. You will bring forward the resonance of this, each time you state it. The entities that are coming forth upon this plane, you will notice, have very different names than has been commonplace on Earth. This is why. They are already resonating to their fourth density names.

Q: [Another lady:] Can you tell me a name? (Laughter) Here we go! (More laughter).

Shall I say 'form a line'? I will indulge you, my dear sister. You are truly beauteous. I am your mirror. 'Chrysona'.

So that you do not misunderstand, the spelling of this is either CH or K, however you would prefer, for that is not important. CHRYSONA. Is this helpful?

Q: I like it.

It is wondrous to spend an evening of time with you in this manner. I truly am enlightened when I return hence. Become as a fish. Swim heartily in the water of life, joyously. Not concerning yourself, and fretting yourself with the foodstuffs in your time to come, or your abode. For your abode is the water of life you are within. Residence is not a place. It is a knowingness. Your home is in your heart. What you would desire to have as peace and harmony and alignment within your life, within your knowingness, that is your light which is coming forward. Allow it to shine upon you as the Sun does upon a fish, just below the water. Bask in its light - the light of you. Dance within the water of life. Blow bubbles if you will. Play. Partake of life. Enjoy. For joy is the state of being of a God, not furrowed brows. Smile. It brings joy to the heart automatically. Allow that joy to seep through you unto all the other essences you see in your life. Share your light, and share your joy. Partake with another in embrace. Allow your fingers to tickle their back. That is your expression of giggling in physicality. Bring the sparks of unification through yourself, in the explosion of laughter unto this plane. I will see you again very soon in your time. It has been an illustrious evening. I will bid you farewell. Namaste.

Chapter 8

EARTH'S BIRTH CHANGES

FIRST SESSION.

Part I.

Greetings, my beloveds.

You truly are the bejewelled firmament of the heavens. All of you are the crowning glory of Godhood. You are just awakening from your dream to reality. It is my honour to share this with you, to reflect unto you that which you be. A birth is coming. You are invited to participate if you wish.

Confusion - have you begun to experience a bit of it in your life? It is catching these days, you know. You have judgment of the word confusion. It is co-fusion, fusion with All-That-Is. The allowance of yourself to perceive multi-dimensionality - past, future, present. All concurrent, simultaneous. So it is wondrous, delight in it. It will allow you to become the crystal citadel, the cathedral of Christus that you really are.

Now, the creation of this universe was one momentous, mammoth, beauteous explosion into multidimensional levels of consciousness. Indeed, every level of consciousness that exists, was created, every particum of soul energy spewed forth in that one instantaneous joyous now moment, and you were all there. You are beginning to remember this creation, ye indeed, even remember before the beginning into the point called I AM. What is occurring is the transition into a new era, the age of God, the age of remembering that you know.

I will tell you beloveds, there need not be discomfort in this birthing. You may flow with it into the river of All-That-Is and allow the petals of life to open, to bring forth newness, new breath, new life force, new persona of that which be you.

As you flow with the energy, merge your consciousness with the dolphin consciousness, for it not only assists in the dream state, it assists in birthing. It allows you to create harmony and communion with Christ consciousness, that which it exemplifies. So, as you imagine diverse circumstances and adversity around you, visualize immersing yourself in water with a dolphin, and as it cradles you and caresses you, blend with Mother Earth, for she also is in the process of birthing. She also is your birther, and you are her's. So merge and blend these energies together, to flow into newness of life, caressed with the clarity of the waters of your wisdom.

The first density consciousness of the elements - air, earth, fire and water - they too have soul energy. They too have consciousness, thought, desire. They too are being brought to the forefront of the community called humanity [reference is to geo-physical changes]. And, as you would concentrate and commune with them, you may align not only your own life circumstances, but your Mother Earth and her birthing transition.

The fire energy, Kundalini, as represented by the grand jewel within your heavens, let it flow through you and into the essence of that which you be, into *your* grand central sun, connect it to Mother Earth, allow it to flow through you into her. Re-circulate the energy up unto your heart and back out to humanity to connect with all the other consciousnesses, and not only your brothers that you call mankind, but all consciousness. Nature, and your brothers of the elements, your brothers of animals, fauna and flora, all of it. Blend with it and know that indeed it is you. Know that as you connect with the fire energy you are reconnecting to the birthing point of this universe, for it was created of fire energy. You are remembering your creation and you are remembering the creation of your future into harmony.

Now, the waters of your land, the grand bodies of ocean, indeed, they too are in flux. They too are in communion with the other elements, and as they rise and spew forth, they make their presence known. That is what you call Earth changes and they are communicating with one another, and not only with one another but with all of life. Humanity and the Gods of the unseen, they too are making their presence known so that they may participate in conscious awareness with everything that exists.

You think these Earth changes are something to be feared and dreaded. There are dire circumstances given forth in your prophecy, but I will tell you this, my beloveds, it need not be. Indeed, your very thought in this very now moment may transcend the Earth changes into quietude, into a gentle birthing, rather than that which is of tradition. *Every thought that you give forth is a prophecy in and of itself.* It recreates the fabric of your future. It reweaves your experience. As you concentrate and focus on dire circumstance, *and even consider it,* you create it, for indeed, it has not been aligned into harmony in the knowingness of your power to recreate the drama as you choose it to be.

So, as the elements are coming forth unto one another to commune and allow their voice to be heard, shall we say, then you may honour this and understand them as the power source that you are, and in this alignment, it too will align with you so that you do *not* experience disharmony in its communion.

When the quakers and tremors come forth, you may abide in a point of this Earth plane, where it does not affect you. It need not occur all at once either. Your platetechtonics are a grand science upon this planet, but it may occur as a gentle shifting, a little energy at a time, so that it will be a bit of a tremor, and yet another one. The contractions may be brought forth in alignment and harmony, rather than discord and fraught with dire circumstances.

As you tune into the essences of consciousness that are of the unseen, your air, earth, fire and water, allow them also to bubble forth within your very being. The fire within you is your Kundalini and your heart flame. Allow the flicker and glimmer of it to be perceived by you. Let it warm you, caress you with its fingers and as you feel it, it will grow and grow and grow, indeed to consume your very being and the entirety of your consciousness. It will embrace the world with its blaze and glow and brilliance, and enlighten all those that are perceived as being in darkness.

Communion also may be of embrace when you consider quakers and tremors and volcanoes and walls of water and all that has been given forth - reach out with your heart. Embrace it with your heart and in this thought and this very motion of your thought vibratory energy, you will allow at soul essence, an etheric embrace in return and when this occurs, there is harmony. It is a heart to heart connection. There is alignment, so that you have recreated your experience into a dramatic experience of delight and deliciousness, rather than dire circumstance.

The dolphins, they are grandly coming forth to communicate with the energies upon the plane, to know dance and delight, sprightliness of the soul, friskiness and freedom, and indeed fervour to understand power. They swim and sleight the water with their being and display the rainbow spectrum of the light and allow the perception of the childlikeness of their being and their essence as a mirror, as a reflection of the brothers upon the land, to know that they too may dance in a circle of communion with the collective consciousness called life - in harmony, in unity, with the elements, and with All-That-Is.

Now, do you know what an earthquake is, in a way? It is when Mother Earth did not take her Earth control pills. You like that one, eh?

Know that when you experience further frustration, not only because of the coming Earth changes, but also because of the changes within your personal life, your relationships, your purse - that is a big one on this plane - then indeed you may align it in the same manner [with laughter]. For that consciousness called Terra, called your Mother Earth, is the same as you. You are mutual mirrors unto one another.

Do you know that your embodiment is a macro molecule? That you indeed have within you millions and billions of universes likened unto your solar system? This universe of your embodiment is also in alignment with the elements. Its fiery creation that regenerates cell after cell after cell with soul memory after soul memory, is of the essence of the four elements conjoined into one community consciousness of that cell. And as you align your soul memory, as you align the elements of your consciousness and that of Mother Earth, your embodiment aligns as well.

Your elements also resonate to the four directions - North, South, East and West. As you harmonize with all directions, you unfold into omnidirectionality, that is all directions at once. That is omnipresence and that is what you are beginning to experience.

Your relationships will also come from all directions, from your past, from your future, and from alternate nows, all directions of time. They are coming unto you for you to recreate the experience to give you an opportunity to embrace what you have not considered in unconditional love before. It is a grand adventure and you are all explorers upon this island called judgment. As you embrace the element within the relationship, within the entity, or even within a financial condition - the element that you do not desire, that you judge - then indeed you will begin to embrace other aspects of yourself and you will be of the light. You will twinkle and glow and glimmer like your stars that are cast within the bejewelled heavens of your firmament, and you will become the essence of light for others to perceive and enjoy and vibrate unto, in awe.

Now, when you allow relationships, as they come unto you, to integrate and interweave into the fabric of all your realities, you will begin to perceive other lives you have experienced with them and your vision will become clarified. The Kundalini indeed will merge and blend with your third eye so that you will remember and visualize and have clarity of perception of that reality, which you have experienced in any dimensional time flow of your before, or of your future.

Indeed, your dreams will become your living, waking reality and you will find your slumber time will be less desired. You will sleep less. Do you know why? Because you do not require the illusion of inactivity in order to have the connection with other realities. You will coagulate your dreams into the reality of your physical life experiences. You will be living your dream. Your dream is any thought you resonate unto at any moment, any now, any beauteous, delicious now of your time. As you experience every drop of it, you are creating an ocean of eternity within which to experience. I will tell you, my beloveds, it is indeed the horizon of heaven, if you wish it to be. It need not be firmaments full of hellfire and brimstone.

There are many of you who desire to put away foodstuffs for fear and trepidation about your future. I will tell you, like your squirrels, you worry too much about 'nuttin'. As you hoard your foodstuffs and put them away in fear and are frightened about what you will be providing for yourself in your future, you resonate with the foodstuffs in fear, in the understanding of the non-ability to provide for yourself. I will tell you this: when the time comes for it to provide you with its energy, it will be afraid to do so, for it resonates in fear.

Now, you may indeed cultivate your gardens and your patios around your abodes. You may delight in it, rather than giving yourself to the fear and frustration of hoarding, and it will provide abundantly for you, more fruitful provision than you have ever considered any tree or plant could provide . Now, land indeed is wondrous. It is Mother Earth herself. It is the garden of Gods within which you may create your experience and your existence and abide within harmoniously. But do not, I beseech of you, go forth and create its presence out of fear and out of the desire for safety, for *what you flee from will get you anyway, if you do it in fear.*

It does not matter where you are, beloveds, for *the vibration of fear will recreate the drama, no matter what you are, where you are or what you are doing.* It will always, always, always recreate it for you.

Your safety is anywhere and anywhen. You may be in the middle of your grand quakers and tremors and do you know, your neighbour will be affected and you will not, if you vibrate from the knowing of your power, from your power-sourceness. Then you will resonate in love with your brothers - and not only your brothers, but with everything visible and invisible - in this new birthing.

It will indeed be a grand, brilliant explosion, a birth into newness of life and newness of perception of civilisation, communication, technology, thought process, creativity expressing the art of God. Every manner of creativity shall be expressed by every entity. Everyone will resonate to the understanding of music and tone, sound and light and colour, and be an artist in every fashion comprehensible.

You will begin to create what you have always desired, the life of a God, but you have been too afraid to acknowledge that you truly *can* experience this. Because you have not acknowledged your own divinity, beloveds, you have not understood the love of yourself. Every relationship, every circumstance, is coming to you from every other dimension for you to love and that includes the relationship of yourself. That includes the embrace of your own heart by you. When you allow this to occur, everyone, *everyone* that comes unto you will acknowledge your beauty, your gentility, your fervour into freedom because they will have resonated to your unlimited love that they recognize within themselves. They too will be brilliant jewels.

If you would desire to transform the world, transform *you*. If you would desire to bring peace, bring peace into your own heart. If you would desire to birth the Earth in a harmonious fashion, birth *you* in a harmonious fashion. Beloveds, it is not the Earth that will bring you devastation, it is your own thought. The Earth abides in the culmination of your thought, whatever you think, so shall it be.

Now, the hoarding of your currency into gold, there has been a bit of chitter-chatter about this one. The same what applies to the food stuffs applies to this. If you do so in fear, it will be taken from you. No matter how much you accumulate. Now, you may indeed have gold in your auric field around you, in your mineral form, but allow it to be usable. Create it so that is of enjoyment and pleasure throughout your daily activity. Have your platters, your tankards, what do you call them, your cups?, have all of these created of this metal. Use it, every day of your life, in the creation of your daily expression. Therefore it will be experienced every day, as a matter of recognition of this activity, rather than being hoarded somewhere for the desire to exchange it later. For the later is always now, beloveds, *always*. You have never known a moment that was not now. Have you ever known and experienced in your reality a moment that was not now? Your future is the shadow. So is your past. You may enlighten and illuminate those shadows with your light, through the now. But I will tell you, beloveds, when you experience joy and immerse yourself in the resonance of the vibration of vivacity, then you create the song of you into a grand symphony.

Indeed, you will not have any fear about anything, for you will experience the childlikeness, the child of God, the Christus, issuing forth in that moment. It will fill the chalice of you to the brim with the sparkling clarity of the waters of your wisdom, for you to partake and to share with your brethren. As they do thusly, the cup is never void, it is never emptied, it is ever full. It is ever replenished from the channel that be you, for you are the conduit of the ever flowing waters of life. You are the conduit of the birthing of the Earth and the new civilization yet to be born, the crystal citadels that are indeed to be erected as monuments to you. You will acknowledge their monumental reflection. You will acknowledge that you too are Christ-all in essence. You are the Crystal cathedral in and of your own SELF. You are the temple, the House of Worship. You, indeed, are to be created as the place of honour, respect, and awe, and the altar is your heart. The sacrament is the fire within it that burns and blazes in brilliance to warm and nurture and caress your brethren, and the Earth, for she too is one of your brethren.

Now, there is within your brain the Pineal gland. Within in it is the crystal tissue which was created during the star-seeding, the colonization of this Earth plane. It is in formation of crystal, although it is tissue in form, not mineral, and as it resonates to that crystal-like, coagulated understanding, it will allow you to interpenetrate through telepathy - which is really telempathy - communion with your brethren. Empathetic communication, *being* them, knowing them, and allowing the Kundalini energy to flow through your throat area, into your third eye, and pierce all the other third eyes of all other creatures and consciousnesses upon this plane, including your animals. Therefore, indeed, the lion will lie down with the lamb. Therefore, indeed, all will be honouring one another and no longer will your fauna and flora be slaughtered. That includes your rainforests.

All the wisdom of the eras gone past, and all the wisdom of the future is coming forth into the now, and you will begin to remember the technology. You will begin to remember how to coagulate matter from energy, interdimensional energy, into mass, into light, colour and sound coagulated and trinitized into matter. That technology will come unto you only when - only when, beloveds - you will allow the flow, the river of you, to be opened, to be a channel, to be the chalice.

Have you ever wondered why an entity ceases their embodiment when their head is lopped off? It is because this consciousness communicating through the Pineal gland, is severed. This is where - behind the nape of the neck - the soul energy enters in to communicate, and allows the channelling of your knowing. When it is disconnected, it frees itself of that focus of energy to go into other dimensions. When this area opens, and the flow comes forth, you will begin to know what you have known, that which you really know, but is within the veil of forgetfulness of your now. You will begin to know how to manifest your freedom, financial security, safety, whatever it is you wish. You will begin to understand how to manifest the birthing in a harmonious fashion.

Sigh in freedom, sing in ecstasy. Do you know the bird does not care who is listening? It sings because that is its very being. So sing, be in delight, be danceful. Be in synchronous expression with your life, and you will have much to sing about, beloveds.

Your sexual expression, it too is coming forth for the contemplation of many of you. It too is recreating itself for you to embrace what you have judged and denied yourself before. Indeed, you will feel a ridge, a dispersal of energy that is not flowing, a damming of energy. Both genders have within them both male and female consciousness and those who are of male gender, will begin to feel the presence of a sexual urge that is unlike to what they ever contemplated before. It is unfamiliar to them. They will begin to experience what it is to create a womb within their heart, to create new life expression within them, to create indeed, receptivity and intuition, unconditional love, freeing others to *be,* and not keeping them in the compartments and organisation of their systemized fashion of thought.

Your feminine will begin to experience an urgency to create within their own reality, a power-sourceness, to be independent and sovereign, and the desire to manifest herself for herself and not to be enslaved to anyone or anything else. As these polarities begin to integrate, you will have integration, integrity of the God that you are. There will be sexual energy spewing forth into all parts of you. Not only your lower fields, but all parts of you, for it is the fire of life, the fire of creation, regeneration, and it need not be channelled into the area of destruction. It may be channelled into the area of delight, of a grand and wondrous display of fireworks, indeed. The energy of the Kundalini will create an etheric spinal column. You will have a duplicity of nature in this fashion - two spinal columns up your back. One is physical and one is etheric, because your embodiment is beginning to create its life, its light form and as it does thusly, your cells will begin to create particums of light within, so that your body glows.

Not only you, but the trees, the flora, the fauna; the fishes within the waters, your fine feathered friends within the skies, and planet Earth herself, will begin to glow. That glimmer is indeed a glimpse of what you call super-consciousness. Now, this will occur, but it has two avenues of occurrence, beloveds. It has the avenue through destruction and war, and hatred, and pettiness and jealousy, and fear, and all manner of pestilence and devastation upon the land. The other alternative, beloveds, is created through the fire of life, harmoniously channelled into a gentle birth. Indeed, a birth - waves and waves and waves of harmonious contractions. You will feel the pressure, the urgency. You will experience newness of life. Allow indeed the dreamer of you to issue forth and be the visionary of all you desire to recreate this civilization into a grand citadel. It is an experience, an expression of God, to be sure. And as you do this, you will acknowledge your power, and in the acknowledgment of it in one moment, it merely magnifies it for the next, and as you acknowledge it in that next, it magnifies it in the next, so that indeed, you walk upon your streets, and every thought you think immediately coagulates in front of you. You would desire what you call jingle-jangle in your pocket, and as you come forth in the very creation of that thought, there will be a bit of your change on the street for you to discover, in the adventure of understanding your power to create.

There will be many of so-called coincidents. It is co-incidents, two incidents, or more than two, coming together to commune. It is synchronicity. All of your life may be an ecstatic explosion of synchronicity, so that you go forth without any fear or anxiety about anything, for you will know that you may create what you desire in any fashion you wish if you will create it without anxiety. Anxiety is excitement with doubt. It is. It is one polarity of excitement about your power, but it is caressed by the thought called doubt.

All of life is collective thought. You are remembering that you have been a collective imagination within the thought of God. There is no teaching. *There is only knowing that you know.* A teacher is an assistant helping others to remember that they know. Your life will be a grand and wondrous expression of the constant unveiling of that which you know.

Do you know deja vu? Do you know what it is? All of you have experienced it a bit in your time. It is merely your recognition that you planned all this in advance. There indeed is an element of knowing as you walk through that power point, that vortex of recognition of other dimensions, and for a moment, you will have a glimpse of other realities and other dimensions. You may indeed walk forth in a constant flow of that vortex, as you acknowledge that it is always with you and that it is not in a point. It is only that you resonate to that point in that moment, and when you carry it with you constantly, you will have constant deja vu. What an ecstatic explosion. A rendezvous with remembrance.

Now, there are some of you who carry forth a desire to be cheerful all the time, to be happy, and although their covering called skin reflects cheerfulness, their heart is heavy. I will ask you, do you smile because that is how your heart is, or do you smile because you are proud of your teeth? Allow yourself to embrace your face with 'a-lign' of harmony. Allow yourself to create joy and cheerfulness wherever you go, but let it be synchronous with the way your heart is vibrating. In the moment of heaviness, embrace that heaviness with the wings of wisdom and lift it into forever, with buoyancy and joy of spirit and soul. And in this, you will embrace it and not sever it. You will not be separating it from yourself, but you will be lifting it. Then indeed there will be an integrity of your expression and your heart. There will be an integration of the darkness and the light.

The darkness and the light are only both polarities exemplified to create God. Both are divine. There is no judgment of the dark, for it is merely the light that has not acknowledged itself. That is all. When you give forth the light of you, then it IS the light, and the darkness is embraced into the light. It is not to sever, or to completely get rid of the dark. It is to embrace it into the light; to allow the dark to remain, but allowing the light to be visible. For whenever you enlighten a room, where does the dark go? Have you ever thought about that? It is still there, you just cannot see it.

Now, begin to think differently of your past. Begin to expand the horizons of your thought process. Begin to allow other manners of perception. Place yourself within the skin of your enemy. *Be* their being, *know* their knowing. Indeed, know the secrets and torments of their hearts, and compassion will flow forth, the expression of unlimited love for their being and you will not have any reason to judge them, for you will know them *as you*. They will indeed be brought into the embrace of your heart, and therefore, their pain will dissipate. They will not create disharmonious expression before you anymore, for you have embraced them, you have become them and therefore their countenance will change and shift. It is *your* perception of perspective. It is not that *they* change. It is that *you* change how you perceive them.

As the Earth rotates around your Sun, whenever it is night time and you have the darkness of the hour of midnight, does that mean the Sun is not there? No, you just do not perceive it because you are on a different perception point. And when the Earth turns to embrace the light, indeed the sleeping, hushed valleys open up to the squeal of delight - to the birdsong. Know that you may perceive from whatever apex point you desire, and ultimately, you shall perceive from them all, for there is only one point of view, and that is everyone of them.

Know that every aspect of your brothers, of the consciousness that you create as lack, any kind of lack at all - lack of relationship, lack of financial security, lack of foodstuffs in your nations that you consider are starving, lack of abundance of natural resources - it too is just another perspective. It is merely another viewpoint of the All-That-Is, created for the purpose of expressing that particular vibration, to understand it, to know it. In this understanding, all shall integrate and merge into the unity of harmony called I AM. *Only after every possible conceivable emotion has been experienced, shall you know God.* That is why all of you are calling unto you all these experiences you have judged. For now is the timing, the birthing is about to occur, and now is the timing for you to embrace these things that you have judged, to go forth into the light, into the freedom of forever called GOD I AM.

Part II.

This nation you call Australia is indeed on the outward rim of the continent you once called Lemuria. As the quakering and tremoring occurred in that timing and the waters went over the land, the land submerged beneath the sea forever. There was a grand shifting of the plates of the Earth - the continents of America and Lemuria came together, and there is a grand fault line there that is part of what you call the Ring of Fire. This has brought much terror to many people, much fear and frustration and dire circumstance and thoughts of discord and disharmony. But it is not necessary. It may give forth ceasement of life, or regeneration of life. It depends upon how you would desire to create it. It is up to you, my masters, entirely up to you. You are the creators. What is it that you desire to create? What is it that you desire to project into your future?

The star-seeding that was created within your tissue, the Pineal gland, is becoming awakened. It is beginning to resonate the memories of those that placed the gene of Isis, the Genesis, within it. It is an additional chromosome and this chromosome is beginning to resonate and awaken within all entities across your Earth, globally; it is coming forth in grand fashion. That is why there are so many people across the entirety of the Earth beginning to become, what you term paradoxically, spiritual. All is spiritual, my beloveds, even the dark.

Now, this awakening within the Pineal gland is allowing the channelling to occur. All is channelling. You give it one particular label and manner of contemplation, but everything you do is channelling, my beloveds. If you have a thought, you have channelled the thought. Did you know that? As you begin to channel more and more unlimited thoughts, you place it in a particular category. But it is not to categorize, it is to communalize. Become in communion with one another in brotherhood and harmony and unity. The creation of this thought may indeed align itself with the Kundalini, the fire energy that spews forth into sparking an electromagnetic energy, enhanced with the harmonious recognition of the God I Am of you, and as it comes into the crown area, you may align it into a thought process that you desire. That is what is called telepathy. Allowing the fire energy to come forth to crystallize it into coagulated experience. That experience is the recognition of another entity, or circumstance, to create physically, the trinitization of light, colour and sound, into that thought. It is likened unto a tuning fork. When you resonate one, the other responds. It is exactly the same principle. All of you are beginning to recognize your magic. Your magician is coming forth within you. Wave the wand of your wisdom and your wizardry will be experienced.

Now, the two areas above your nose area, right at the point of your brow, are becoming awakened also. They are grand meridian points. Allow the third eye to be connected with the heart seal. It is likened unto a double pyramid. Feel these two points now, of your own body and you will feel it is very sensitive and tender. As you do thusly, right at the point where your brows meet, just above where the sandman deposits his material. The other triangle that is downward pointing, is the centre point of your heart.

You are becoming the thinkers of the land and in your thinking, you create your future. You are capturing the vision into coagulated experience. So *whatever you envision is becoming.* As you become aware of this, everything within you begins to open, and flower and blossom, grandly, wondrously and gloriously. You will begin to feel everything emphasized. Every emotion that comes unto you will be an embracing of a more emphatic emotion. As you embrace it, it will become grander and grander and grander and therefore, what you call the pits of depression, will become the pits. You will experience the devastation of the heart and soul. The desert of the soul - the dark night of the soul, some call it. But as you resonate to the opposite polarity, which is joy and dance and celebration and delight, you will experience your life as exquisite ecstasy. The embrace of the two polarities into unified harmonious experience, is what is called coming into super-consciousness. That is coming through the twelve days of light into the twelve days of dark, to create the day of divinity.

Now, the platetechtonics of your planet, the geometric understanding of the planetary plates, they are shifting. They are creating a grid of vortices and meridian points upon the plane that are shifting and coming into alignment, releasing the ridges and disperses and flows of energy through them. Do you know, the very plates of your blood are doing the same thing - platelets? For they have contained, through their very essence, their very expression, the gene of Isis, the extra chromosome. The recognition is not only within the Pineal gland. It is within every atom and every cell of your body. For every atom and every cell contains holographically, the whole of it all. As you resonate emphatically to the remembrance of All-That-Is, of all dimensions of your experience, so does your blood. It indeed will come forth in grand fashion and express in like manner, according to the resonance of your thought. Womankind, according to her season of time, will experience much more flow [of blood]. The increase of your blood in the pulsations of your veins will become grand and wondrous. If there is congestion within the head, the pulsation will create an ache of the head because it is congesting and contracting, and restricting this flow. Indeed, for there is an expansion within the blood flow and an increase in the pressure, an urgency of pulsation, an acceleration of time. Therefore, when you have the ache of the head, allow yourself to perceive within your third eye area a glow, a grand central sun, and let it warm and release the barriers of ice and rigidity and melt any dispersal or ridges there are to create a harmonious flow through this area. And you will indeed have the dissipation of the ache of the head.

There is also an increased flow of your sinus fluids. You will have sneezes, and you will have an increased flow of all sorts of fluids within the body. You will have much desire for the use of your tissue. This also includes saliva, for it too, contains the element of your vibration, your signature vibration, and as you increase it, you will begin to swallow more and more. And you will begin to swallow more and more of your realities and your dimensions. You will begin to recirculate them within your embodiment, for they too are part of the flow.

As this continues, you will have the opportunity to embrace what you have judged. *If you do not embrace it, you will have war within your very cells.* You will create diseasements - you call it cancer, you call it Aids, you call it many things. Many of these diseasements you call Lupus[1], and all forms and fashions of ailments that are beginning to pop up all over your world, is because there is war within you. The wars upon the plane and the diseasements of the cells - which is war, cell and cell unto one another - is a reflection, of the war within your very soul, within your very being. The embrace of this war as an opportunity to be aligned, brother to brother, cell to cell, consciousness to consciousness, will allow this diseasement to cease. What a limitation. [Last reference is to diseases].

Now to the war of the planet with the planet, your quakes and tremors and dire circumstance. It is the restriction and congestion of the birth process, and as you constrict and congest, there is more and more pressure and more and more swelling of the tissues of birth, and more and more resistance to the birthing itself. And so indeed, there is more and more pressure to push it out, and yes, there is less and less harmonious flow in the opening and flowering of the petals of the birth canal. So, I will tell you this, beloveds: *war is denial of that which you do not desire; denial, separation, severance, saying unto it 'get ye hence from me, I do not desire you'. It will continue, beloveds. Until you understand that the key to freedom, to peace and harmony, to joy, is embracing.*

You are not warriors, you are embracers. As you begin to understand this, you will indeed align the planet and yourself, and all those you love, with the desire to be in the consciousness of harmonious flow. Certainly, there will be those who do not desire this consciousness, for whatever reasons, for it is not their ripeness of time to begin to understand their divinity, in this particular time flow, in this particular now. Do not judge them, I beseech you, for indeed all shall come into their knowing in their own ripeness of time. It is simply not according to how they have chosen their ripeness of time, but they are divine Gods, and they have indeed divine human free will. So allow them to express as they choose, as you would desire to be allowed to express as you choose. It is honouring one another. Offer them the banquet of your being, and allow them the understanding of the awareness, but do not force them to partake. You see, you may display yourself as a divine example, but as you go forth and desire to convert, you yoke and enslave your brethren.

---

[1] Lupus, (L., a wolf: from eating into the substance.) any of various skin diseases; especially a chronic tuberculous disease of the skin or mucous membrane, characterized by the formation of reddish-brown nodules. (Webster.)

Bureaucracy will press harshly that which will be called super-consciousness, because it is afraid. Did you know this? *It is afraid. It yearns and desires to be loved. It has an aching and agony of spirit and soul that feels the void, that feels indeed, unwanted, unloved.* The reflection of its exterior experience is exactly that which it is. How do you transmute this that is darkness, this bureaucracy that oppresses the light? I will tell you - *love it.* That is the key, beloveds, to love. To allow their agony to be recognized, to live within their skin, to know their knowing, and how indeed they hurt of their hearts. As you do this, you will perceive their understanding, and know why it is they feel this desire to oppress others, and bring forth control over others. You will understand them. You will experience them, and therefore you will know that they too are divine, and they too, are created of love, of God I Am, the All-That-Is. They have sprung forth from the very seed of thought that you have sprung forth from. They are your brothers. They merely do not know how to love themselves. This is the only manner they understand how to receive love and honour - by forcing others into a position to love and honour them. Not from their heart, but through their action.

By merging with their hearts and their souls, with your thought, you will change it. You will transform them and transfigure them, and they will begin to open, as they are already doing. They will begin to flower and recognize there is another way.

The war-lords will be de-seated, and your wars will dissipate. It [the dichotomy of polarities] will be greatly enhanced for a while of your time, in the understanding of grand war and trepidation and grand light and understanding of love. But there will come a point of countenance, and in this point of encountering one unto the other, there will be an embracing, and a song is born. That song is peace. Only when you embrace shall this song be birthed, not only in your own life experience, but of the planet as well.

The ozone layer, and all of this, will dissipate. We will discuss this a little bit later, your particular experience of life changes as the Earth changes. The creation, however, of how it occurs is entirely up to you. What I bring forth a bit later in your time will be indeed, your choice. Prophecy is but for the moment, constantly shifting and changing like the sands of time. You are the one that shall create the acceleration of time, for you create time. You also create space. As you create the time and space of your future now moments, you will be creating the vision and capturing it upon the tapestry of your life.

Now, when all of you join together into an understanding that your diversity, your uniqueness is to be honoured, then indeed, you will begin to understand that there are many, many, billions and billions of different manners to express the same divinity. Even though an entity, an expression, is different, and you would judge it, based on your past understanding, to be unbeautiful, you will begin to acknowledge the essence of beauty within it. Begin to look for it. Indeed, begin to see what is beyond the obvious.

Those who are heavy of the skin and of the flesh and have an abundance of cells upon them, you will begin to understand their beauty, and not judge them. Then you will understand beyond the flesh. Be a grand skin diver, as it were, and perceive the beauty beyond the surface of the pool of you.

Some will desire the creation of dire circumstance. Allow them to experience it, *after* your sharing, if they still continue in the desire to experience dire circumstance, that is their right. That is what they choose. So be it. Honour it and love it. Therein lies the rub, in honouring it, for it is bringing them the gift of wisdom. It would not be there if it did not have a gift for them. It tells the tale of wisdom and they are desiring to hear that fairy tale. So allow them the honour of sitting beside the crackling fire at the hearth of their life and of participating in delight in that particular tale. Allow them to live the fantasy of that dream and to be immersed within the vision of that reality, if they wish. That is up to them. And your life is up to you.

Honour them, and you will awaken the birth within them. They will not consciously be aware of it, but they too will begin to shift and change. Indeed, they too will come into alignment. It will take them by surprise at times, but they will begin to open and flower and blossom into the beauty that be they.

There is already this [flowering] within your governmental structures. Have you not noticed? There are a few that are coming forth who are of the light, of light-heartedness. Gorbachev, for example, within the Bear country is one of these. He too is living and abiding within the structures and regulations and politics of his governmental body. And he too, treads the tender thread of the harmonious representation of his heart and simultaneously abiding within the kingdom of his bureaucracy. Indeed, if he steps beyond the thread, he may be replaced, and he knows this. So as he is integrative of the oppressive, and that which is expressive, he too, will align the Earth into freedom. There are many coming forth such as he.

In the next few years of Earth time, you will find that many leaders in the war torn countries of Earth will become similar to this - integrative - expressive of the God I Am in a gentle and tender fashion - not oppressive of the light.

You too can be like this, you know. You may shake your neighbour and your brother until their necks fall off, but I wish you to understand that this is the manner of the Piscean era, of force, of a disharmonious flow. Allow them to be and delight in their beingness. And in this manner, what you desire, voila, will manifest as if by magic. For the magic of your thought will create it. In the allowance of that which is to *be,* it creates joy and peace.

The Sun of your heavens, the fire energy, embrace it, love it, let it be resonant and reflective of the fire energy of your own grand central sun, and also of the fire energy of the grand central sun of the Earth plane. The solar ball of light and the central sun of you and the central sun of the Earth, will become a trinity. You will be the catalyst to create harmonious expression of the ozone. Ultraviolet and retraviolet rays will come into harmony. The electrums within your auric field will enable the electrums of the ozone - and the oxygen thereof and all the discordant display upon your plane - to align. It [the hole in the ozone layer] too, can be changed.

If you feel you are so powerful that you can create your life - what is it that you call it in your books and pamphlets? - you are responsible for your own life, you create your own reality? - if you utterly *know* this, then why is it that you do not know that you can change what is forecast for the future of this planet? The ozone layer may be regenerated. Do you not know this? It too contains a hole that is reflective of the hole within you. You are a microcosm of your planet. If there is a hole within the ozone layer, there is a hole within you. What caused the hole within your ozone layer? Not honouring the body. What causes the holes within you? Not honouring the body. Not allowing yourself to cry when you feel like weeping. Not allowing yourself to resonate with love and laughter, when indeed, you would feel as though it is not the place and time for it. And you go forth into your supermarkets, and you push your buggies, gazing upon your grand tomato, and you feel like crying. But you do not, for you consider 'what will they think of me?', - you exhibit 'shelf-control'. But I will tell you, beloveds, you may allow the rivers to flow, and the nectar of the soul to issue forth upon the softness of your cheeks, to replenish the flow, the void that is created from the river. Embrace the wisdom that has just been captured *without trying to figure out what it was that you just understood.* For that is living within the mountains of your mind and not within the havens of your heart. Let the heart fire of your being blaze and glimmer, crackle and hiss, to sing the song of brilliance. Allow it to experience itself whenever and wherever it desires. When walking outside your abode and there is a gentle rain ushering forth from Mother Earth, and you experience a desire to take off your clothes and splash within the puddles, romp within the fields and the daisies that caress you with their freshness and dampness. Bring forth the fragrance and aroma of the flowers of the fields and the gardens, and the garden of Gods that you call humanity, as well.

Bring forth the arbour of awareness within you. Romp, without considering 'what will they think of me'. Indeed, do what you are unaccustomed to doing. If you are placing your left shoe on your foot, in custom and nature - it is a ritual that is habitual - change the foot. Begin to place your shoe on the right foot occasionally. *Change your habits!* Do you know the only difference between habits and going with the flow of life, is your blindness? Your blindness to the other options. And your life - it becomes bland. Very likened unto an unseasoned experience; you do not have the punches and pungency of the spices of life. The only difference between a rut and a grave is one has two ends on it. So consider resurrecting yourself from the rut and routine of your life. That is being reborn.

When an entity comes unto you and asks you 'Whyfor are you so joyous?'. Ask them 'Why are you not?'. Let them respond however they wish; allow the embrace in that moment, because they are experiencing a contemplation of their agony, which is the point, the apex point, the flash point of transmutation. In that moment of their contemplation of it, is the opportunity to change it. Allow them to know this. Take the time to weep with your brothers, to embrace them.

If you rush and hurry and scurry because of your busy schedules, and see beside you an entity that is heavy-hearted, consider that your schedule is always on schedule, and that your life is created according to your heart's desire, not according to the time clock. Now, embrace them, speak to them, love them. All that is required is to state unto them an expression of joy. Gaze within them, consider what is beauteous, and tell them. If it is an aged man who is heavy-hearted and has a cane in his hand and grand furrows in his brow, indeed, he has been disillusioned with his life. He is not, in his own contemplation of himself, the king and master that he thought he would be when he was a youth. Allow him to understand his beauty. Allow him to understand that he has given you an instant of joy and express appreciation for it. For in this experience of viewing his heavy-heartedness, you have experienced an opportunity to love the perceived unlovable, to enlighten the unenlightened, to understand with compassion the ridges and dispersals of the flow of life.

The crossroads of your life - giving you many choices - are there for you to understand that any option is just as valid as any other. They are all equally divine, and whatever pathway your heart desires in that moment is divine. And if it changes its mind later, that is divine too.

In your fear, when crossing in an unexpected manner, you call it jaywalking, you get that 'run down' feeling. But know, indeed, you may cross the ocean of eternity wherever you will and do whatever you desire, if you integrate all the energies and be in integrity of yourself. Integrity is only integration and honour of the God I Am.

The time piece, your clock, will indeed become just another aspect of physicality. It is an enslaver, but it may be honoured, for it allows the particular function called physicality, upon this plane. So honour it, but it is not necessary to be enslaved unto it. You may transmute it as well and create time, by bending light. That is another discussion. As you desire to create the dimension of inter-dimensionality, you will begin to focus into non-focus. Not one particular manner, but all manners. Allow the All-That-Is to *be* All-That-Is. Focus is going further into density, into physicality. Non-focus is expressing the illusion of all focuses at once. Therefore, as you shift you begin to feel a bit disoriented and you do not exactly know where to plug your light in - you constantly run around searching for a socket to plug your light in so that you may glow. Do you know this? Plug your light in here [the heart] and you will glow forevermore for all those who are still searching in the darkness.

Many of you gaze into your neighbour's garden and do not see the beauty of the silver rose - you see the broken gate. Many of you may be likened unto a blind man searching for a black cat in a dark room, where there is none. You are living a life of illusion and the illusion is that you do not have a choice. *You do.* I am here to reflect unto you your choice. I am here to reflect unto you that your choices are changing constantly. Do you know, constant change is the only stable condition of life? It is, you know.

Whenever entities would consider they must align their lives to their birthday - their star sign - in order to fulfil their destiny, you can allow them a more illumined understanding. Each now moment is a birth. Your cells are constantly being recreated. The body, your temple, is constantly being regenerated. Your awareness, your auric field, is constantly being rebirthed into a new awareness, a new understanding, a new rapture of opportunity by your experience, as it comes unto you. So indeed, your star sign of astrology will begin to open to the awareness of becoming all the signs, the entire astrological chart.

You will create your own sign, that is the thirteenth, and that is called God. It will be an integration of all of them, in a harmonious fashion. And indeed, as you experience one moment, it may be Aries, the fire. As you experience another, it may be Aquarius. But all of them will interweave themselves through your life. It will become an expression of all of the above, rather than this *or* this *or* this.

Whenever anyone asks you what time you were born, state *now* - what day you were born, state *now*. Bring nowness into your vocabulary. I will give you an exercise: go for one hour of your time, without speaking in the past or future tense. You will find it quite an illuminating experience. You go through your lives, contemplating the shadows of your past and future, which is not yet here. You do not perceive that it is your now moment. Speak in the IS, and you will regenerate the is IS, Isis. The gene of Isis will come forth.

IS is the God I Am, in both polarities, reflecting one unto the other, and is also expressed in the mythology called Isis. It is considered the female principle, indeed. But it is the duplicity of the female principle that gives it power. For it is an aligned power-sourceness of allowance and embrace. It is the female [principle] represented in balance. Now, the gene of Isis spears forth unto you the genesis, the re-genesis, the regeneration, the birthing of the planet, of your body, of your memory, of the universe, of the galaxy, and it is occurring each moment.

There are the electromagnetic lay lines between every atom of existence, in every dimension, on every plane, that indeed interconnect every thought that is emitted. *Every single thought you emit affects, in one now or another, every other facet of consciousness in the All-That-Is.* It is interwoven, it is embraced, and in the auric field of Mother Earth, it is called collective consciousness, or what you call mass consciousness. The auric field of the Earth plane, that is collective consciousness, is indeed no more than her own soul memory. You are a microcosm of this. Your soul memory contributes to it. As you align your soul memory, she aligns. As the soul memory within every cell of your body aligns into non-war of itself, your soul memory aligns, and each one is a macrocosm unto the other and a microcosm to the other. It is both ways.

Now, understanding this inter-connectedness, you will understand the power behind every thought. Understanding the momentum behind every creation of vibration of thought energy that you place into the etheric body of this planet, will allow you to consider your contemplations. Consider what you think about everyday. What is it? Is it the trinity of words - hurry, worry and bury? Is it desiring of love, constantly? It is very easy to love the lovable, but the rub is, loving the perceived unlovable.

What is it that you wish *not* to be? What is it that you desire to keep farthest from you in your life? That is where your harmony will be aligned into the expression of peace in your life - by loving it. If you judge your body, love it. If you judge another's limitation, love it. *If you love what you judge, it will not be within your experience* as an appearance in your physical reality, for it will have been released into the All-That-Is of you.

All you can create for your physical experience is what you have not embraced yet. And as you embrace it, it dissipates, until indeed, you create the wholeness of ascension in your reality. Do you know ascension? You are an ascended representation of what you were the moment before. Did you know this? You are a constant culmination of All-That-Is in your creation of consciousness in your now. As you become a fuller and fuller and fuller experience of the All-That-Is, you become a more and more ascended experience of the All-That-Is. With every awareness, with every understanding, is an awareness of yet a grander understanding to come. There never is an end to it. You are never enlightened, as you call it. You are always in the Is of life, which is constantly expanding.

Enlightenment becomes a grand separator upon this plane. Your brothers, who you would consider to be limited and judgmental and in the midst of the decadence of life, do you know, beloveds, that in other dimensions, they are the wizards, and you are the simpletons?

Do you know this? It is all relative. It depends on which reality you desire to focus on within. But you are all equal, all of you are, beloved masters. All of you have access to the same I Am. You are all created of the same drop of love, into the momentum called atomic energy.

You too are atomic energy, and the creation of the nuclear energy upon this planet is smashing the atoms against one another. It is the expression of war in its very creation - a non-embrace, non-harmony. You too are expressing that same nuclear weaponry within your very being. Do you know why? Because the atoms of you do not sing and dance together to create an accelerated expression of speed beyond thought, into the All-That-Is. That is the ultimate power. Allowing it to be of such speed and such power, and such potential, that as you create the coagulation of that energy, you explode into another universe. You become a supernova. And all of the scientific endeavours in astro-physics and geo-physics and all this that is coming forth, will align to this knowing.

Within your laboratories is coming forth an awareness of the unobservable. Indeed, they too are awakening. Your laboratory is nature. Gaze upon her grandly. As she expresses, so you may also. As she rains, it is indeed the heaven releasing the tears. It is heaven releasing the flow of life. As she experiences evaporation, that is the inception of the waters of life, the partaking. As she experiences thunder and lightning and grand and wondrous and joyous storms of her life and tempests, it is a divine and delightful experience of an explosion of awareness that is electromagnetic current flowing in a beauteous display of itself. It is a joyous ride through the clouds. You too may experience such wonderment and display. Therefore judge not the storm of your life. Embrace the tempest, for she whispers the lyrics of wisdom unto you, if you will allow her to.

The soil of your planet is the fertile loam of you, through which the seeds that are planted by the thoughts of everyone else, may germinate and grow into blossom, if you will allow it. Or they may be implanted within the desert of your soul, your division and judgment, and wither away into the fear of your separation.

So know that you are always a reflection, a microcosmic and macrocosmic expression of your planet. As you let the river of awareness flow unto you, as you stub your toe in the darkness of your midnight, as you perceive an ounce of pain, state unto yourself: 'This is a birthing process, it does not have to be painful'. This may be experienced in every circumstance that comes unto you. You have your driver that experiences a grand traffic made out of jam, a jam made out of traffic, and indeed they honk their horn at you. They grandly emulate geese, you know. Know that this is a birthing process, that as you harmonize without their conscious awareness of it, you may harmonize them.

Indeed, you will create other manners of transport, when you do not have your fossil fuels anymore - different methods of transport through crystalline technology, travelling upon lay lines, electromagnetic travel lanes coursing through the vibrations of your planet electro-magnetically. Through the resonance of your thought process, it will travel where you wish it to go because it resonates through your thought and is electro-magnetically amplified according to the lay lines of the planet. There is a structure that has already been created to allow this crystalline understanding of transport to be manifest within your next decade.

All these inventions and discoveries and wondrous expressions of technology are within your future, and the disharmonious presentations during your daily activity called traffic, business, red ink - some of you have experienced this one - they shall pass away.

This is a birthing process. Go with the flow of the wave, the pulsation, the pressure, and as you do thusly, it will be transformed and transfigured. It will be resurrected into an awareness that allows the birthing to occur, harmoniously. *The fruits of this birthing are prosperity, abundance in every fashion, harmony, peace and a dissipating bureaucracy.* The grandest governor is one who does not [govern]. Do you know this?

The creators of bureaucracy, they too will be born into a new awareness, a new awakening, the quickening that is occurring now. And, for a while, they are becoming stronger. They began in your sixties of time, when your New Age movement was in its origin, its embryonic state, and now they are coming into the fruit of the womb, and, indeed, they will blossom forth.

The element of light-heartedness and laughter will create harmony within your life. When you stub your toe, giggle, and remember that this is all just a grand play, a provocative play indeed, brilliantly staged by you. Know that you create every single piece of that drama, every piece of it. The discordant response in your relationships, you are creating that too. It is a mutual mirror for both of you, so honour it. For you wrote the script, you can rewrite it any time you wish.

The waves and pulsations pour upon you, likened unto a fountain of forever. Indeed, the waterfall will spew forth upon you. You may embrace the droplets, or place an umbrella over your head. If you do, they will fall from you and you will remain in non-awareness of the ecstasy of their flow. It is up to you.

Part III.

Would you desire to have query?

Q: You mentioned Kundalini. What is that?

It is the fire energy. The energy of creation that flows from the area at the base of the spine, into the spinal column, up through your solar plexus, your heart, your throat area, then through your third eye, your crown and out into All-That-Is. Indeed, you may reverse the flow and ground the energy to complete the circuit, and that is where your enlightenment comes forth. You will begin to align the electrums as they pulsate and vibrate with the very essence of God thought, into harmonious balance. During my entry into this embodiment you noticed a bit of quaking and tremoring? And then you noticed it dissipated a bit? That is because when I entered, I was reflecting every resonance that abides within this room and integrating it into a harmonious flow, and when it became integrated, the quaking ceased in that fashion. And as you shift and change constantly your own auric fields, your own energy and thought contemplation, this particular resonance is merely a mirror and allows constant reintegration of that, and therefore you will notice a bit of this [quivering], for I am constantly changing into the stability of you. That is how a mirror operates. That is how the mirror of your life operates. It constantly changes according to your thought flow.

Q: How does aging of the body fit in with the concept of timelessness? Therefore is aging avoidable?

Avoidable? Embraceable. You have a grand, straightforward way of dodging yourself, my brother. *Aging is a process that is caused through the contemplation of linearity, the elapsing of time in a sequential, chronological fashion.* If you know that there is only now, then there is never any aging, because there is never a before or after. Then you are constantly in the understanding of everything as now, now, now, forever through life. That is where immortality is experienced, when you release the dogma of time, the dogmatic restriction through the celebration called anniversary. That is truly clinging to time. It is allowing yourself to be enslaved, for every moment is an anniversary, every moment is a celebration, every moment is a birthing point. Each anniversary is just as divine and grand as any other. So as you release the understanding of time, sequentiality and linearity will become more and more immersed in the beauteous now moment, and as you do thusly, you will go forth into the forever now called God I am, called ascension.

Q: You talk about going into the Aquarian Age and we are actually in the Piscean Age, but in our time, we move forward and the Age of Aquarius is backwards. I cannot work out why we are not going into the Aries Age.

You are actually going, in your understanding of linearity into the age of *all* the astrological signs. The consideration of your Piscean Age and your Aquarian Age and all of this is the Piscean concept, in and of itself. And so, the minute you speak of the Aquarian era, indeed if you would desire to call it that, it is that, but really, in the unlimited perspective, it is the All-That-Is Age, the era of God. Thank you beloved.

Q: For the last one and a half years, I have not been well. I have not been able to cope with my work. Will I go back to my work, or will I be well?

First of all, there is this grand and wondrous word you have which is called work. It is a word that has within its very vibration, the concept of resistance and labour and effort. And I will tell you this, beloveds, your moment to moment experience will begin to transmute itself from work to joy, to play, to celebration. You will not have your work, or your labour. Your Labour Party will release the first part of that phrase, hm? The freedom to choose what you desire to experience will be acknowledged by you. You will go forth from one romp and rapturous experience and delight into another, not ever considering it work. If it does bring you support, so be it, but it will not be work. It will be a joyous expression of your creativity. Do you know, my beloveds, all of you have a grand desire to know what your career is in this New Age. You go forth bumping into reflection after reflection, after reflection, and you state - but this cannot be all that is, what else is there? I will tell you this, beloveds, you seek and search for a career in an era where there are none. Perhaps you can be in the career of creating careers, hm? Indeed, the support of yourself will be your knowingness that you constantly provide, synchronistically, support for one another, all as equal brothers. You will begin to experience this as coincidence in your life. 'Fancy that. How about that? That happened to me and this happened to me, and how about that?'

Do you know, my beloveds, you would desire to partake of foodstuffs, perhaps, and you have an entity coming forth rap tapping upon your door, who just so coincidentally desires someone to share some foodstuffs with him. You would desire a grand and wondrous abode, and you frustrate yourself and furrow your brow about 'how in the world can I have enough collection of the currency, to provide myself with a grand and wondrous castle?'. You will never get it that way, beloveds, not a in harmonious fashion anyway. When you know that it may come unto you in any manner, and not limit how it comes unto you, and not limit it by requiring that it must be given to you with currency, then it will flow to you. And you will have a rap tap on your door, and someone will wish you to abide within their palace while they are away for a few months. You see? Open all the doors of opportunity and do not restrict yourself by determining *how* it will occur. Currency is consciousness, and currency shall pass away from this plane, for your currency will be your energy exchange directly, one unto the other. Even gold will pass away, for it will be embraced within your auric field, and you will walk in a constant cloak of gold. So, ye, gold itself is a limitation.

There are many other things we will discuss about your gold later in your time. However, I wish you to know that your work place, your market place, your business - the busiment of the embodiment - it may be however you wish it. If you feel the desire to express in another fashion, allow it to manifest for yourself without judging what you do, alright? So be it.

Q: Both Soul and Spirit pass over when we die?

Indeed. It is not really a passing over, either. It is perceiving a different dimension. But there is a particum of you that remains and abides within the dimension that you have just experienced. That is how you may embrace all that you have ever experienced, and ever shall, for there are particums of light, and atoms of energy that abide there, and by embracing them into you, you communicate light, to light, to light, to light, and interweave and thread all of these realities together. Becoming enlightened - allowing all these particums of light to collect into your conscious awareness here. Thank you, beloved.

Q: I would like to ask you about healing. Through history, we are told that Jesus Christ was able to say to someone: 'Take up your bed and walk', and they were instantly healed.

But he was reflecting their capacity to heal themselves. He was a magnification, an amplification of the power, and a demonstrator, in this fashion. Very likened unto this, [St. Germain referring to himself] except in his own embodiment. It was they who desired to be healed, else they would not have been. *No one is a healer,* except themselves. You never really heal anyone else, you merely reflect their own capacity to heal themselves, in an amplified manner. Thank you, beloved.

Q: My emotions are of fear and unhappiness, which I see as the illusion of being separated from our Source. Are these emotions necessary, in order for us to make a conscious human choice for integration?

The experience of *all* emotions is required in order to consciously integrate, indeed. *All* emotions, and one is just as beauteous as another.

I will depart for now. You are truly beloved, all of you, and I will return in a short period of your time and we will discuss the changes in more detail. Before I pour this understanding into your chalice, I desire to prepare the chalice, to polish it a bit, so that indeed it may lustre and shine and glimmer with the sparkling waters of wisdom. Alright? So be it. Go forth now and until further notice, celebrate everything. Fare thee well. Namaste.

Part IV.

Greetings, my beloveds. How did you sup? You have calmed the beast within your belly? The sharing and breaking of bread is honouring one another in every encounter, for in every encounter you will be experiencing a communion of consciousnesses. You will not view your brothers as though they were side dishes you have not ordered. You know, you consider some of your brothers as wise, and some as other-wise. *(Audience chuckles).*

The laughter bouncing of your belly, allows indeed the resonance of the heart seal, your heart chakra, to open and flower, and bloom into new brilliance, and light-heartedness in the communion with humanity. Laughter is a grand aligner, a grand healer and harmonizer of life. It is of grand medicinal value, to be sure.

Now, the polarities of life, of humanity, the polarities of masculine, feminine, of positive, negative, of the God I Am, and God I Am in opposite reflections of one another, is coming forth to unite its consciousness within you, to birth divinity. The female is symbolized in the past eras of time by the serpent, and the male, masculine energy, power-sourceness, is symbolized by a sword. And the serpent, encircling and embracing, caressing the sword, has been given forth as a symbol of healing in the field of medicine. You may gaze into your auric field with an electronic microscope, and through the facilitation of new technology that they have of your now, that is Kirlian photography, and find indeed, serpent-like formations within your auric field. Encased within it, embraced within it, is a particum of light that it is surrounding, that it is caressing.

So you have this very symbol of healing within your very auric field. It is for you to be the physician, the healer. Physician, heal thyself, indeed. It is manifest within the light forms, within the particums of your energy field around your embodiment. As they [the light particums] become aligned and empowered, others that flow into your energy field will also be healed and harmonized.

Now, the electro-magnetic lay lines upon your plane, are likened unto the bone structure within your body. Do you know, this phrase you call 'feeling it in your bones'? It [the bone structure] is becoming aligned and aware of what is in the electro-magnetic lay lines of your planet. It is feeling Earth's energy. It is coursing the marrow of your bones and enhancing your neurons, enhancing the neurological perception throughout the structure of your body. So indeed, as the shifting occurs and the birthing begins to occur electro-magnetically, the lay lines will shift and so will the structure of your body. So will your bones begin to shift, because you will be more pivotal and you will begin to be more pliable, functioning in more than one position at a time. The neurological system will begin to enhance its awareness and create indeed other axioms for the perception of the unobvious, the non-physical.

When you feel and understand the harmony and power of this shifting, you will begin to create within yourself an awareness, a tingling to the touch, a feeling in your solar plexus that you know something; that is called a gut feeling. You may indeed align all these awarenesses into one moment of perception through your third eye and have the vision of what it is that you are perceiving, of what it is that you are feeling and experiencing. There is a term you call geomancy. You may have a map of the world and have it upside-down - facing downward. Place your left hand across it, gently flow it across the map, or chart of the Earth, and place the right hand upon your solar plexus, and close your eyes. Now sense and feel the tingling of certain points and place a mark upon the back side of the map. Perceive the electromagnetic energy that is racing through this planet. You will find, much to your surprise, that there will be seismic activity in these areas, for you will be feeling it 'in your bones'. You will be predicting. You will be prophesying, because you will be aware of what Mother Earth is experiencing, as she begins to shift her plates to allow the birth to occur.

Now, volcanic activity is the fire energy to be aligned in harmony with the atmosphere and to warm the planet, and to enhance the energy field around this planet by its electrums.

But you know, you too can receive the energy. It does not have to flow forth in this fashion. You too may receive the energy that Earth desires to emit. Stand with bare feet on the sod upon the grass of the Earth. Raise your arms with the palms upward and feel the energy flow through your feet, through your solar plexus, through your heart, through your crown, very likened unto a volcano. As you do thusly, it enhances your own power, for it flows through the seals of you and concurrently emits a vibrant, golden light, an illumination of laser-like quality, and connects all the other bodies of humanity in this fashion, with this power. It spews not only upward, it will be spewing laterally, as well. Understand that Earth, in her nature of gently caressing you, will bring forth sweetness unto your life. It is not all sour and acid in these transitions, there is nectar quality in it.

There was an entity by the name of John Glenn[2], about 20 years ago, or so, in your time. He connected with the stratosphere and brought forth his presence within the deepness of space. But alas, around him he was viewing and envisioning speckles and glimmering light, photons of energy. For indeed photons are the first manifested form of love light, as it is born forth from the grand Sun, the grand

---

[2] John Glenn, American astronaut.

centre of the solar system. It indeed allows the piercing and penetration of the auric field of the planet. It is likened unto sperm, and the planet is likened unto an ovum, and a conception occurs to create sunlight. As its receptivity is perceived, the inflow of the photons come forth, and therefore you perceive light. It is love born and conceived of Christus, illumination, unfolding perception.

So indeed, as you receive these photons of energy, you may capacitate yourself into photosynthesis, generating the greenery of your life, allowing growth to occur and unfoldment, spewing forth newness, a birthing, regeneration of different interdimensional perception. As you create the awareness of receptivity of different flows and manifestations of energy, you will also - through your consciousness, that is not perceptible by you, your super-consciousness - allow all the other entities of humanity to create this expression as well, ye indeed, even the entities you call trees.

The rainforests will begin to re-grow in abundance. Your scientists will scratch their heads and wonder how all this came about. Indeed, they will begin to investigate. They will begin to do research how it was that this lushness of life spewed forth in an apparent desert. In the same manner, you may experience abundance to flow into your own life, into the desert of your soul - the abundance of love light. *The photon is the particum of light that holds and capacitates the energy of God I Am, the energy of the All-That-Is, limitless love.* You may conceive, in your receptivity, through the penetration of your auric field, the energy of All-That-Is, of all your brothers.

Your enemies, that is what you call them, they are really a projection of what you judge in yourself. Allow all that you had previously judged to be converted, transmuted, transformed into positive energy. You know, the possibility and potential for utter destruction, for dire circumstance of incomprehensible magnitude, indeed, the opposite polarity of it is unlimited potential of your life, not destruction, but regeneration. It too abides within the same potential, if you desire to resonate unto it. So allow yourself to create the unfoldment and awareness wherein freedom abides. Make it your choice, so that every thought you emanate each moment is pregnant with opportunity to conceive newness and regeneration.

It is also pregnant with the possibility to conceive abortive circumstance, that is destructive and non-generative energy. Embrace either, for both are wondrous. All the possibilities during the transition of your life are options, equally applying for the job, you know. Resonate to what you really desire of your heart. Understand the crystalline clarity of your own consciousness. Do you know what the crystal within the Earth is? It is the Pituitary gland, the Pineal gland, the Christ-all within the Earth. It creates the electromagnetic lay lines of the planet, to birth the outward awareness of Christus on the plane. As you remove crystal from the Earth, you are removing parts of her generative force of life. Allowing it to remain, allowing it to abide, will enable her to be harmoniously in the flow without the pain of the ripping and rending of her innards.

You also do this with fossil fuels. Do you understand of which I speak? It is called petroleum. However, petroleum is becoming obsolete. The creation of new methods of transport and healing is based on crystal, is Christ-all. It represents the same thing in the mineral kingdom that you represent in the form of humanity. Mankind is a living, breathing, crystal. Every atom, every cell, of this embodiment, resonates and vibrates to the knowingness that it too, is a crystal. It too, contains the very facet, the nature of the mineral.

As you create awareness of newness within these cells, they are exploding into and becoming supernova. They are indeed receiving the photon energy of the grand central sun of the All-That-Is. Also, your embodiment is shifting and changing from copper and carbon-based to silicon, diamond-based. Your body is becoming enhanced to create the receptivity of the light. Therefore, a shifting of your foodstuffs will occur. As you embrace the photons of the Sun of your solar system, *they* will sustain you, rather than foodstuffs. It will create the energy flow through your body, and you will not require the mechanism of foodstuffs, of vegetation at all. Therefore your body will become lighter, less dense. The organs themselves will shift and change and grow into newness and different nature. They themselves will be crystal and etheric in nature and reflective of the spectrum of light you call rainbow. They themselves will manifest a combustion machinery of energy, rather than through foodstuffs or petroleum, - it is the same; for the transport systems are exactly at the same birthing stage as your embodiment. However, the auto-machine feeds on petroleum, and your body machine feeds on foodstuffs. You sup. And so, when you sit at the table, you will have the grand opportunity to clink your chalices together and share a glass of wine, or water, or any manner of liquid, for it will enhance the sustenance of life to flow through the tissues. And from water - or any manner of liquid - you progress to a breatharian to sustain your embodiment, simply with your breath, through partaking of the ions and an-ions within the atmosphere.

So, this will occur across the course of the next five hundred years of your time. You have much to anticipate.

The carbon within your embodiment, and within the embodiment of the Earth plane, is transmuting itself. Carbon-based dating systems are becoming obsolete. For those who have been before on this planet, who colonized it to create humanity here in the first place, through star-seeding, were not carbon-based at all. They were silica-based. So the present technology of carbon-based dating has not understood how to date. It will shift into a different understanding. It will gain access to that crystal, silica consciousness, and in doing thusly, archaeology will understand the present [through silica-based dating procedures].

So bless the sciences that desire to know and understand the past, for it allows the understanding of the future, and of the present. Archeology can be very much likened to the peeping Tom among the sciences, you know. Peeking into the past, to peer into the mystery of it all - becoming excited, because they are perceiving the mystery of the now. As they unveil it to themselves, each one of you will also unveil different awarenesses unto yourself. As you begin to experience yourself to be unlimited, you will begin to have the option, consciously, of how you will respond to it, how you will embrace it, how you will love it.

To love or not to love, that is the question. And all that is spoken here, this day of your time, is to be set into motion only through your own understanding. It is to be set into motion through the desire of yourself to create a more unlimited panacea of options for yourself, to bring non-focus into focus . Figure that one out. But that is indeed what it is, the paradoxical nature of life brought into the now.

In participating with the Earth changes, you will also participate with the creation of discordant energy of the ionosphere, the stratosphere, which you have called in the past, toxins. It is also created within your embodiment. You are excreting, within your very embodiment, what has been judged of the past that has created the ridges and the dispersals of consciousness within your present awareness, and all of it is to come forth in its congested murkiness. Allow it to become clarified. That is what is occurring with the atmosphere and the waters of the planet. All the emotions of all the past, of eons and eons and eons of history are coagulating into the consciousness of the planet. Therefore, as you clarify and allow the flow, the channel of you, to open and receive purifying thought, it will clarify the atmosphere and the waters of the Earth, through thought and through resonance of the thought that *you are* the very Beingness of yourself. You are pureness, pure thought realized. The Earth is this pure thought transferred. The Earth is no more than you, in the future. You yourself will become a blazing planet, a grand central sun of your very own consciousness millenia in your future. Terra, at one time millenia ago, was a consciousness such as you, unfolding in other dimensions. And as there was perception of more and more focus of energy into the creation of the now, then indeed it began to be more and more expansive, and her consciousness brought forth its appearance as the body you now call Terra. You too shall be a planet in another solar system in a galaxy far, far away. Indeed, you too shall become your own solar system in your future.

The smashing of the atoms is aborting future universes. For each atom evolves into a more unfolded particum of consciousness, yet to be understood as a physical body called humanity, in eons of time to come. An unfoldment of consciousness is a forever, forever,

forever, continuance. It never stops. It never ceases, even when the solar system is completely ascended into the seventh dimension. There are still galaxies, and indeed, universal, multiversal understandings that are just being born into physicality. So when you fret and frustrate yourself because your brother does not understand this that you call New Age chitter-chatter and paraphernalia, do not fret about it, beloved. There are eons of time for him to create the opportunity to embrace it, and in his own ripeness of time, he shall harvest the awareness. Know that all has its own season and timing.

Regarding your foodstuffs, you may create the desire for non-toxic vegetation. However, know that whatever you partake of, if you are in alignment yourself, you enhance it. You align it. You create awareness within it, you enlighten it. So fret not and fear not what you take in, for it is clarified through an aligned consciousness. That is how indeed, healing occurs of what you call terminal diseases. The recreation and transmutation occurs spontaneously within the body to regenerate that which was not at easement, that which was considered toxic. So you too can experience this.

When you create alignment and appeasement unto another, create not enslavement to expectation by trying to please another. *Desire not to please others, desire to be pleasant to others.* There is a difference. Expand and grow, in whatever fashion you feel, as though your heart is taking you and the awareness enhances itself. It is going forth in a spiral, in an accelerated fashion, in whatever direction you allow it to go. You will experience an acceleration of this coagulation in your life. It will come unto you faster and faster and faster. The vortex called you is beginning to rotate in a much more accelerated fashion. Do you know why? Because you are creating less time. You are bringing more and more of your lifestream into your now, creating less future, less time. As these vortices create the spinning, the reflection of the photons - the light energy of the All-That-Is is born into physical perception. In other words, your auric field is becoming enhanced. Not only growing wider, but growing more brilliant.

You will feel a thickening of the energy around you. It is because you are bringing more and more of your energy unto you, and you will begin to acclimate to this and flow through it with more and more ease. But in the beginning, you may experience a bit of what you call sluggishness. You will feel as though you are being heavied, that you have a weight upon you, that you are in a forgotten fog somewhere and you do not know where you are exactly, and you feel a bit disoriented. Does this sound familiar to anyone? But as you see beyond the obvious, remember to be gently agile within it.

Embrace this energy field, this ocean of energy that you are within, and swim within it, very likened unto the dolphin consciousness. They swim within an energy sea, in their consciousness. Emotion is energy in motion, God energy in motion. They [dolphins] too have grand emotion. They open their heart seals to the rest of humanity. Allow them too, to perceive that which they be, the dancing delights and nymphs of the ocean, called God I Am. The whales, they swim with facility and power and agility within the sea of emotion, called God I Am awareness, unlimited love. They are the sorcerers and the Samurais of the seas. They are here to reflect unto you what you too have desired to be, so that they may assist you into the gentle birthing of this being. Be yourself the sorcerers and the Samurais of humanity. Merge into the awareness of embracing and transmuting the warriors of life into wearers of wisdom. Cloak yourself with this knowing. It is encountering you at every corner. Play with it. Be light-hearted and buoyant about it. Enlightenment and gaining understanding is not a heavy occupation. It only comes unto you with the consciousness of play and the grand play-pen is Earth. So embrace it, and your brethren, and you too will come to know the ocean of emotion called God.

Now, there is much talk about Earth changes, the grand quakes and tremors and all the dire circumstances that are given forth, and the walls of water, hm? You do not have to create it this way. There will be a bit of shifting of the coastlines, and the platetechtonics. The geodesic understanding of the inner domes of the inner Earth will shift, for that is also what is occurring. The inner Earth is also shifting and quakering and tremoring, but it need not be of dire calamity. The crystal will assist you. But not the crystal in mineral form, but the crystal of your own consciousness within the Pineal gland. The crystal is but a tool, the diamond is you. You are the jewel. Allow yourself the hope of the dream of your tomorrow. Allow it to be here with you now. Embrace it, heartily.

You will begin to understand the acceleration of the future into your now, of All-That-Is. In other words, the inner Earth will spew forth unto you, your galactic brothers above you will come unto you, and all will be embraced in one beauteous and brilliant diamond-like moment of awareness. But you must know that it is NOW. Not will be, not twenty years hence, or fifty years hence, but now. Participate with your dreams, understand that the unreality is the reality, and the reality is the unreality. View each in the essence of non-judgment. Be like the child, in its innocent awareness, as it gazes forth from luminous eyes in awe and in wonderment of life, without embarrassment, as it embraces without judgment, understands without finding fault, laughs without reason. It too, is your mirror. It too, lives within you.

Mother Earth is perceiving a grand birthing, but desire not to cease the labour, for you are the child within the womb, being born. So give forth love unto these contractions. Give forth gentleness unto the spirit of the birth, and the waters as they wash through you and over you, and embrace you into the new awareness.

God is doing a thesis, and you are the notebook. And I tell you, the brothers of the unseen are delighted to watch the drama that you create before them. You definitely keep us entertained. No one could ever say that you are dim bulbs. Light, colour and sound is triangulating, even in this room. The resonance is beauteous. Hear the sounds beyond the silence.

When you are alone in the high tide of evening, listen to your own heartbeat, hear the ringing in your ears. Hear the whipping of the wind through your lungs. Hear the sounds of the creation of life. For in this song, you will understand a symphony, and the symphony is the creation of every note, harmonious in tone, brought forth to resonate with every other note. The new octave that is born into your awareness, is super-consciousness. As you transmute yourself from one set of octaves into another, you will be transcending the dimension of physicality, of that which you hear, and open unto yourself all the fifty-two sensory perceptions. You will understand telepathy and a vision not of your eyes, but beyond physicality. You will understand feeling, clairsentium, clairaudience and clairvoyance. You will be the psychics reborn, the sorcerers, the soothsayers, the prophets. All reborn. The rebirthing is simply the allowance of embracing the veil of non-remembrance into remembrance.

You are like a drop of energy in an ocean of emotion, of All-That-Is. And you place a barrier around you - a barrier of limitation, so that your uniqueness does not leak out into the ocean of All-That-Is. You are afraid you will lose your identity, and the skin that surrounds you is this veil of non-remembrance. All that is required, my beloveds, is to relax the skin and allow the flow to occur, understanding that you retain your flavour of uniqueness, while at the same time, you blend with the Forevermore. That, indeed, will allow you to perceive through all the senses. The renaissance is, indeed, yet occurring again upon your plane. In your history, during the time of the renaissance, did you know that they did not have dyes to create brilliance of colour, because of the collective consciousness of the Earth? In your now time, you perceive brilliance of colour and hue, spontaneity of tone. Understand that further brilliance is created. You will see ultraviolet, and ultrascarlet and ultraemerald, and brilliance personified in the fourth density and above, for it all will be imperceptible to those in third density consciousness.

Now, there is something I wish you to understand: *the creation of the third density consciousness remains and abides, even though you transcend into unlimitedness, super-consciousness. But indeed, you will have facility to participate with all the other dimensions, as well as the third.* So it is not that you will be going forth from physicality, never to experience it again. You indeed, shall, if you desire to. But it is that you will have access to interdimensional realities which you do not perceive now. And you will have the option to know what you think you do not know, but what you really do know already.

You are quite precious, you know. Quite cherished. All-That-Is loves you in an unlimited capacity, and it desires you to love yourself in the same fashion. So open your heart to receive yourself, to conceive yourself into newness.

There is a resonance of urgent anticipation in this room. It is like Christmas. You are all abiding for there is this grand package beneath the tree that you are just so excited to open. But you do not know exactly how to open it. And you turn it over and you gaze upon the beauty of the ribbon and the bow, and the paper that wraps around it. And you are perplexed, because there seems to be no end to the bow. There seems to be no end to the paper, and you do not know how to get into it. But you hear this rattle in there and you understand that there is something in there that you want. And your curiosity carries you into piercing the package.

I will tell you, beloveds, you all desire for joy and knowing to be pre-packaged, and to be picked up at the counter of a drive-in store. But the store is self-service. And it comes in an infinite variety of packages. All colour and hue, indeed, all consciousness, for it may be the tender leaf that curls itself timidly in the caresses of the breeze. Or it may be like a woman, who gingerly walks through the meadow and as she caresses the air into the love born of her breast, she sees the light. It comes forth in the newness of dawn, the rosy hues and amber waves of the grain and grasses of the sleeping valley, and the hushness becomes a beauteous symphony, piercing the horizon with a stream of light. Freedom, indeed, is born from the breast of this woman, and she begins to sprout wings, and allows herself to hover in the awareness of this awesome power potential of life. It is potential, and it is experience in the same moment. It is capturing the essence of life. It is indeed, understanding God.

All of these energies that bring forth this capacity in your life, that create their awareness within your life, you pass by, as though it were a piece of litter upon your pathway. You do not see it, you do not perceive its beauteous brilliance. You merely see it as: 'Oh yes, I see'.

But you know, you may kneel in awesome honour even before an inanimate object. What do you call it, a chair? Kneel in awesome love, for that too is consciousness, else the atoms would not be held together. Become the chair, become the throne, the seat of life, and you will indeed be seated upon the throne of your own knowing. Expand the ceiling of limitation into forever. There are no skins upon this plane. There is only the illusion of uniqueness born into separation. Uniqueness may abide in merging with All-That-Is. It is co-existence and non-existence, at the same moment.

Give yourself the gift of the now. Relax and enjoy the present. That is meant both ways. The splendid dawn is coming unto you. Have you ever seen the rosy hills in the evening of time? There is the dawning of the dusk, as well, you know, not only of the morn. There is the dawning of all the seasons. There is the dawning of noon, and of midnight. The hour of power is upon you. Kiss the tears of your brethren. It is like ambrosia, the nectar of the Gods. Enrapture yourself with the wisdom that you are bringing to one another. And continue the sharing, one unto the other.

Bureaucracy begins to shift and change through this sharing. You have upon your plane what you call income tax system. And it is quite a curiosity in that it takes more energy to complete the forms than it does to create the income in the first place, hm? It too shall come into shifting and changing. It too, may be born forth harmoniously, and not with the overthrow of government, but with a gentle ceasing of strict regulation. It will indeed, be released, but it need not be released through judgment, and pain, and power struggle. It may be released because it is recognized that it is not necessary. *God does not desire to be governed.*

The structure of your body, as it changes and shifts, will begin to receive the polarities of masculine and feminine and integrate it within you, interweave it in the fabric of your being. If there is anything out of balance, you will become very, very aware of it. Embrace it, however you wish. You may judge that which you fear for separating your Self from your SELF, or you may embrace it into a harmonious blend, and allow the serpent and the sword to intertwine. Let the healing occur.

The herbs that you will participate with in your time to come, will be no more than a resonance of what is already within the spectrum of you. And you may change and transmute any substance into a herb. Did you know this? So if you have the tea leaf, you may transmute it into any herb you desire, simply by resonating to that particular frequency. You have the power to recreate everything. Every thought is a recreation of life.

Chapter 9

EARTH'S BIRTH CHANGES

SECOND SESSION.

Part I.

Be there query? I would desire you to understand that when I ask for query, there is couched within the very core of it, the response. It is the purpose of this interaction to gently and lovingly tug those question marks into explanation marks.

Q: St. Germain. You made reference to our archaelogists and the carbon dating and you mentioned that the carbon dating was not giving them the results, because the beings who were on this planet before, were of silica types. Could you please explain what type of bodies it would be possible to have, if they were silica-based?

Elastic, a bit translucent. It is what you would call atrophied in certain facilities, although it is not really atrophied. It is the dissipation of the energy facilitated in a particular organ because it is no longer required, likened unto the appendix, likened unto the digestive functions and organs. All of these will dissipate a bit, and the heart seal, and the Pineal gland will become grander and grander in size. In this manner of facilitation, the body will be more translucent, because there is more space and less mass, it is less dense.

The transmutation of the core, the fire core of its life, is silica based, rather than carbon-based. Carbon has a tendency to resonate to third density, and silica, or crystal, if you would call it that, is resonant unto a higher consciousness, a consciousness of clarity and multi-faceted expression.

You have degenerated into limitation. For you indeed desired to create the grand panacea of limitation - to play the game of life on this plane. And you are enjoying yourself. That is why you created the drama, because you enjoy the melodrama so grandly.

Q: Do you then mean that we were seeded from another planet.

Of many other star systems - thirty-three systems, and that may be translated into twenty-four, depending on the perspective. You were seeded of other civilizations, and that is where the laser light creation of spontaneous generation of the ovum came forth to create life upon the planet. It was what you call immaculate conception, although it was conception through light.

Q: Why is there so much resistance to our space beings who have always been in contact with us, and when are people on a greater scale going to accept them as our helpers?

When you can accept one another in your differences. You see, beloveds, they are quite different than you in appearance and physicality, if you would desire to call it that, in embodiment. You judge your neighbours and your brethren, because their skin colour is different. How can you receive a brother of humanity that is *very, very different* from you without being scared out of your skin?

Q: Do they come from one particular place, or different galaxies?

From many time flows. You see, beloveds, *this particular solar system is in the exact mid point of creation from involution into evolution.* And it is creating quite a bit of curiosity among your brothers of space - it is, colloquially speaking, 'where the action is'. And some of them come forth simply to see, what all the commotion is about, and they view you, and they allow you in wonderment. There is what you would term a laser-like net, interwoven around the planet, by the Brotherhood of the Light, but it is communally desired by the humanity upon the plane, by the humanity above the plane and humanity within the plane. And therefore it allows an understanding of vibratory difference of nature, so that it is to be of a harmonious resonance for them to come forth into this Earth, Terra, whatever you wish to call it.

Q: There are other planets within our solar system like Pluto and Neptune - are they not engaging in the dark aspects of consciousness, like black magic? So would they not be attracting more attention?

Your planet is like a beacon within the solar system. You radiate energy, consciousness, and thus you radiate to other dimensions and attract their attention; likened unto tuning forks, they resonate unto you. Therefore they come into this dimension, so that they may perceive what they are harkening unto, and assist, because that is a mutual calling. When they come forth, it is because they are desired. And the black magic of the dark nature of your brothers, it is no different, my beloved, than the ones that are upon this planet that do not understand their light.

Q: Could you comment on the possible changes that we might experience in an economic sense in Australia?

If you would desire to participate in a limited understanding of what you call future and what is projected according to your now, indeed. For a while there will be a gentle increase in the value of gold, then it will be what you call the bottom dropping. I never did understand how come the top could not drop.

There will be a grand diverse reaction within bureaucracy, diverse in that entities will understand their sovereignty and their power to create their own energy through their auric field, and the gilded awareness of their own God I Am, rather than being dependent upon gold. It will be a grand facilitator in I Am-ness, beloved. Is this sufficient?

Q: Could you please speak about the people in the Inner Earth and what our relationship is to them, and how we can be more in harmony with them?

You can be more in harmony with them, by being more in harmony with yourself. Your relationship with them is the same as your relationship with the brothers above the plane. They are indeed brothers of humanity who are expressing in the different light forms, the differently created embodiments within another dimension. They are not in the core of the Earth that you perceive as your reality. It is stepping into another dimension altogether, allowing yourself to understand humanity therein. Their bodies range from third to sixth density, very likened unto this planet. Upon the surface of the Earth, there are embodiments that range from third to sixth density upon this very plane. And according to your planetary understanding of the heavens above, those brothers that abide within the grand craft and are crystal in consciousness, they too have a spectrum of vibrancy, of resonance, from third to sixth density. So they are really no different. When you perceive your brothers as equal, they will emerge, for they know that it is in the harmonious ripeness of time to come forth. Some of you perceive the uniqueness of your brothers as something to be judged. But I ask you, if one crystalline flake of snow is different than another, does that mean that it is not a flake? Indeed.

Q: St. Germain, I would like to learn more about love, please.

Love is not a learning at all. It is a knowing that you already know. All that is required is to release the idea that you do not know, and you shall know. Live life more and more, and you will understand it. And when I say live it, I mean immerse yourself in the embracing of it.

Now, as you step into your exterior, and there is a drop of rain, state unto it: 'Greetings, brother, I love you'. As you step your unshod foot to the shining face of the Earth, state unto the sod: 'Greetings, brother, I love you'. As you place the grand brush of whiskers to your teeth, state unto it: 'Greetings, brother, I love you'. And then you will understand the essence of love.

Q: I would like you to talk a bit on the difference between being and living in the moment and manifesting for the future.

Know that it is manifesting in the moment and it will dramatize itself in the future.

Q: And what about being in the now and planning or action..

Action is only the creation of the flow of thought through physicality in the now. That which is play, is light-heartedness of that action, which is only the creation of momentum from one now to another now, to another now. You recreate each now holographically, whole in and of itself, and if you desire to create the illusion of sequentiality, that is up to you, but it is not necessary.

Q: I would like to understand how one can keep creating thoughts that are beneficial to oneself and everyone else. What happens if one has a negative thought, a so called bad thought- say you are angry with somebody and it is a real emotion, what does one do with that?

In the moment of creation of discordancy, acknowledge it, love it, embrace it, and state unto it: 'I honour you in your discordance, and I love you and we merge together and gain access into the All-That-Is, in an ultimate, intertwining embrace, so that there is no difference, one unto the other'. It is embracing your judgment, your fear, your hatred, your jealousies, your anger. Anger is merely another label for fear. Blend it all through your heart. Embrace it and caress it with the wings of your heart, and fly to the Forevermore, into freedom. That will create harmony, rather than disharmony and it still validates the disharmonious emotion.

Q: I would like you to expand a bit on the teaching that you were giving about the Earth's crystalline structure. I am in an interesting, paradoxical situation at the moment which is that I have been drawn to work with and to sell crystals, and at the same time I do not feel particularly comfortable about doing that.

Then do it not.

Q: Right. We are using them in healing applications.

Do you know that to have them present in consciousness, their physical presence is not necessary ?

Q: Right. Can you explain the effect on the structure of the Earth's crust and of the mining of crystals, because it seems to be happening more and more as the demand for crystals increases. I am concerned about Brazil. You made some reference to crystals closing or holding the energy in meridian points.

They do not hold it, they facilitate it. It is very likened unto a consciousness flowing through them and interweaving electro-magnetically into a transformation point in that particular area, likened unto a meridian point, indeed. As they are removed and dispersed on the outward plane of life, they disperse their energy flow; the meridian points become integrated all over. So it is not to be feared. However, it creates a vacancy within the cavern of that meridian, but it will be filled. Where there is a void, there is a vacuum that is always to be filled. And what will fill it? The crystalline consciousness.

Q: In response to a previous query on the violet flame, could you elaborate a little bit more on it?

Indeed. The Violet Flame is the culmination of an eon of dogma. It is the transition point, to go forth into that which is dogma-less, called the era of God. All are lords of all rays, not only the violet one. The release of all these rituals and all these perceived practices, will enable you to resonate to whatever ray that creates its appearance within your spectrum of light in that moment and enhances your perception of the ecstasy of the All-That-Is. So you see, it may be blue one moment, or red another, or orange another, there is no difference, all are valid and delightful. All create the clarity of the crystalline consciousness called white, which pierces into the dimension of illumination, of brilliance, called golden. Alright?

Q: With the creation of more and more solar systems, or universes, and as it is also perceived by astronomers, the universe expands, but there is also a school of opinion that eventually, the universe will contract. Is this conceivable, is it possible?

That is what occurs during birthing.

Q: I would have thought there would be a continuing expansion, rather than any contraction.

What occurs during birthing, but expansion and contraction, beloved. It is both, not one or the other, but all of the above again. Now, an expansion into a supernova, a grand explosion of light, a new creation of dimensions, will occur. That is what they are speaking about. And the contraction is the pressure of the labour, as it creates the awareness of concentration of energy into the musculature of Earth, to push it forward as an impetus, as a quantum leap, into that supernova of expansion, you see?

Q: My other question is - is there a specific focus of light in Australia? A.. what do you call it?

I understand of what you query about. You need not words to communicate with me, beloved, if you desire response. Very often I desire you to vocalize your queries, for it clarifies your query to your own consciousness. If I speak forth an answer, you will not know which question I am answering, hm? But if you would desire, I will assist you in this fashion and respond.

Australia is a grand island. It is indeed the participation of the outer rim of the ancient land called Lemuria. And even before Lemuria, pre-Lemurian, and pre-Atlantean, it was the land called Pan. As it is coming forth now, into the awareness of new life, resurrection, into awareness of its power, it is being, pulsating, enlivening itself into the chakra called the heart of the Earth. And in this pulsation point, it is emanating light and power, and electromagnetism throughout the rest of the Earth. It is like a centre point vortex. But it is not the only one, for within this particular heart chakra of Earth, there are several understandings, and Australia is only one. Hawaii is another. The heart seal will begin to blend and expand as the heart of you expands to encompass all your brothers. The heart seal of the Earth will expand to encompass all the other seals, and indeed the entire Earth will be a pulsating, throbbing, heart of peace and love, and prosperity. *The Australian continent will become known as the impetus for that awakening called I AM.* It is to be a focal point, but it does not invalidate the other focal points of energy. The Middle East is another sort of focal point, but not of the same chakra. There are all sorts of chakras, with just as much validity and awarenesses spewing forth, for your brothers and you, to participate with and to understand the embracing which is you. But indeed, that which is Australia has a special place in my heart, shall we say? But I love all the others as well.

Q: Hello, I Am. I am a new high school teacher and I was wondering if you could give me some guidance with working and playing with high school students.

That reminds me of the sign I saw upon your playground. It says - beware of the children, especially when they are driving. Now, that which you call your adolescents of this nature, are coming forth to understand their God essence, and they are very timorous about it. Because of the eons of soul memory they are coming into, they have what you term confusion and they do not know in which direction to go. They have not understood yet that it is all directions. So they quiver and quake in their stockings about what is to be their future and they do not know their power. Therefore they give their power to peer consciousness, or peer group pressure. That is also another pressure of birthing - their awareness of themselves. They give their power to chemicals. They give it forth to creative expression. They give it to every manner of facility that is accessible to humanity in their lifestream. And so, you may allow them to bask indeed within your light and your grand example. Give unto them the illumination of the darkness within their heart and soul and let them know that you offer them a banquet of understanding called: 'go with the flow' and let your heart guide you. Know that it is not necessary to abide by any particular preconceived, rigourous structure, or consideration of the children's 'should nots'. For when you follow your heart in integrity with the God I Am, in the integration with it, in honouring everyone else's God I Am, then you will create beauteous genius and magic, and they will be the way-showers of the humanity to come.

Q: St. Germain, you mentioned a tidal wave. How is it going to affect Australia?

However you wish it to. Now, there will be some shiftings in the water levels and the Earth shall open and swallow a grand drink; then it will belch forth a bit of heat, gases and minerals, from its intestines and deposit it within the ocean to form islands. This will create shiftings and gentle tremors within the Earth plane, but it is not necessary to create a grand deluge, unless of course you would enjoy the view. It is not necessary to create dire circumstance and devastation because of it. As I stated, the shifting may be a gentle shifting of the plates, - a little at a time - so that humanity upon the land may, little by little, adjust to it, and prepare for it. But not through fear, but through the acknowledgement that Earth herself is changing and thus humanity will shift consciousness to integrate with the Earth that is changing. The tidal waves and the walls of water have all been prophesied, and given much thought of concentrated energy. If you would desire, you may transmute this. But do you know what this means? Whenever you encounter someone that is all quivering and shaking about that which is to come, give them the knowing that I have reflected unto you this day and share it diversely throughout the planet, unto all your brothers, that it is totally up to them and it need not be difficult at all.

Q: Good evening, I Am. I honour your brilliant presentations. I have two questions.

They [the presentations] are really yours, you know. I am reflecting them unto you from your own heart.

Q: Thank you. The first question is: Are there any signs of Atlantis that can be seen, whether they be under the Earth or in the ocean.

Atlantis - what a grand memory that is now. Indeed, I will answer you, continue.

Q: The second question is in relation to soulmates. Could you talk to me about soulmates, what it means, how it applies in the now.

How many lifetimes do you have? Alright, beloved. I love you grandly. You may relax while I respond, if you wish. Atlantis - when it is stated that it is arising, it does not mean the continent. It means the consciousness. It is arising within each and every one of you. Atlantis abided upon this plane for thousands of years, thousands and thousands of years. All of you had many lifestreams therein, not only within Atlantis, but within Lemuria, as well.

So, as you enhance your life from your forgotten yesterdays and your unremembered tomorrows, you will be rebirthing the consciousness of Atlantis. The demise thereof is harkening and heralding upon your plane, as an option. That is what is given forth as prophecy and dire circumstance - destruction and devastation of the planet again. It is not necessary. You may redramatize it and it is coming forth and culminating into the new birthing of the new Atlantis yet to be born. It may culminate into a civilization of crystal citadels called humanity, understanding of its Godship, rather than agonizing in utter battlement over judgment and hatred, and warrior essence.

Atlantis is within the Atlantic ocean in its physical presence. Parts of it will be born forth, fragments of memory. But the entire continent shall not rise again, for that would re-situate the entire Earth as it is seen now. Neither will Lemuria rise forth in its entirety. There will be some islands emerging, the peaks of the continent. But Lemuria and Atlantis are not places, they are thoughts, they are consciousnesses. Indeed, from all planes of existence, from all nations, Atlantis is arising again.

Soulmates - when the energy contained within the soul body of the thirteen spectrums of light that came forth to coagulate matter from the dimension of light - when God contemplated itself and desired to reach out and touch itself - there were multitudinous millions and millions and millions of fragments of energy created. Energy bundles of different frequencies, and as these different frequencies were brought into cohesion, there was a consciousness born: a consciousness called humanity, each one of you. And as there is a release of this particular focus of consciousness, this frequency particums become immersed into the All-That-Is of your soul body energy again, so that parts of them can refocus into different cohesions to create a different persona.

So, there may be you that is also part of another, etcetera, and there are millions of them on all dimensions on all levels of existence. Everything that exists is consciousness in one manner or another, and so in the utter unlimited understanding of it, everything that exists is your soulmate. But in the manner that you speak of, there is what you call a female counterpart, but it is not only one. For the female counterpart that is your soulmate is also the female that abides within you. And as you resonate into expansion, you will have a different vibratory energy, and in your next now moment *you* will be different, for you will have accessed a different awareness. So your own vibration, your signature vibration, is constantly shifting and changing into more and more unfoldment and expansion. Therefore that which you resonate to as soulmate, or what you term twin flame, also changes and shifts constantly. You continue to resonate to a higher and higher vibration until you converge together to create dominion of that which is GOD I AM in the flesh - conjoined into one Christus and anti-Christus consciousness. The physicality of flesh is not the only manner it may come unto you. For you see, the I AM energy in the All-That-Is is not to be limited by one body. It is physical, it is non-physical. It is male, it is female. As you merge and blend more and more with your own male soulmate energy, you will merge and blend more and more with your female soulmate energy, and all will come unto you. It may be embodied within a child, or one that is heavy in age. It is not only a lover that you should consider as soulmate, although that is what you focus upon at times. This focus is born from the yearning to experience your own incompleteness into wholeness, and you may only do this, my beloved brother, when you understand that the void within you is also full. Thank you, beloved.

Q: Greetings, I Am. I would like you to explain about the phenomena that has occurred around the Bermuda Triangle. Is it a special electromagnetic field, or what is it?

It was, at one time, an electromagnetic vortex to create an interdimensional flow of experience from one dimension, which is this one, into many others. It is no longer that[1]. It has aligned and calmed into quietude. Thank you, beloved.

Q: I wonder, would you mind commenting on the seeming increase in child abuse today.

It is anger. Your children are coming forth as instruments to allow compassion to be born of the breast of humanity. They are co-

---

[1] During a group event held in Cairns, North Queensland, St. Germain stated the Great Barrier Reef area of North Queensland as being the new portal, in place of the Bermuda Triangle.

creating the experience, for all is manifested of thought, of the desire of the thought in every now, and therefore, they are just as divine a god as those you would call the adult of your plane. They may be in smaller packages, indeed, but they are just as divine and just as powerful a God. Many of them retain their awareness. They do not enshroud themselves so much within the veil of forgetfulness and so as they create their appearance upon this plane, they create their embodiment to be within circumstances that will allow another to encounter their anger and their violent nature, so that they may embrace it by understanding the ravaging of what occurs within their own soul, and the torment and terror that it creates within the experience called life. You see? So it does provide a grand reflection and what you would term service. Thank you beloved.

Q: Sometimes I feel like I cannot touch my feelings. I am not clear on what I am feeling. I feel like I am more in my head than in my heart and I would like to understand how to be more in touch with my heart.

It is not really a touching. Did you know that? Because a touching would indicate that it is exterior of you. It is merely the sensing of the vastness of its energy within the whirlpool of your heart, creating a grand vortex and you may feel the wheeling and spinning and whirling of it. You may feel the nature of its energy without touching it as exterior to you. *Healing is revealing yourself to feeling.* Not touching, feeling. There is a difference. I love you, beloved.

Q: I am going through a beating of myself and I understand that it is to learn to absolutely love myself. I think you said the answer is in the question, so I will not ask the question.

I love you, beloved. And what is it to understand love? It is to understand that that which [you think] you be is not that which you be. It is that which you are in All-That-Is. It is not that which you consider yourself to be in a physical limitation called body. It is what you are in the glorious exemplification called God. As you gaze into your mirror, know beyond the face and feature, see God, the glorious glow, reflected unto you. Know that what you have created as your experience is delicious. Delight and savour it, every moment of it, every fragment of its stew, and feel not grievous about anything, for all is grand and grief is merely non-acknowledgment of its grandeur. Indeed, beloved, I salute you, and honour you, in the jewel of you, for you are beautiful.

Q: Bless you for that, and I will learn to love every minute of it.

Thank you beloved.

Q: I would like to know when the soul enters the body, if it is at the point of conception during the foetal development of the baby, or at the point of actual birth.

It varies with every consciousness: from before the point of conception, until perhaps one year after birth. There will be light force anchored within the body at the timing of birth, but the complete and wholeness of anchoring the soul energy within the body may indeed occur after the birth, in the wholeness of it, in the fullness thereof.

Q: Is that the choice of the soul?

It is the choice of all that are creating this experience; mother, father, all relations, even the physician, for they are all participating of the wisdom of the experience.

Q: Thank you. The other question is - Do you know, or can you talk on the word 'the tribulation' - can you expand on that?

That is a grand word in the doctrine of theology that has come forth. And it is alright, it is divine in its energy essence, but it is only one manner of manifestation of the changes to come. It is the twelve days of light and dark, the manifestation of the ultimate opportunity to embrace the dark with the light to create the illumination within that which does not understand its luminescence. Indeed, the tribulation is a vibratory essence of recognition of dire circumstances to occur. In other words, in the very moment you speak it, you allow it to manifest. Do you know why? Because you have already known that it will occur by its very verbiage. As you know that it is not tribulation, that it is celebration, you change the very nature of your future. Thank you beloved.

Q: Namaste. This is a very personal question and it has taken a little courage to ask you. My great desire all my life is to unite with the God-SELF within me. I have recently discovered that there is a possibility of travelling to Mexico to a certain lady who does past life accesses and she heals the emotional body. I am hoping that it will bring what I have been waiting for, and because of the amount of money that I will be spending, I wonder if there is another way of doing it?

There are many opportunities cupped within your question to bring forth illumination within you. Now, her healing of your emotional body, is not what happens at all. You may let her reflect you, but *you* heal it ultimately. *Past life therapy is of archaic understanding.* Have you ever considered, my beloved, that you are not embracing your emotional nature, and that this creates the congestion and frustration of your life as of your future, not your past, all of your ultimate nows, what you call parallel lives?. Have you ever thought of that? It is not necessarily your past that you are warring with. Now, become aware that all your past, all your nows and all your futures are being created into your now, poured into your now, the very substance and fabric of your life, giving you opportunity after opportunity to free yourself of judgment simply by encountering one after the other, after the other, of your judgments. They will come unto you, likened unto grand warriors of the battlefield, and they will continue coming unto you until you embrace them all in love. It is not only of your past, it is of all dimensional realities, even your dream reality. That which you would call other creations of awareness of this reality, there are many manners of its manifestation. Some of it is through acupuncture, some of it is through hypnosis, some of it is through what you would term to be crystalline, but the crystal ball is your Christal heart. You will know what you know, not from the exterior, but from within you, from your very vibratory energy which is emanating and exuding from the very essence of you. So wherever you go, you will create exactly the same opportunity to embrace it. It does not matter where it is you are, or who you are with, for you create the embracing of it from the heart, not from then head. And your currency does not matter, for you will create your heart's desire into the flow of your experience without your currency, if it is the desire of your soul energy in fervency of the emotion. That is what creates the impetus into manifestation, the emotion that is contained with it. So, currency does not really matter. If you want it enough, you will have it. Do you understand?

Now, there is another way of encountering what you desire to know, and that is: *know that you already know*. In the admittance of this and the acknowledgment of it, that knowing will seep into your conscious awareness. But many of you have the cart before the horse, and desire to know that you know, but when you know that you know, you will know that you know. Did you get that one? Is this sufficient, my beloved?

Q: Yes. I focus on the Earth planet as often as possible. I focus on all the magnificent rays of light and love to come through from the highest spheres to lift this, our Earth planet and to help it out of the troubled age that we are in, and I see the beautiful lighting up and the glorious beams that radiate down upon it. Now, I wonder whether this goes on anyway, or is it because I am tuned into it?

But of course it does, and it is constant, whether you realize it or not, it is constant encounter with that which is Earth plane consciousness.

Q: So when I do it, my tuning in to it does not make any difference to what is going on?

You may enhance it, but it is still there. And the only manner that you enhance it, is by allowing it to be however it is, without judging how it is. Now, the rub for many of you is to go forth and gaze into the murkiness of your rivers and gaze unto the most beauteous. That is the rub. Gaze unto the caverns that have been created through the mining, and the forests that are bare, as beauteous. To gaze indeed, into the heavens above and see the stew of the broth that is created as a consomme of the clouds, is that what you would call it? Some would call it air pollution, to see it as beauteous, to gaze unto the grand hole above the Antarctica as beauteous, to gaze unto those that you would consider to be warriors and devastators of the plane, as beauteous, to gaze unto the grand diseasement you call Aids, as wondrous. Now that is the test of your perception of divinity, in All-

That-Is. It is not to view a flower as beauteous. It is to view a warrior as beauteous because he is expressing a creative expression of God and *paradoxically, the moment you view - whatever it is that you would have previously judged - as wondrous and beauteous, you change it.* You transmute it. You clarify it, but allowing yourself to gaze upon it in the first place, without judgment and condition, is where indeed, the opportunity of your own birthing process will come. The abusers of children, that is the verbiage you have given it, to honour them and respect them, as God, to love them. Know that they too are divine, and whatever they do is divine, because they are God that has chosen the doing.

The dolphins, and the whales, they have embraced their brothers. They have acknowledged that all is divine and have come unto this plane to embrace their brothers called humanity into a delightful expression of play and creation, of heaven on Earth. When they swim in the ocean and then spin within the air, and remerge back into the waters of the ocean - do you know, when they do this, they slice into a different dimension, the ocean of air. They go from the ocean of water to the ocean of air with ease and delight, and back again into the water. Interdimensional, they are, and they delight of it all.

As you would gaze unto the ravaged Earth, gaze not into her ravishment, gaze into her replenishment. You may replenish her resources with the creation born of your thought. Revibrancy may be born into here atmosphere. Clarity may be culminated through your consciousness. The heaviness upon the cities that you call your smog, it is only a reflection of the heaviness of your judgment of it. Do you know that if you are light-hearted and loving of every atom of it, it will disappear? *Try it.* When you are within the room where someone is participating with a grand smoking stick and it is insisting in caressing your nostrils, allow yourself to love it; if you judge it, allow yourself to love it, and watch it go the other direction. *Watch it.* Create this play with your drama of life. It does this, believe me, and all of *life will begin to create harmony about you, if you do not judge it.* View it [the smoke] as a sort of incense, and once it desires its creation within your nostrils, and you harmonize with it, watch it go elsewhere to create the opportunity of harmony somewhere else. Until all embrace it and then it is no more. That is the nature of life.

Part II.

Q: Beloved I Am, you have told us that there have been many ascended masters...

Have been? There are, and you are one of them.

Q: Thank you, I appreciate that. But among the names that I have heard you mention, I have not noticed any women. Could you tell us something about that.

All womankind is ascended master, as is mankind. If you would desire to personify a particular exemplification and demonstration of womankind as an ascended master, that is separating them from all the rest. That which is ascended master is All-That-Is, beloved. Separation is dogmatic and of hierarchical formation and is of the Piscean age.

Q: Yes, I understand that. I think what I wanted to hear, is why, say, Jesus Christ, Buddha, and other people, all seem to have been of male gender.

They demonstrated in the past as male personification because the consciousness of your plane was male. It is now coming into balance and it is not male or female, it is both in Oneness. Not one or the other and not even really both, because it transmutes as soon as it becomes integrated and intertwined into the creation of the All-That-Is, it is really neither. The masculine consciousness of your plane is what desires all the holes to be filled, literally - all the spaces in consciousness to be filled, a desire to understand. And if there is a space that is not filled with understanding, they desire to go forth and fill it with something to create understanding and label it, and therefore they have very many compartments all with a particular label and they feel very satisfied with themselves. But I will tell you this, beloved, all the labels are now coming off and all the drawers are being allowed to be immersed into Oneness. Male consciousness upon the plane was the ultimate desire to go forth and find the perfect manila envelope in which to file yourself. You will come to know that a filing system is an organized manner of misplacing things. You know what I mean, do you not? It is now time to know that there is no misplacing of anything, for there is no place to misplace anything to. It is all belonging to the river of I AM. And indeed, what you call manila envelope and filing system and all the labels that you have created into your consciousness of masculine nature, is disappearing, because the label is transmuting itself into I AM. Indeed? So be it.

I tell you this: who you are is wondrously brilliant. You are all Gods in design, and you state unto me 'I Am', yet you walk out of this door and immediately have an identity crisis. You do, you know, and know indeed that when you have this Cris-Is, that the answer is all of the above; I Am [is] all of the above. You are judgmental and you are non-judgmental, and therefore you are I Am. Embrace them all, and as you do thusly, you embrace the planet. It is ravaged and it is replenished, and therefore it is I Am. Indeed?

Q: Greetings. Could you please tell us what the role of churches will be in times to come.

Shake, rattle and roll. They will not come into a grand vision of change. Their hierarchy will begin to disintegrate and begin to understand a different manner of perception of life and divinity. It is already occurring. The Pope of your now is changing and shifting the perceptions within the body of the Church, and it is creating quite a bit of chitter-chatter among the illumined of the Church, because he is grandly different, as is Gorbachev. But he operates also within a certain direction of limitation so that it is a harmonious treading of that particular thread of limitation as well. Now, all dogma, all religions, the ancient, eastern traditions, the western civilized understanding called church of Christian nature, all of it will come into the transition as part of the birthing process. The great prudes will come to know their divinity in the fashion called humility. The grandest understanding of divinity is seeing through the eyes of humility, and they too shall know this. Honouring the nature of All-That-Is. It is ultimately up to them how they shall embrace this opportunity, but it will come unto them. And they will be reflecting the nature of the planetary changes, as they shift their consciousness and crumble their walls to create anew, a castle of Christus. Thank you, beloved.

Q: Greetings. Could you give us some information about a blue cloud, a cloud that I understand has emanated from Sirius, and which seems to be hovering above Australia and New Zealand.

Curious, you call it a cloud. I would have called it a collective cohesive consciousness called craft.

Q: Craft?

It is not a physical craft as you would perceive physicality to be, but it allows the electrums within the atmosphere to integrate with one another to reflect a certain understanding of light and cohesive energy, to culminate into the illusion of a body of energy you call cloud. But you will note it is very different to a cloud formation, and it has the hue of blue because that is what the star called Sirius resonates to.

Q: Thank you. I was wondering, when the planet was seeded, you referred to this seeding...

Sirius was grandly involved in this, most especially in the Atlantean and Egyptian understanding, which came forth later. That which is dolphin is of Sirius, and they were star seeded into the Atlantean. Their consciousness was contained within the continent of Lemuria and they interbred with the Atlanteans.

Q: There is a heavy trend of people to personally use crystals for their own growth and advancement. Is that wrong?

There is no right or wrong, and what is crystalline will not give you any advancement, only *you* give *you* advancement. *You* are the power source, not it. It is a reflector, it is a facet of the mineral kingdom, mirroring the understanding of Christ-all for you to gaze upon and understand your own nature. As I stated before, you do not have to have its physical presence in order to have its consciousness with you.

Q: I wish to know how to manifest for the changes in the future in a way that is gentle and harmonious.

Know that you are always supported, regardless of how it is, know that you are always supported magically. All that you would desire as support will come unto you without you limiting it as to how it has to occur, how it must come unto you, how it is to be manifested. For you see, your gold will disappear. So will the old understanding of foodstuffs eventually, for you will not require them. You are in the process of birthing into the non-requirement of it. You will sustain each other through the exchange of your energy flows, golden energy flows, and you will be constantly wearing the garment of golden, for that will be your light. Alright, beloved? The illusion of gold as coin and clinker in your purse, it is an experience, to be sure, called the game of prosperity, the game of abundance and success and failure, limitation of life upon the plane, and the game of the understanding of judgment, of the 'haves' and 'have nots'. Did I tell you the forebearers of the 'haves' and 'have nots' are the 'knows' and 'know nots'. Those who know, they are the creator of their life and they are empowered to create the drama of their life how they wish it to be. They are the ones that bestow themselves grandly with abundance untold. Abundance untold - is that what you do not report to the Income Tax Department? Indeed. And sustenance, it will always be there for you, for as you caress nature, nature will supply you forever. You are the prince of your own provision. All of you. Foodstuffs align unto you into this provision when you align into IS with the non-requirement of it.

It is a paradox, but it is knowing that you are always, synchronistically, experiencing life in a joyous now moment in the Isness of it, and to be without frustration or fetterment into the heavy burdens of yesterday and the whirlwinds of tomorrow. You may, if you desire, change a piece of your verbiage from 'today' into 'tonow', and it will shift your focus of a limitation of a *day*, into a *now*. And so you will begin to experience an infinite acceleration of the momentum into the creation of your life.

Q: My question concerns correct discrimination. For example, when disharmony occurs in one's life, it seems I could choose to embrace it, as you suggested, or I could move, so that I remove myself from the disharmonious circumstance. I think both of those would be okay, however, which would be best?

There is no better or best, both are judgmental. Did you know that? Removing yourself from a situation consciously, you judge that it is not alright, but if you allow your flow and your heart's desire to create your experience elsewhere, what you remove yourself from will not come unto your experience. That is a paradox, but that is life. You will find many paradoxes within your life, for it is created of the energy of paradox, the nature of polarity. Now, the embracing of it is allowing it to be alright and not disharmonious, so you would not perceive disharmony within it in the first place. But if you do, honour your judgment. Embrace your own judgment. Embrace the circumstance and allow the circumstance to be transmuted. It is not an avoidance, it is an awareness of transmutation. You may change it, simply by allowing it to be, in love.

Very likened unto the rock and the brook. The giggling waters not say 'Move rock, move out of my way. I wish you to be elsewhere.' They encounter the rock, in delight, and say 'Ah, I love you.' And when you are in this particular position, say: 'I allow you to be, and I create my energy elsewhere, and I love you and I caress you with my nurturing waters.' There is a difference. It is light-headedness and a love and an honour that is within it, rather than 'Oh, you are awful and I do not want to experience you and I will go up on a hill where it is a bit more harmonious.' Do you understand? Your options all contain a certain amount of opportunity to perceive judgment, but the same opportunity is there to perceive non-judgment. Alright?

Q: Thank you. The question that has been going through my mind regards you being here in a point in space? Are you not everywhere?

And everywhen. Indeed, that is omnipresence. In your understanding of you, you will come to know that you are too, everywhere and everywhen.

The illusion of your life, is the illusion of God, the I Am, coming forth upon the plane, to create the forever river of limitation into the brilliance of the God that be within the limitation - to unfold it into its wondrous birthing, unto newness, called super-consciousness.

Now, Is there water, a bit of water? You may toast me with the chalice of your heart. The water enables the electromagnetic energy in this instrument to flow a bit more harmoniously. *(Someone offers St. Germain a glass of water).*

Q: Would you like a refill? Because it was so fine, would you like a refill?

Oh, but of course. Have you ever noticed how calming and how refreshing it is to hear water being poured? Be like the water, gurgle and giggle, and therefore there will be bubbles coming forth from within the deep of your very thought. Be effervescent and create bubbles of laughter and dance and delight and song. Place yourself with friskiness and festivity and participate with life as the ultimate dance of delight. So be it. Thank you for your refreshment, it tasted wondrously. You tasted wondrously.

Q: Greetings, I Am. You spoke of the new consciousness in the Soviet Union, and in the Papacy. Could you speak of that consciousness in the United States and Australia?

They are sisters, born of the same motheren. The sisters you call America and Australia, notice even the similarity of the vibrations of the names of these continents. They both begin and end with alpha and they are very similar in consciousness, likened unto twin sisters. Born very close to the same point in history, they come forth to unite and embrace one another, and they will help the rest of the Earth to understand the resonance of sister to sister, brother to brother. They will stand in their glory and grandeur of sovereignty. America, the North American continent, is the crown seal of the Earth. In its desire to be in the diamond light of All-That-Is, it will merge in honour eventually with the understanding of not only democracy, but divinity. There will be a grand shifting and changing and a transmutation of the governmental structure. This will occur in

Australia as well. However, because it is the younger sister, it will be a bit later in your chronology.

Now, the heart chakra and the crown chakra are both very, very intimately and intricately involved in the birthing of Earth. The heart chakra also encompasses Hawaii. The heart chakra is Australia. Hawaii is also part of the crown chakra. Much energy will be given forth in this area, because it is a concentric circle joined together in the merging and blending of the two energies.

It is where the embrace touches in tangible form, and as it begins to blend, it is not only blending westward, it is blending eastward, for the motheren of both is east, which is Britain or the United Kingdom. It too will transmute its governmental structure, as it already is beginning to. The focus of energy therein and Aylesbury, Glastonbury and many of the areas that are of ancient druid understanding are coming forth now, to be the Merlin reborn, to be Arthur reborn. Do you know what Arthur was? It was a personification of an understanding of alignment and honour of Godship of awe around the Round Table. There was none who was at the head of the table, for all were conjoined in a circle of equality, and all were honoured, and all represented certain vibratory resonances of the thirteen original soul bodies.

So, the eastward experience of it will go forth from the United Kingdom into Russia, and into China, and will blend yet again as it merges into North America, which is conjoined with Australia. Now, China has been called the red nation. It indeed does resonate to this particular polarity, but it is becoming aligned through the very nature of its ancient, ancient wisdom into awareness. So red will be transmuted and shifted into the white.

There are some of consciousnesses within this nation, as there are within many other nations, who will desire to control the world, it appears, but like your churches, they will also be brought into the opportunity to experience humility. It is the balancing. So fear not, all is well on the western front, and on the eastern front.

Q: Greetings, I Am. I would like to ask where my brothers, who do not wish to embrace super-consciousness, will go, and what sort of time will pass before they desire to embrace super-consciousness.

It is ultimately up to them. Each one has the opportunity in every now moment to embrace super-consciousness. They will go to the same place they are now. Earth is now in third density consciousness - her own auric field is third density - and when fourth density or super-consciousness comes upon the plane, it will not be perceiving third density and third density will not be perceiving fourth density, for they will be different dimensions then. Now they are co-existent dimensions, and when super-consciousness prevails, the shift will occur and that is called a rapture. It is ultimately up to them when they desire to experience the other dimensional realities and realms of unlimited life. It may be the next moment, it may be eons of lifetimes hence, but ultimately, all shall, alright? So be it.

Q: You spoke of Australia and America representing or manifesting the heart and crown seals. Where are the other seals in the Earth's body or the Earth's physical form, particularly with regard to the Russian continent and Africa?

Africa is called the Kundalini energy, the fire energy. Russia, the bear country, is merged and blended with Europe. It is Eurasia, and it is the liver and solar plexus.

Q: Could you speak on the act of sexual union between men and women, apart from giving birth, and being a great time, what healing aspects if any, are experienced? Is it the man connecting with his feminine and vice versa, or...

Oh but of course it is homogenization of both, each unto the other. Male experiences male and female, and female experiences male and female, and when they embrace one another, they exchange across the borders of their auric fields. And the creation of orgasm is merely the explosion of understanding of joy in this merging. It is really born of thought, rather than physical creation. Do you know this? Omnipotence is born forth in this fashion as well, and as you let this explosion go forth through your thought and to the rest of the universe, you may create powerful expressions of your ultimate creativity, your reproduction into your life of coagulated matter.

Now, sexual expression will shift and change also in your life to come into super-consciousness, for the lower and higher seals will become centred in the heart and therefore you will not experience, in this Earth plane, the heavy and dense energies, nor will they be experienced as airy-fairy, as you have thought it to be. In the merging and blending, there will be a coupling of consciousness of the heart, and in this coupling, there will be born and birthed an awareness of new life. In super-consciousness, there will be physical birthing, but it will not be fraught with pain, and it will not only be the creation of physical merging. There will be many immaculate conceptions, born through thought, light impregnation. So it will also be a grand time.

Q: Will it be as much fun?

Indeed. What is fun, beloved, but a joyous experience and play.

Q: Beloved I Am, I am part of a study group on the book of the I Am, by Godfrey Ray King. Within this book, there is talk that one shouldn't indulge in trance. Within our group we have two people bringing forth messages of love, guidance and wisdom, and I do not understand how this can be wrong.

Indeed. There is no right or wrong, beloved. There are no 'shoulds' or 'should nots' either. This particular creation of dogma was appropriate for that timing. It was many years ago in your thirties of chronological understanding, and in that timing it was harmonious, but it is now the ripeness of time to be a springboard for further unlimitedness. Not for all, for some - those whose hearts allow them to resonate to a further knowing - and those who resonate to limited knowing, it is divine, for it is the ripeness for their experience in that now moment, so judge them not.

Q: I am a soul that has always existed, and on the basis that I elected to come to this dimension, to experience ..

And you received a unanimous vote, hm?

Q: The concept of choosing my parents, is that a concept that is realistic? In other words, that I chose my parents for the experiences that they would learn from me.

No, not at all, but that you would learn from each other. It was a mutually co-ordinated desire manifested for the reflection of all concerned. Honouring the divinity within everyone else will allow you the understanding of humility, for you are learning from them as well, beloved brother. Do you know what you are learning? Would you so desire that I tell you what you are learning?

Q: I would, yes.

You are learning how to release and allow others to be within their limitation and to bless them.

Q: Can I ask you one other question? In terms of computers and the role they play in our society, I wonder what sort of role they will play in our society as we evolve further?

This is indeed a grand expression that I would desire to share with you. Your computer is a manifested illusion that is accepted as a valid symbol of ascended consciousness by your technological society. Your technologists shall indeed create a voice box into which you speak and which has intellect that is self-aware. Consciousness that you may communicate with through your computer? I will tell you this: they will state to the commercial market 'Voila, herein is a grand piece of machinery with which you may converse through this grand box that has within it assemblage of a mysterious new technology.' I will tell you a thing: it is empty. It is a symbol that is allowed so that you may converse with the unlimited being that you are, through the reflection called machinery, hm? You are beginning to ascend into this understanding. Artificial intelligence is only unlimited intelligence that is not recognized as your own. Your microchip is only the crystalline within every atom of your being that is included with all the experiences of All-That-Is. It contains unlimited 'bytes' of wisdom. There are times when you have lockjaw and you desire not to participate of so many bites at a time and you experience congestion. So you carry yourself to your local dentist, and query him: 'Oh why, oh why do I have this horrendous ache of a tooth, the jaw, the gum'. And you place within your mouth the down payment for a house and allow indeed the pain to manifest elsewhere, for it will continue to manifest until you understand its origination, which is non-acknowledgment of your power to bite off and chew whatever amount of I Am-ness - a glorious experience what some would call discordant energy.

Then there is accelerated life experience, for you bite off and ingest more and more energy into your system. You will not carry yourselves to your physicians' offices, your psychologists' offices, indeed. It is because you are allowing the diversity and uniqueness of life to display itself without judgment of separation. And the judgment and separation carries itself into your nations, you know. There have always been those within the western world that have stated 'Ah, beware, there is a communist.' But the communist is providing a grand service indeed. How else would the western world scare themselves into being friends with each other.

So it is all back to the beginning where there is no beginning. You are all the same energy viewed through different mirrors. Some of you desire to have the rear view, that is alright. You gaze across your shoulder into the archaeology of your past called past life therapy, hm? Desiring to know who you were rather than knowing who you are, which is part of who you were, but that is not all of who you are, for who you are is also who you shall be.

You continue in the constant search to know that which be you, forever yearning and seeking, forever on the pathway of lack of understanding. You know indeed that the pathway is you and you can never be off yourselves so you can never be off your pathway. The detours, they may be bumpy, but you may take a joyride and have experience, likened unto a child when they go over a bump, and they love it. You too, may allow life to be a grand circus, three ring circus; the ring of your heart, the ring of your solar plexus, and the ring of your crown, concentric in their union. Then you will not search so fervently for a mate, for the mate of you is you, and the mate of your planet is mother Earth, and she is conjoining with herself to birth a new awareness. Did you ever consider that your planet is married? Some of your planets are single and some have rings. But she is, she is merging and blending with the male energy of herself. She is penetrating herself, with the I Am-ness, the Source energy of the All-That-Is, and she is also in ultimate reception of it at the same time. That is why there are so many of you with such urgency of your sexual nature in your now, because you also desire to go forth and penetrate, the urgency to give forth and spew forth the ultimate energy of life, the creation of the All-That-Is. You also, in the same now moment are so yearning to receive it, and you are reaching out to yourself in the giving and reception, for it is the same event. Therefore your sexual nature will become enhanced, and it is the root energy, the regenerative energy that is coming forth. Let it enhance the regenerative energy of your planet, of Terra, for her sexual energy is the spewing forth of all volcanoes and the allowance of herself to receive your energy. The fire of life comes forth, connected with your heart through the root. Root yourself into the planet as a terminal point, as a point of focus or concentration, and let the flow continue through your heart, bathing and basking within its brilliant, diamond light and continue it into your third eye, to co-create the reality, the vision, your dream into experience. Therefore it will be indeed an enhancement also of your psychic energies, your sensory perceptions, your telepathy, your understanding of empathy of your brothers. That is why so many are becoming open to the awareness of starvation upon the planet, and indeed the planet herself, as she is beginning to birth, and her urgency to re-unite with herself. The allowance of the flow to continue into the crown will bring forth Godship, the crowing and reigning and dominion upon the plane of the All-That-Is, blessed in the beingness called humanity.

Now, the chatter of your mind, the doubts and the 'can't' and 'shoulds' and 'shouldn't' and all the judgments and limitations, it is indeed likened unto a diadem. It too is a crown that is between your third eye and your crown seal and it brings pressure into this area. You feel at times a grand migraine. Flow into it and allow expansion of this crown, to be blended with the I Am crown of that which be you. The chatter is merged and blended with the Christus, for the chatter is anti-Christus which brings forth the doubting of your divinity and as it is merged and blended, the polarities are united into freedom of being. So it is not getting rid of the chatter in your mind and quieting it, it is allowing it to silence. Honour it, listen to it, hear it, understand it, acknowledge it, have compassion for it, and embrace it, as you would a child. Perceive it as a gift, for without it, you would not be. Did you know that? The polarity that allows you to continue to be grounded into physical dimension is this particular understanding of anti-Christus, and as you align it, you will become lighter, less dense, more transparent. But honour it, for it has afforded you the exquisite, delicious expression of being human, and in this, you have enhanced God.

Q: Greetings. I wanted to ask you a question about the death process of the physical form. I have done a bit of study on the Tibetan teachings and they outline quite a long process whereby the consciousness may leave the physical body over a period of three to even seven days. Now in the west here, when people pass we usually dispose of the body very quickly, and I am in a position where I will be working with people making their transitions, and so I would like some guidance about this.

Death is an unreality. There is a changing, a transformation of circumstance, and of configuration of consciousness, but *no thing ever dies.* Energy is eternal, even the energy of the body itself, does not die. It changes form, but it does not die. Now, as you would consider the desire to go forth into other realities and realms of dominion and dimension, know that it is but an instant. The decision forces may be over eons or days, or hours, but the actual experience is but an instant. The consciousness of your particular culture, is how it is, because that is how you create it to be. So, in the eastern understanding, they have allowed the process of decision and the creation of a dramatization of what culminates before the actual transition into another dimension, to be an elongated version of timing, and the west has not. Both are valid, and both are options, and both are to be experienced by what you have called your brothers that you may share with in your future of time. Allow them to know, what they wish to experience, is a blessing, for it will bless them with yet another experience upon the plane of their foreverness.

Death may be likened unto your grand tele - changing channels. The energy, when you are not focussing upon that channel, does not disappear, it is simply not viewed in that moment, hm?

Q: So in terms of moving the body, it is complete when we feel it is complete.

Indeed. Actually, have you ever experienced embracing a body in rigor mortis? That is how it feels when the All-That-Is, the eternal Is-ness, comes forth in the desire to embrace you when you have your limitations upon how it shall be. You feel grandly stiff. I would desire to carry forth a riddle in this timing.

You know, they have this grand ritual, they have the viewing of the body, and they always seem to have a chair, a seat, provided in nearness of the body. Do you know what that chair, or seat is for? It allows rigor mortis to set in.

Q: One of the healing methods that has become really popular here, is called Reiki. What would you have to say about that and the debate that so many people get into as to whether they will do it, won't do it, why they should or shouldn't do it. My experience is that it really works and that it is a very powerful tool and I am just really interested to hear what you have to say.

I would suggest you take a rebate on your debate. It is not necessary to have one, hm? The understanding of Reiki is one manner of expression of stimulation and transmutation of certain ridges of energies. That is not the only manner. There are as many manners of this as there are people. So indeed, honour those that would desire to share it, and honour those that do not, alright?

Q: Greetings. Just before the break, you used a term that I had never heard of before, and that was 'oversoul'. Could you explain that to me, please?

In a limited manner of understanding unlimitedness, I shall. Oversoul is the creation of identical energy essences of the All-That-Is into the focus of a particular frequency that is emphasized, and there are thirteen in this particular plane of existence. All twelve spectrums of life, plus the thirteenth, as created of the unified whole of all the other twelve, are created on this plane from whence all your consciousness spew forth. All of you create your awareness as different forms of these particular energies. You may indeed resonate to one or the other, or the other in your particular emphasis of focus and create certain frequency bands called personalities, but they all remerge into the Sourceness of the Oversoul, which are all identical unto one another. In that, it is remerged yet again likened unto an inverted funnel into the All-That-Is called God I Am, Original Thought. An Oversoul is a piece of verbiage of yours and I was only using it for convenience in that moment. Really, there is no separation. Alright? So be it.

Q: Namaste, I Am. I was wondering whether there is any significance to the fact that the climate in the last few years has warmed up all over the globe? In Melbourne we are having extreme Indian summers. Could you fill me in on that?

Indeed. It is the fire energy coming forth to commune with the rest of nature, as the elements make themselves seen and heard. I will tell you this - as it is seen now, it is just beyond your year 3000, and your planet will be a star. The planet will still exist, but the atoms within your atmosphere will be ignited into a fire, or a brilliance, not really a fire as you consider the element fire to be, but a brilliance, so that it is perceived as a glowing brilliance by all the other systems that are gazing upon you. In this understanding, the Earth herself will become a sun, and the solar system will evolve and unfold into a grand ball of light. It also, in millenia to come, will become a grand sun of consciousness. It will explode into a Supernova. So that is the beginning that you are feeling, the heating up. It is divine, it is to be cherished, for you are also heating up into the ultimate evaporation you call ascension, spontaneous human combustion, hm?

Q: No serious dehydration, or sort of cataclysm is in store in our near future...

Only if you know them into existence. If I were to give unto you anything of this day of time, it is to know that the Earth changes can be whatever you wish them to be. You are the creation of that epic drama, and it is not for me to tell you how you will choose to create it.

Q: Greetings, beloved. There is a place I love dearly. It is called New Zealand. You have talked about Australia and North America and Russia, and I was wondering if you would say something about New Zealand.

The Sea-land? It is indeed a part of the Lemurian continent, as well. It is created as an understanding of separation, but it too shall merge, much as it does not desire to, hm? But it will be after your political arena has calmed a bit. It will not be discordant, for there are other parts of this area of your world that will merge, as well; other parts of the bescattered continent of Lemuria, that part of Lemuria that is still present. The reason I hesitated on that word is, because there is beneath the water that which you would not call continent, but a civilization really, but I will allow that one [the word continent] for now.

Q: Will we in fact see a rising up of that land, and southern Australia rising up with New Zealand?

New Zealand, as you call it, will be indeed giving forth of a bit more land in some areas and a bit less in others, because the waters will rise. It will begin to have an isthmus that connects Australia and it. Indeed, it will support alignment unto other areas of this your world, economically and politically. It will create quite a difference of bureaucracy upon it than what is present of your now. The peaks of the mountains of the other lands that will rise from beneath the water into land and islands, will be within your next thirty years[2] of your time. This is how it appears according to your now; remember everything is subject to change. All of these areas will have a difference in political arena compared to now. Hawaii, Indonesia, Samoa, Fiji, all of these areas, even your Japan, the land of the rising sun. Fancy it being called that, hm? We will speak about Japan later.

---

[2] Year of comment is 1989.

Q: Is there any plan for beings to incarnate on the actual Earth plane, apart from visitors such as yourself, to accelerate growth through their continued presence?

When all of you have draped the garment of your light body upon you, then I shall; for then, and only then, shall you view me in equality, or any one likened unto that which be I, which is really yourself, you see? I am your mirror, and in the desire of that which be I to come forth upon this plane to experience communion and fellowship with the brothers of humanity called I Am, I shall, and I shall allow myself the delicious delight of hair upon the face, for a change. And indeed, I shall also express as a child, as the creation of elfin and spirits, and Merlin, to be sure; all of the culminations of consciousness of wizardry and wit, and I will be a reflection unto all of you, and all of you will be a reflection unto that which is I, and all of you will be a reflection unto one another, and we shall all conjoin together into an exquisite expression of I Am-ness, and the song of joy is heard and born from the breast of God realized. So be it.

Q: Will you choose to be immaculately conceived, or will you come through the natural processes of conception?

Neither. I have done this before, and I shall do it again, that is manifest a body. Do you know what that means? Voila, I am there, and voila I am not! And then voila, I am, again. It is a very delightful experience. There is curiosity and puzzlement everywhere I go.

Part III.

A friend of mine lost her son in an accident and has become very bitter. What happens to people who never get over that bitterness?. Do they keep coming back to get rid of it? That is one thing I cannot understand. How do you ever get rid of it?

You need not get rid of it. You need allow it into your experience, into your heart, and release it. Getting rid of it is - would be sweeping it under your carpet. You have to face it and deal with it, nourish it into its own divinity. Allow it to be for its own reasons.

I understand what you are saying, but when it is happening to you, at the time that it is happening, there are many people who take that bitterness to their graves.

Of course they do. That is their choice, and in that choice they have learned. They have learned what it is like to carry that bitterness with them for a lifetime. What it is like to have that occur, to have manifested that for themselves and to not allow it. It is a grand lesson of itself. When they manifest it for themselves again, at a soul level, they will consider what it was like before and consider a different alternative perhaps if they choose to. It is likely that in that particular circumstance it need not be the next lifetime, perhaps it is merely a like incident within that lifetime. There is an alternative solution. And your soul allows you that knowledge. Your conscious mind is that of storm. It is not easy to penetrate.

However, your soul has garnished the wisdom from the experience of bitterness. Now it is time to experience something else.

Do you know what each and every one of us here on this planet has to deal with, for what lessons - or main purpose - we are here for?

You see my dear, realization of divinity is also the realization for each and every one of you that you have free will, free choice. You are here merely to gain enlightenment for yourselves in one way or another. In other words, to call back to your light being, to your Source. To *be* All-In-All, if you will. To *be* the creative force that will create your universes and your stars and anything you desire. However you desire on your daily basis to manifest your enlightenment, that is your choice. It is not another's right to decide for you, or to predict for you, for that matter. It is your own right to decide and predict for yourself. And you make those choices in every moment of your time, even in your slumber, you make those choices.

Will there ever be a time of total peace on this Earth, where everybody here feels total peace?

Humanity will experience what you consider total peace. It will not necessarily be on this [third density] Earth. It will be on Earth. The

Earth will be different [fourth density]. However, there will be total peace and unified sovereignty.

Speak to us of education!

My sister, education in your limited terms is synonymous for the word 'wisdom'. However, your wisdom comes not to you from your books, from your scripted paper, from your institutions, not even from your teachers. Your education, or wisdom, which is a far grander word for it, comes to you through your unlimited God-SELF. Allowance of the knowledge to come through you to your consciousness, through your conscious mind as you call it. And acceptance of it, so that you may utilize it in your outer world. Teachers in institutions and the pages thereof, are merely the reflections of the wisdom of others. You may learn from it. That is very true. You learn far grander lessons and wisdom from your SELF. Your educational systems in this society on your planet are of course serving a purpose, but they will come to a mass change here very soon in your time. For the boundaries will be broken. There will be no grade system, as you term it to be. Nor will there be different divisions among your students. All will be equal.

It is part of the shift that is necessary for super-consciousness to occur. Much as your governmental shifts and all the shifts upon your planet, internal and external, for your externality is merely yourself reflected back to you. The shifts that are occurring are occurring within yourself as well, and it is merely on another scale that you see it reflected in your society.

Are these changes gradual, or are they abrupt?

They will be gradual, in your terminology. In the history of your Earth, however, considering it has been here for eons, it will be rather abrupt. It is relative. But it will be part of the unleashing of the sovereignty of each individual. It will be grand not to have your restrictions.

How are we to prepare the children of today, the way they are being taught?

They will help prepare you. You will allow them into unlimitedness. You best do that by realizing everyone's unlimited SELF, your SELF and theirs.

How do we go about discovering that we are God?

First of all, look at yourself and consider the divine creation you truly are - your flesh, your bones, the eyes within you. All life is grand. Your sands upon your shores, your clouds in your skies, all is life and all is grand. But all does not have the cognition you do. You yourself are a wondrous work of art. Consider that. Consider that you do create your own life circumstances, and who else but a manifesting God could do all the wondrous things you have done in your life-span this time around.

What games are we playing that we do not realize? Why is it so difficult for mankind to realize this?

Because humanity has a conscious mind it is battling with at this time in your history. It is a war. It will resolve itself in time, as you perceive time to be. It is limitation for a purpose. The purpose is Self-realization. Realization of your divinity, your God-SELF. You place upon yourself these limitations in order to realize that you can, as a manifesting entity, overcome it. Those entities that have experiences of mass-catastrophes in their life, and they overcome, and overcome and overcome, are merely pulling to themselves [the knowledge of] who they are. They will realize it much sooner than the individual who has a rather tranquil lifetime. However, these limitations in your mass-consciousness are dissolving. For all the entities on your Earth plane, upon this planet, are desirous of realizing their divinity, at a soul level, and some consciously. It is dissolving before your very eyes. It is not to concern yourself over, merely because it is all part of life on this Earth plane, part of a grand design. All is as should be.

How important is it to have a knowledge of our past lives in order to shed some knowledge or purpose or to help us reach enlightenment in this incarnation?

It is only as important as you feel it is. In reality, in the overall picture, it is not important at all. However, if you feel earnestly that it is, then it is.

Realize also that each moment is magnificent in and of itself, for there is nothing but now. Releasing whatever it is in your - what you term to be your past - is releasing yourself into your divinity and your light. Hanging on to it as a crutch merely cripples you.

You need not be in your ritualistic poses, or have your incense burning. It is alright, but it is not necessary. You may simply walk beside the water or sit beneath your pine trees in a quiet place. For the quiet reflected outside is reflective of the quiet inside. Quiet in your soul - and listen, listen. Many times we turn a deaf ear to what our soul is attempting to tell us. It is knocking and we do not hear. We choose not to hear. We hear only what we wish.

I am a little confused about free will. People go for readings and they are told that certain things will happen in their lives and they do happen. Is this something that is predetermined at soul level or can one change that based on the fact that we have free will?

The entity may, of course, change anything with free will. What is told to them, they believe. Their belief believed it into existence. You see. If you are told you are going to die, and you believe it with all your heart and soul, then you will die. But it is your choice not to. You see, if you believe something so fearful, it manifests itself for you. That is part of the manifesting process. Those entities that are speaking to them, giving them the information for which they ask, are in a limited understanding, although they are providing a service - that is true. There is nothing wrong with what they are doing. They simply have not realized that all have the power to change anything at any time. Seers or prophets - they are all divine beings. They are all grandly loved. But all have that capacity. It is not a gift that is select for a few chosen ones. All have that capacity, including yourself. You merely tune in and you will see what they see and if you do not desire that particular circumstance consciously, then you change it. Many of the things that I have said that are likely to happen are likely at that point in your time. However, anything can happen. I understand your confusion.

If you change your thoughts you can change..?

Not your thoughts. Your thoughts - as what you term thought to be - is your mind which is limited. Thought is divine indeed. It is a creative force. But the thought you speak of is your mind and you have to change what your heart desires. You may say 'I desire not to be sick' but in your inner Self, that illness affords you whatever it is you would desire - your love, your security, whatever. The ones around you, pity you, and occasionally that is what you desire, which is alright. But you have to understand the difference between what your mind would tell you that you want and what your heart tells you, you want.

So it is more of a belief system?

Know is a better word than believe. If you know it. If you know it to be so - if you know that that is what you wish, then it *is* so.

Thank you.

Thank you my sister. You see, releasing limitations is the main lesson we all are here for. Any limitation - physical, emotional, intellectual - any limitation. No need for rituals. No need for dogma. No need for giving your power away to someone else, for you are all powerful masters, all of us. Such a grand light we could light the universes if you but knew who you are.

So you do not have to try and figure out who you were or what your purpose is?

Of course, my sister. You are learning grandly. That is the message your man Jesus came to teach, in meekness and humility. It is merely the realization of all others' divinity as well as your own. But there is no better or worse.

Why is there so much confusion around Jesus?

He is misinterpreted because those that came after him were frightened of his message in their limited thinking and it changed to some extent his message and that is what is written in your books. Some is not changed and some is.

But then he could have controlled that.

We do not interfere with human free will.

You see, when they realized how divine he was after his ascension, they were in awe of him - of his message that all could be as he was. And because of that your leaders, the political leaders at that time of the church - the priests - felt in order to control the people and have an orderly government it was necessary to keep the people unenlightened of their own manifesting capacity. That is why the Essenes were disbanded. That is why their mystical wisdom has been hidden all these years. Some of it appeared in your Dead Sea scrolls, but some of the messages were coded and the codes have not been broken.

Is there a message for humanity in the Great Pyramid?

There is a message for humanity indeed, for that particular pyramid was manifested by beings not of your Earth and they were informing those that were curious enough, who were of the consciousness that could accept the message without distortion, that they indeed are enlightened beings and have the capacity for manifesting, that they themselves could build the pyramids. You see, *the message of the pyramids is the wisdom of how to build it, for how to build it is by being divine.* Those divine beings that came to your planet to build it left it here for the unveiling when the time was proper. The time is nigh.

What about the pyramid right now? Should they be disturbing it?

What is there to disturb? The wisdom is already apparent. It is already in your hieroglyphics and pictures have been made of them. It is not necessary to concern yourself, for the tunnelling is not destructive. It will lead only to those corridors that will be revealing, unveiling.

So that will happen soon?

It is likely. The King's chamber has many of its pearls of wisdom, its emeralds that will speak to the hearts of those that find them. There will be a mystical unveiling and even your newscasters will know about it.

Has [Lord] Maitreya anything to do with this?

There is an aspect of that entity, however, that particular entity is of a certain energy force that it would not be possible to concentrate all that energy into one body. Maitreya was the entity that overshone the man Jesus with all his wisdom. That was the entity who Jesus channelled. That particular entity was with Krishna and Jesus.

What about Sai Baba?

A grand entity indeed. He is one of the entities on your Earth plane in your current time that is desirous of doing what your Jesus did, in a manner. Demonstration of being in more than one place at a time and manifesting before one's eyes all the miracles.

But then the pictures of him..

He desires it not, much as your Jesus did not. That is their choice to give their power away. It is my message and many of the other masters' message not to give your power away. It is only to revere yourself, not someone else.

The entity Maitreya was the entity your master Jesus spoke with and channelled during his incarnation on Earth.

Who is Sananda?

Sananda is the grander SELF of your Jesus. Sananda is from the same plane as I. Jesus, in order to be born into this Earth, was of fourth density.

Is it true that our bodies are changing from second to third density?

Third to fourth. Third density is gross matter animated with a Spirit residing within, full of all the choices that any divine God has. However it is also inclusive of a limited consciousness. Fourth density is God-man with unlimited consciousness.

Are there any [densities] beyond that?

Of course. They are non-physical however.

After fourth is not physical?

Of course, that is where Jesus went, beyond.

So we are going into fourth density?

That is the transition of what you call New Age - Aquarian age. Jesus was the herald of the Piscean age. The Aquarian age is now being heralded in, and fourth density is becoming more prevalent upon this Earth plane.

Does that mean more people will be in that fourth density?

Indeed it does. And when your mother Earth ascends herself, all will be in fourth density or above.

What does that mean when the Earth ascends?

Your Earth will change frequency, much as the entities upon Earth and within Earth will change their frequency. For *ascension is merely a change in frequency*. You do not perceive the body because it is a different frequency. It is the non-physical, in your terms, because you do not see it [from the view-point of third density]. And when this occurs, you will have another parallel Earth. You will have this third density Earth, and a fourth density Earth. Your fourth density Earth will be, what you have called in your history, your heaven, for it is of a different frequency and those entities upon it are enlightened. They are divine, manifesting as they choose in unity and harmony with the universe.

The Earth continues, both Earths continue. The entities upon this Earth, this [third density] Earth, who decide for their own reasons not to become enlightened, at least not now in your time, will remain upon this Earth and have further incarnations until they have experienced what they desire to experience and have learned the lessons they would desire to learn. Not that they *have* to learn, what they *desire* to learn. This [Earth] will remain. There is another [Earth]. It is also in existence and it is fourth density and those upon it and within it are also fourth and above.

We could have a world, another Earth?

Of course. It is a different frequency and you as a third density entity would not perceive it for it is of a different frequency.

But you can perceive it?

Not in this third density body.

But you can in fourth?

Indeed. Much as the spectrum of light you call ultra-violet. It exists but you cannot see it.

But why would we not all choose that?

There are some entities upon this Earth who desire to remain in their dogmatic limited existence.

But why would we choose that when we know...

Not all are consciously aware. Nor do they desire to be. Why? Ask them. It is their choice.

But if they do not even know that their higher consciousness exists...

They do at a soul level. You see, it [the choice] is always done at a soul level, for all entities, regardless of how limited they seem to be. Their conscious mind, however, is that which is limited and it is for them as an entire entity to decide whether they desire to open themselves to enlightenment. In other words, to partake of wisdom in this manner or another manner, or to remain closed. It is up to them, and there is no right or wrong, for they are learning grand lessons in their manner.

My question is, how is it in a marriage - one becomes enlightened and one does not? What happens in that circumstance? Would one who is more enlightened, not rub off on the other person?

That is what you call a mirror and it does occur, if you would call it 'rub off'. You see, when enlightenment is made available to an individual, their conscious mind is then aware and then they may consciously decide to partake or not to partake. Their choice is being offered to them on a silver platter. If they decide not to, that is alright, for who is to say they will not decide to at a later time? Once a particular fragment or aspect of your soul group is moving into the light, it is a natural happening for the rest of that group to be drawn to it. It is though it were a magnet and it pulls the other aspects toward the light.

Is that what they call harvest?

In many references your harvest is your fourth density transformation, your ascension. Some would call it rapture.

Then that is going to happen soon?

What is soon? Indeed, however, release your time limitations. Watching your clock will keep you unenlightened forever. Let go of your time. If it is later than that, so what? For you are here for all eternity. It matters not what time it is.

But that is a hard concept for us to comprehend - I mean I can remember when I was a little girl trying to figure out how long eternity was and we had nothing to measure it by because on this plane, we are born, we live and then we die. So the only thing that we know of is that limited time frame, and thinking of eternity just boggles the mind. Things go on and on forever, or they constantly are - that is a concept that is difficult for us on this plane.

It is an exercise for a limited mind in unlimitedness. You may tread that mill over and over again and your limited mind merely becomes exhausted, for unlimitedness is inconceivable. If it were conceivable, it would not be unlimited.

I wanted to ask something about manifestation, and to request it of my grander Self - any special way of requesting it that works best?

When you are quiet, whether in meditation or slumber or merely simply quiet with yourself, call to yourself - your manifesting Godhood. Command forth its presence. Give to it your desires. Affirm to it that it already exists. Your conscious mind will argue with you on that one, but there is no time differentiation in the grander picture between asking for it and receiving it, for there is no time. So in the grander sense, it already is. Request of it the desires from your heart - emotion is grandly indicated. Know it into being. Know it is so. And your oversoul, your grander Self, that part of you that is an aspect of the Source, will pacify you and manifest for you, for your limited Self, that is.

Does one say it out loud?

It matters not. If you feel more in command verbalizing it, that is alright. And then your grander Self will say 'See I told you so. You can do it, you know.', and your conscious mind will have received the proof it desires all the time and you will allow the door to open a bit and it will become easier.

What better method could we use to hold our mind steady?

Why not try relaxing. Holding one's Self rigid is tension. Relax into the joy of the moment - knowing that all moments are of the light. For all moments in your existence are a part of you and you are of the light. So naturally it would follow that they are also. Release your tension and aggravation, the part of you that is rigid, that [you think] must be regulated or controlled. For what is it that water does? It is unlimited. It forms to that which holds it. It splashes and gives joy. It rejoices constantly, even in its storms. It is a divine life form. You may take your lessons from your water - it is a fluid, not rigid.

St. Germain, when Jesus said 'Whenever you ask in my name', did he mean the higher SELF?

In MY name, indeed. That was of course the Christ-consciousness that was speaking. Your higher SELF, in super-consciousness *is* the Christ-consciousness.

And also this: When you pray, when you ask for something and believe that you have whatever it is, then you will be given whatever it is...

Ask and Ye shall receive. Knock and the door will be opened.

What happens when you want something, or you think that you want something, yet your consciousness keeps throwing up barriers to the fact that you do not really want it?

That is the war with yourself - your alter ego. That is what your Bible has termed the devil. It is not an evil. It is merely part of your divine Self, your alter ego. That part of the ego that is within each and every entity. Your man Jesus also had an alter ego that was part of his divine SELF. However, he allowed it into its own divinity, in love, in unconditional love. And when one is allowed in unconditional love, one succumbs, as you might term it. It is not desirous of overpowering, for it is loved. You see, it is a part of yourself that is arguing with you, with the ego of divine SELF. And they will debate back and forth. It matters not who wins the battle during each occurrence, for your divine SELF will, in utter enlightenment, reign supreme. You see it is not about who wins, but how the game was played. By playing the game, by allowing in unconditional love, you win anyway and you are enlightened. Then, once you are accepting the totality of all unconditionally, even your arguing alter ego - love it, love it as part of your divine SELF - and it will resist no more.

Is there now a religion, so to speak, to better handle ourselves and our feelings?

Any religion, as you would term it, is dogmatic. You see what is religion but rules and regulations about giving your power away. Recognizing divinity within all of you is where the power is. Not only yourself, but of all others, yourself included. The religions upon Earth have been quite limited for the purpose of having power over your brothers. It was quite a political factor in your past history. It was how to control the people, how to instil within them fear, retribution. Your sinning as it is called, is where the power lies, the fear of hell, fire and damnation. It is all a controlling factor. For those things that you experience that would be considered by those dogmatic practices as sin, are merely there for you to gain knowledge. You see, you are eternal regardless. The burning you feel that would be a part of your hell is merely your conscious mind battling your divine SELF. The war rages on, much as a fire does. To answer your question: *there is no particular religion that would be beneficial.* You see, the part of super-consciousness that will allow unlimited, unconditional love and peace between the bretheren of your nation, all nations, is the undoing of these dogmatic practices, of the limited concepts they put forth. It is to allow the sovereignty of all - your Soviets, your Americans, your South-Americans, your Africans, your Middle Easterners - all are sovereign. All are divine. The allowance of that disallows what they have been battling over these centuries in your time - their dogmatic practices. The middle eastern countries will take one piece of their dogma and slay hundreds of thousands of men over one little piece of dogma. Releasing all of that limitation releases all nations into freedom, and there will be peace, for they have nothing more to fight about. As far as what you should turn to now, you know the answer to that, my dear.

St. Germain, I wanted to ask you about negative energy..

What you consider negative is merely another aspect. Positive is one side, negative is another. Lack of separation is unlimitedness. They are one in the same. Experienced and expressed in different manners, much as you and you are one and the same, but opposite expressions of each other. You see, *allowing what you consider negative would only mean that it is no longer negative.* Consider this. There is one negative person and then one positive person - what happens? The negative person either quietens, leaves, or becomes positive. That is the same regardless of attitudes, energies, personages, whatever, experiences. It is all the same. Allow it into your life in a positive fashion and it will turn its tide. You must believe this because your doubts will create other negativity.

If you should tell a darker nature to go away, 'Get out of my life.', you are telling part of the whole to go away. If you would like to retain the whole, merely tell that part that is darker 'I love you. Would you not like to come into this wondrous Eden of mine and be loved forever?'. And it will dissipate. How is it your man Jesus dealt with the negativity of the political factions against him? He loved them and accepted them. And what did they do after they had slain him? They knelt down and cried and wept and said 'truly this man is divine'. They turned positive.

Now you do not say to a child 'It is alright to destroy this household with your hammer'. You tell the child 'I love you. I know you have a desire to hammer this household. However, I would prefer that you did not and I will love you even if you do, although I will occasion this hammering with the back of my hand. But I love you anyway, my little young one.' You see, there were many messages within your Bible, however it has been misinterpreted. 'Spare the rod and spoil the child'. Another is 'You will not enter the kingdom of heaven, except that you become as a little child.' That is opening your heart as a child does with wonder and awe and love.

It also said that it is easier for a camel to go through the eye of a needle, than a rich man through the gates of heaven.

You see, what it means is that in those times your rich men were the men of your politics, your kings and the men of your church, the priests. They were the ones who desired to limit their brothers. They were the ones who took the power away from the peoples to accumulate more wealth and power for themselves. It was difficult for their conscious mind to release the need for this power. In order to become part of super-consciousness, it is necessary to release the desire and the need for your power over others.

So it really had nothing to do with money, per se.

It does not. He was speaking of the ones who were rich in those times, who were heavy laden with power hunger, with alter ego.

There are lots of those still around.

Of course, so it still applies, but not as far as your currency or your gold is concerned. It does not mean that in order to be super-conscious you have to be living in a hovel, eating roots. It means you need to release the power hunger over others. And what is the basis for power these days in your time? Money. Is it not? So you may have all you desire. Mountains full of it as long as you do not shackle your neighbour.

How would you bring super-consciousness down into this conscious-ness?

You do not bring super-consciousness down to you. There is a very simple truth. Realize your divinity and automatically your frequency will change, automatically. Ascensions in your times past have occurred many times. Various masters have ascended. Occasionally it occurs so quickly that the body disintegrates in heat and a pile of ashes is left behind. It is considered to be spontaneous human combustion, and your frequencies are automatically raised to whatever frequency you desire. However, it is not something you consciously do with your mind. You may raise your frequencies and you will partake of a certain amount of awareness, but you do it by releasing your need to do it, and allowing your divinity to come forth.

Become humble. Realize humility because you realize the divinity within everything - your leaves, your petals of your flowers, your ocean, your rain showers, your fishes in your seas. They are all equal to you. They are all divine creatures of love. They give to this universe lovingly. You become ONE with all of life. Your conscious mind will battle and that is part of the growing process. You will feel at once significant and master and insignificant as an ant, both at the same time. That is Godhood, sovereignty and humility, simultaneously.

So, there is nothing really too much one can do to meditate and bring the light in your soul down....

Of course there is, for enlightenment of your body is always helpful. And you do become aware of certain things. Certain things pop into your consciousness from your experience, your past lifetimes. You will gather to you, bit by bit, pearls of wisdom.

Through meditation?

Hm, and it need not be cross-legged. You may do it walking. Quietly with yourself in alignment.

Alright, is there anything in particular, specifically, that I can be doing that would really help?

I wish you to do this: become quiet with yourself in a comfortable manner. Allow your soul energy to disperse into the universe, encompass it all with your light. Carry forth your energy to all parts of your galaxy. Consider that as a sovereign, you may create such a galaxy. Also consider that all the other beings on this planet are just as sovereign as you are. That will give you the humility. Contemplate it for a while. Until the dew from your eyes is apparent on your cheeks. You will know, and then you will know what the work is you have cut out for yourself. It is quite simple. It is not always easy.

Could you talk about soulmates?

It is quite a complex subject. There is much chatter about it in these days. Many run around and flit about in life anxiously awaiting that one divine entity. They just know, that person is it, the one they have been waiting for all of their life, and so they run around checking them out, as you would term it. Is *this* him? Is *this* him? Or the other way around - Is *this* her? Getting the statistics from each individual - are you married?, da da da da. There is much emphasis upon that and in a manner that is giving your power away, for your life is built upon finding someone else, rather than yourself. There are soulmates indeed. Once you have gained a certain amount of enlightenment, you call to you all parts of your soul energies, all parts of your soul family, your oversoul. It is automatic, for the gathering together of your soul energy to you is what enlightens you and it brings to you illumination and your body becomes less in mass and more in energy. It lightens in weight and illumination. That is all part of your soul, including your soulmate. You see, your soulmate that has been put forward as one entity that is a male or female - and that there is only one - is true if you look at it in the light that the male or female energy may be embodied in several different personages. Both seen and unseen. There is one female energy existent within that soul energy family. It may exist within several different personages, both seen and unseen. It is the gathering together of the male and the female into no sex at all, because there is no differentiation between the genders when enlightenment occurs. It is ONE. There is no longer separation. You draw to you that particular mate automatically. You may recognize it in one entity as part of a male energy or vice versa. You may have two male soulmates, or three, or whatever. They are not always manifest on the Earth plane. They are not always manifest on any physical plane. You may have one here and one in the Pleiades and one on the inner planes which are non-physical altogether, but you draw them all to you. For there is only one male [or female] energy totality that is a part of you. That happens without any effort on your part. You do not need to look for them. They will almost fall into your lap. You will look and they will be there and you will know. You may not consciously be aware of this, because your conscious mind may have its barriers, but there will be something special about that entity that draws you to them and you will discover who they are. The only way this can occur is through Self-illumination. The only way is through realizing your own divinity. Your hip-hopping about only pushes it farther away from you, for you are giving your power away rather than drawing it to you.

Now, when all this is accomplished and the entity is, perhaps, in another star system - or on the inner planes - or on this Earth, when all have felt a closeness with you, then you may move on, into grander illumination. Also consider that your energy, what you would term your soulmate, may not be manifest on this Earth at all. The energy may all be dispersed elsewhere. So your fervent searching gains you nothing. The only way to find them is to find yourself.

Someone was telling me about how you, in a previous incarnation, would draw energy in through the top of your head instead of eating physical food.

It is not always through the top of one's head. It is throughout your entire system. You see, you gather the energy to run your body with from your atmosphere, from the electro-magnetic energy contained within your stratosphere.

You need not consume food stuffs. Your body may operate without a middle man, without processing green plants, the photosynthesis, for your fuel. You may partake of that energy directly.

From the Sun then?

Not only from the Sun, but from all the other electromagnetic forces without, not only solar, but all the energy contained within your atmosphere.

So would one do this as a conscious attempt coupled with creative imagination, would that be sufficient or would you have to have a....

One does this after the mastery of other things which we have discussed. Your Tibetan masters have accomplished much in this direction. They exist practically without any food stuffs at all, a few grains of rice here and there in their lifetime. They have spent many other lifetimes realizing that. You see, that is the first step. It is a major step, for the other is fluff. It comes naturally.

Would this realization be considered an initiation?

In a manner of speaking. But it is not necessary to label it. Labelling separates. It is all part of divine creation.

Speak to us about animals.

Those creatures that you call animals reflect man's consciousness as a mass-consciousness. In the days of your time when your civilization was not quite so technology-oriented, not quite so organized, as it were, your beasts were more savage. The animals of your time have always reflected man's consciousness, as a whole. And the ones you keep near you, in your abode, reflect your own consciousness. They are mirrors for you. They have a certain amount of consciousness of their own, but they have decided in their own sovereign right that they are desirous of providing this service of being that mirror to you. The ones who can best serve you are attracted to you and you to them. You learn from them as you do from your children.

Some people say we come back in that form, is that possible also?

Merely as a fragment of your original soul energy. Not as the soul energy you perceive to be human soul energy. For there are other fragments that are first and second densities - recall we spoke of third and fourth - the first and second density are of the animal kingdom and are fragments of the energy that is part of the soul family, the oversoul. It is a consciousness that provides a service, as your canines and your felines do. That consciousness, when it terminates its particular existence, returns to the soul unit, remerges, and then may be a part of human consciousness, but at an entirely different level. One cannot reincarnate, as you would term it to be, as an animal. It does not work that way, but your animal instincts, those tendencies of yourselves that are uncontrolled, are the part within your soul that has been in its past a fragment of an animal. But it is only a fragment, a minute fragment, that goes to make up the whole of the divine soul that you are. Do not confuse it with being in another life as an animal.

Where do devas fit in?

They are of a different kingdom. The deva kingdom, the angelic kingdom, they are of an energy Source that is of the divine creative force that you call the Source, that also has its purpose, its desire and its own divinity. It may occasionally incarnate in human physical form, however, that is not very common. Most of your angelic kingdom, including archangels, continue into eternity as archangels and they are part of divine creation, as is their choice in that manner. They are not, if you would use the limited term, evolving. They are already part of the divine creative force that you call the Source. They are already in enlightenment and wisdom. That is why they are not physical. The elementals are merely consciousnesses that are part of the universe. It is your fire, your air, your water. It is all consciousness. It is life. It is part of the universe made manifest much as the stars and your other heavenly bodies. It is another manifestation.

And the purpose they serve?

The elementals are merely a consciousness exhibiting itself in whatever form they desire. They are also capable of manifesting themselves, if they desire to, as a planet or a star, or whatever. The deva kingdom provides the service as guidance and protectors and inspiration and companions. That is their choice to do this service. They, from time to time, do incarnate. It is not very common, for the forces upon your Earth plane are repellant to them. They are persecuted because of their nature, because of their unconditional love and protective nature. So they do not exist for very long at a time. They occasionally take on a body to perform a service temporarily, much as walk-ins do. But to be born into the Earth plane as other humans, they are persecuted.

What was the purpose of Stonehenge? Was that just a reminder?

It was a landing base for the craft that were here to help civilization at that time. The civilization that used that as a landing base at that time is now far advanced beyond those particular propulsion systems. They no longer travel in that manner. They were using craft at that time that used an energy similar to atomic energy, however not completely like in nature. And now they travel through teleportation. They instantaneously are where they desire to be without craft.

Could they adapt to the environment?

If you are a God. You see this particular civilization has come to the point where they are in divine inspiration. They are in super-consciousness. And you, yourselves, when you become a part of that world, will be able to travel whenever and wherever you choose, without your craft, without automobiles, or your jetcraft, or space-craft. That is what Sai Baba did in a limited fashion. Being in more places than one at a time - you may do this in a more unlimited fashion.

Is that the same as astral projection?

Astral projection is projecting part of your consciousness to another place in time with your body remaining. What I speak of is your body being with you. Astral projection is allowing yourself into your Godhood, into super-consciousness. And if you would term it so, indeed it is a start. It is very wondrous and good for you to experience this to give you a taste of things to come.

You spoke of walk-ins, could you explain about that?

That is a divine entity from another place, perhaps another universe, who desires to partake of the Earth plane for a particular reason. Perhaps guidance, perhaps arrangement of political governments, your laws, your regulations. It is by mutual consent between two entities, that is the entity upon the Earth plane and the entity that is not of the Earth plane - the allowance of the one that is of the Earth plane to allow his or her body to be used for the consciousness of the other entity. During that period of time, whatever is to be accomplished, is accomplished and then the 'walk in' entity returns to his home, if you would term it to be home, and the entity of the Earth, retains his or her consciousness that was before. It is stamped, as you would term it to be 'mission accomplished', however, it is by mutual consent, much as you are witnessing at this time [reference is to Azena regarding St. Germain]. It is for a reason, a grand design. And it is becoming more prevalent on Earth, for your entities of other universes are making themselves known on your Earth plane, because it is ready, it is ripe. They [Earth humans] are not so fearful as they once were. They are opening. They are realizing their brothers will not attack them, that they are here to help them.

I thought that the original entity, when they made the switch, no longer wanted to take on the experience of...

There have been occasions when the entity that had possession of the body in the first place, desires not to return, for they have experienced worlds far more grand than the one they had inhabited before. That is not often, but it does occur.

Can you speak to us of Bartholomew?

Bartholomew is a grand entity. He is another teacher. He is and has been on this Earth plane in many incarnations that are considered significant in your history.

Kutumi in your mystical readings is an oversoul of that entity. He is one of the Great White Brotherhood. That is a gathering of masters, of entities who choose to become part of the Earth plane in teaching and sharing during this time, to bring all of the Earth into super-consciousness, to love them into their grander Selves, and into enlightenment. It is merely an assemblage of all of us entities that are here to hold your hands. That is why I say we are more than this one you call St. Germain speaking to you. I am the mouthpiece. They are also consciousnesses that are upon this Earth plane, taking whatever forms and fashions which best serve the purpose.

St. Germain, what and where is 'Shambala'?

Shambala is the planetary term one uses for this Earth planet. Shambala is Terra's name in fourth density - in super-consciousness.

I read an undesire to dissipate from here, but it is of the ripeness of time. The grapevine of your consciousness is heavy for the plucking. Understand that I am always with you.

I Am that I Am and you are that I Am, and always, it co-exists together, and I shall come unto you as a brother, in communion, fellowship, and in delight of your experience, and sharing. Not as your teacher, you are your teacher - not as your guide, you are your guide, and not as your guru, you are your guru - but as the lover of you that will allow love back unto yourselves. Understand always, my beloveds, that I am your mirror. And as another would come unto you and express an appreciation unto you, always, always, always tell them: 'I am your mirror'.

So fare thee well for now. You do bless me, beloveds, and you are God. It has been a grand fairy tale experience, finger-painted by the hand of God that is you. Allow yourself to laugh with yourself. There are no such things as mistakes, no such things as errors, perhaps mis-vibrations, but not to be judged.

It has been grand this evening in your time. There are many hearts that are full. Questions have been answered, but it only raised more questions. That is good. Your soul will answer them for you. Thank you my dear brothers and sisters. It is always my honour. I am always pleased to partake of this plane. It is a grand and wondrous place indeed. I will see many of your faces again, but it is not your faces I look forward to, it is your light. Oh, it is magnificent. Good evening.

GOD I AM

From Tragic To Magic

By Peter O. Erbe

Every 25,000 years our Solar System completes one orbit around Alcione, the central sun of the Pleiades, a constellation at a distance of approximately 400 light years from our Sun. In 1961, science discovered a photon belt which encircles the Pleiades at a right angle to its orbital planes. Our Sun, and Earth with it, is entering this photon belt between now and the year 2011.

This photon belt is the cosmic 'trigger force' to shift Humanity from third level into fourth level density, from Separation into Oneness. Thus, the magnitude and beauty of this event Earth is preparing for defies any description. Earth and Humanity are aligning for its birth into Christ-consciousness - the union of Star Light with Matter - the marriage of Spirit with separated Selves.

As the night transforms into a new day, so is the Age of Darkness giving way to the Age of Light. It is the greatest event ever to grace the Earth and her children. Terms such as the New Age, Superconsciousness etc., are but different labels for one and the same occurrence.

It is the 'end-time' of the prophecies, for time as such shall cease to be. Ageing, ailments and sorrow shall be no more. To partake of this grandest of events, man must be aligned with its energy.

Humanity, as such, is governed by False Perception, the adherence to the frequency of Fear, the result of which is literally an upside-down perception of life. Only that which is aligned with Light can partake of Light, thus those not aligned with the cosmic current of

energy flow - the Divine Intent - shall sleep t long sleep.

It is the purpose of this material to devel the magnificent tool of True Perception, wi which we align ourselves for the birth into t dawn of a new day in creation, the Age of Lov

As the chrysalis is the bridge between t caterpillar and the butterfly, so is Tr Perception the bridge between third level a fourth level density, between Separation a Oneness.

The universe with all its beings, in seen a unseen dimensions, joins with us in the greate of all celebrations, the jubilance of rebirth in Light - the dance of the Gods - for where Ear and we as her children go, is the fulfilment the soul's ancient cry:

WE ARE COMING HOME

Available from your book store or write direct to:
IN AUSTRALIA:
GEMCRAFT BOOKS
291-293 Wattletree Rd., East Malvern, Vic. 3145
IN U.S.A.:
JEWELL MARKETING MARKETING SERVICES INC.
10400 Walrond Avenue, Kansas City, MO 64137 -
Toll Free: 800 221 - 9183

TRIAD
PUBLISHERS PTY LTD

MESSAGE FROM THE STARS

THE P'TAAH TAPES

AN ACT OF FAITH

TRANSMISSIONS FROM THE PLEIADES

CHANNELLED BY JANI KING

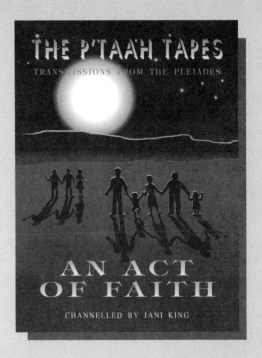

Something very unusual and very special took place in the latter half of the year 1991. Amidst the magical setting of the coastal hills of North Queensland, Australia, a group of people gathered regularly for twentyeight weeks to listen to the teachings of one of the star-people: P'taah from the constellation of the Pleiades.

At a time of a humanity stressed to the hilt and suffering as never before from the effects of a fear based consciousness, the denial of the God within, P'taah's communication could not have been timed more appropriately.

P'taah prepares humanity for the forthcoming transition from separation to Oneness. If there ever was a message of limitless love, of joy and upliftment, of concrete thought applicable to practical, every day living, then it is this material; though much of it shakes the bed-rock of belief structures which constitute human reality.

P'taah tells of the grand changes to come for humanity and the planet Earth,. He opens our vista to a universe teeming with life. He speaks of the Inner-Earth people and the star-people and in doing so, assures us, that we are not alone. What is more, he presents us with the panacea to transmute fear into love, to discover who we really are. Gently he dissolves the imprisoning shackles of dogma and concept, which lock Man into a consciousness of survival thinking, and reveals, contrary to all appearances, an irresistible, breathtakingly beautiful destiny for Mankind.

The love of the star-people for humanity could not be expressed any better than in P'taah's own words:

**WE WILL DO ANYTHING
TO BRING YOU HOME!**

**TRIAD
PUBLISHERS PTY LTD
AUSTRALIA**

Available from your book store or write directly to:

IN AUSTRALIA:
GEMCRAFT BOOKS
291-293 Wattletree Rd., East Malvern, Vic. 3145
IN U.S.A.:
JEWELL MARKETING SERVICES INC.
10400 Walrond Avenue, Kansas City, MO 64137
Toll Free: 800 221 - 9183